WHAT THE BIBLE TEACHES ABOUT
SPIRITUAL WARFARE

ROBERT DEAN JR.
and THOMAS ICE

kregel
PUBLICATIONS

Grand Rapids, MI 49501

What the Bible Teaches About Spiritual Warfare

Previously published as *Overrun by Demons: The Church's New Preoccupation with the Demonic.*

© 1990, 2000 by Robert Dean Jr. and Thomas Ice
Second Edition

Published by Kregel Publications, a division of Kregel, Inc., P.O. Box 2607, Grand Rapids, MI 49501. Kregel Publications provides trusted, biblical publications for Christian growth and service. For more information about Kregel Publications, visit our web site: www.kregel.com

Library of Congress Cataloging-in-Publication Data
Dean, Robert, Jr.
     What the Bible teaches about spiritual warfare / by Robert Dean Jr. and Thomas Ice
          p.   cm.
     Includes bibliographical references.
     1. Spiritual warfare—Biblical teaching. 2. Devil—Biblical teaching. 3. Demonology—Biblical teaching.
I. Ice, Thomas.   II. Title.
BS680.S73 D43   2000   235'.4—dc21   00-030376
                                                        CIP

ISBN 0-8254-2487-9

Printed in the United States of America

2 3 4 5 / 04 03 02 01

To our parents—
Alton and Vesta Ice,
Bob and Gloria Dean—
who fought the good fight by
leading us to a saving knowledge
of Jesus Christ, and whose love
and support through the years has
enabled us to fight the good fight.
We love you.

Train up a child in the way he should go, even when he is old he will not depart from it.

—*Proverbs 22:6*

CONTENTS

ACKNOWLEDGMENTS

No book is ever produced without the help and support of a number of people. Dr. Charles Ryrie provided helpful suggestions and was someone with whom to talk as we sought to refine our understanding of the Scriptures. We are also grateful to our respective churches for giving us the freedom and time to work on this book. Finally, we wish to thank Grace Bible Church in San Marcos, as well as Gordon and David Whitelock and the folks at Camp Peniel, who provided us with places to retreat from the pressing demands of our churches so we could write. Without the help of all of these people, we would still be on chapter one!

1

THE GREAT WAR

*For though we walk in the flesh, we do not war according
to the flesh, for the weapons of our warfare are not of the
flesh, but divinely powerful for the destruction of fortresses.
We are destroying speculations and every lofty thing raised
up against the knowledge of God, and we are taking every
thought captive to the obedience of Christ.*

—*2 Corinthians 10:3–5*

Another long, miserable day at work, and now this! Someone's
car had overheated and blocked one of the two lanes left open
on the freeway while the other three lanes were under construction.
Sue was steamed. Not only had her day at the office been an absolute
disaster but she now had to put up with this. She was going to be at
least an hour late getting to the daycare center to pick up her three-
year-old son, Joey, but the extra bills from the air-conditioner repair
had left her with no extra money to eat out. After a day like this, Sue
dreaded having to fix dinner when she got home. She felt so trapped.
She couldn't understand why life wasn't going better now that she
was a born-again Christian.

For the last several months so many things seemed to have gone
wrong. First, the car needed a valve job, then Joey broke his arm so
badly that it needed to be surgically set. Then the compressor on her
air conditioner went out. She could not believe how the bills had

snowballed. It would take her at least a year, maybe two, to get all of these bills paid off. And she knew that other unexpected expenses were sure to come up in the meantime. She desperately needed something to perk up her spirits.

While she was waiting in traffic, she decided to turn on the radio; maybe that would help. That's when she heard it—an advertisement for the new steak restaurant that had just opened. As she thought about it, she dreamed of how wonderful it would be if she could just pick up Joey and go there for a nice, big steak and a good, rich, chocolate dessert. But she knew she couldn't afford a meal like this and ought to put it out of her mind. But that gnawing voice inside her said that she was worth it. After all, what difference would another thirty dollars or so on her credit card mean? She was worth it! She would face the money problems later.

Is this a valid response to the pressures and circumstances in life? Or could it be that the small voice is really the influence of the world system? What could Sue do to avoid this kind of thinking?

Can Prayer Exorcise a City?

José and Maria had been born-again Christians for only two years. During that time, they had become quite involved in their church. For several months, the pastor had been teaching about spiritual warfare, especially prayer. One of his major emphases was that Satan and his demons held sway over certain territories and that in Miami (where they lived) one of the reasons for the high incidence of drug traffic, prostitution, and violence was the demonic oppression of the city. If Miami were ever to be freed from the dominion of these demons, then Christians must gather together and pray. Only through the effective prayer of the Christians would the holy angels have the power to gain victory over the demons and enable Miami to experience spiritual revival.

The series on spiritual warfare culminated with a week-long prayer marathon. People in the church had been encouraged and challenged to join six- and ten-hour prayer vigils and to pray and fast around the clock. At the end of the week, words of prophecy were spoken in the church, encouraging the people that their prayers had been effective and that many of the demons had been routed.

José and Maria lived in the Colombian sector of Miami, and many of their friends and family members were involved in the drug trade. José and Maria were excited that this deliverance would finally give them the opportunity to witness to family members without hindrance from satanic opposition.

When their words of witness were met with the same familiar hostility, they did not question God but waited in faith. Yet, as the days went by, they noticed that there was very little difference in the moral climate of Miami. The drug traffic continued, immorality was just as rampant, and gunfire continued to punctuate the night air.

Can prayer deliver a city or neighborhood from the influence of demons?

Can Christians Be Demon Possessed?

Julia was in her mid-forties. She was divorced, and she struggled to raise her two children on a single income. Yet, she was always confident that God would provide. Life had been difficult, but the one hope that carried her through was her sincere faith in God. Despite this confidence, she had struggled for more than ten years with bouts of depression and had finally started visiting counselors. Although she had seen three counselors during the last five years, the depression continued.

One weekend, a visiting speaker at her church taught that Christians could be demon possessed. Julia had always been taught that a Christian could not be possessed, but the speaker said that depression could be a sign of possession. She left church that night with a mixed sense of relief and fear—relief because now she might know her real problem and fear because now she believed that her depression might be the result of demonic possession. But she was not sure just what to do about all of this.

Can Christians be demon possessed? What is the difference between demon *possession* and demon *influence*?

Can Christians Be Cursed?

Frank and Martha were finally getting away for a weekend "second honeymoon" together, although doing so meant leaving their high-school-aged daughter at home alone. They trusted Linda because she had never given them any real reason to doubt her. Now that she was about to graduate from high school, they believed that the time had come to give her the opportunity to show her maturity. But unknown to them, Linda had planned to have a party the whole time they were gone. During the party, a group of her friends who were involved in both a satanic rock music group and a cult hid a pentagram in a junk drawer in the kitchen and placed a curse on the family.

Several days after Frank and Martha returned home, they sensed that something was different about their life, but could not put their finger on what it was. During the following weeks, they noticed a deterioration in the circumstances of their lives. Several things went wrong with their car, and the air conditioner in their home had to be replaced. They also began to notice more bickering among the family members and a certain spiritual confusion in the family.

About this time Frank heard from his neighbor that there had been quite a bit of traffic in and out of their house while they had been away. Eventually, the entire story came out, including the identification of some of the kids as members of a Satanist cult. When Frank told a friend about all of this, his friend suggested that the reason things were not going well for the family was because the Satanists had probably put a curse on the house, and the family would have to undergo some sort of exorcism before they could be delivered. To Frank, this suggestion sounded more like superstitious nonsense than sensible advice, but he began to wonder what the Bible taught about demons, curses, and spells.

Can Christians be victims of occultic curses?

Will Mind Control Help You?

Carl was a very successful salesman. At twenty-five years of age, his commissions for the past year had earned him almost two hundred thousand dollars. Furthermore, he was being considered for a sales manager position. Carl was overwhelmed by God's blessing in his life.

One day, the senior manager of his division called him into his office. He praised Carl for his work and ambition and saw nothing but the best for him. However, he suggested one particular seminar that Carl should attend if he was ever to reach his goals. He implied that Carl would probably not receive the promotion unless he attended. As Carl questioned his manager about the seminar, he discovered that it was designed to teach him mind-control principles, improve his memory, and enable him to influence other people positively. One of the most important results of the seminar, Carl's manager told him, was that he would be introduced to a spiritual counselor upon whom he could rely and who would give him an edge over his competition.

Is Carl on the verge of being involved in occultic practices disguised as sales techniques? Is mind control (positive mental attitude) a biblical approach to handling life's challenges? Or is it an open door to demonism?

Can Demons Make You Sin?

Bob and his sister Susan had grown up in a Christian home and had been well trained in the Scriptures. When Susan was in college, however, she began to lose her spiritual bearings and became lukewarm toward God. For several years, Bob had been praying for her, and God seemed to have answered his prayers. Susan had joined a new church that was quite alive, and she was more turned on to Jesus then ever before.

This so impressed Bob that he, too, soon joined this same church. He was impressed that these people seemed to act aggressively on their faith and truly expected God to perform miracles and signs and wonders, just as He had done in the New Testament. At first, Bob was skeptical, but he heard so many glowing testimonies from Christians who had been delivered from demons and were now free from sins that had plagued them that he, too, was thinking that perhaps the problems he faced with sin were the result of demonic influence in his life.

Can demons—"spirits of lust, murder, anger, gluttony"—cause Christians to sin, or is sin simply the result of choosing to follow our own sin nature?

Can You Have a Demon of Lust?

Bill had been introduced to pornography as a young teen. Through the years, it had become more and more of an obsession. This obsession intensified in college when he began looking for more ways to get his sexual thrills and discovered adult peep shows. While he was a senior in college, he was led to the Lord through a campus ministry, and for several years the pornography problem no longer bothered him. But after he was married he again found himself tempted by the pleasures of the pornography palace and the massage parlor. What made this situation so difficult for him was that he was in his second year of seminary, studying to be a pastor. He just couldn't understand why he could not overcome this sin.

Finally the guilt became so intense that Bill went to one of his seminary professors for advice. This professor suggested that he very likely was being influenced by a demon of lust and that he should go through a deliverance session to gain freedom from this demon.

Do demons cause specific sins in people's lives? How are Christians to have victory over the sins with which they continuously struggle?

Can Pagan Objects Haunt You?

Fred and Linda had been on the missionary committee at their church for twenty years. Now that Fred was finally retired, they went overseas to visit several of the church missionaries. When they returned home, they brought with them a number of artifacts with which they hoped to help people in their church to understand the various cultures where their missionaries served. So they included these objects in a mission display in the basement of the church. But soon a lady in the church confronted them, saying that some of the objects that they had brought back were used in pagan rituals or were idols and that Fred and Linda should destroy these things and cleanse the church before they became victims of the demons that are associated with them.

Can Christians who are obediently walking with the Lord innocently or unknowingly pick up demons through objects that are associated with occult practices? If so, what should they do about it?

Can You Inherit a Demon?

Sandy had grown up in a family that was deeply entrenched in occult practices and witchcraft. Both of her parents were in a coven that her grandfather had founded. Her mother was also a palm reader and astrologer. Her father had on a number of occasions served as a channel for the spirit of a man who had allegedly lived in India twenty thousand years ago. Because of Sandy's upbringing, this was all she knew about religion.

When Sandy left home in her late teen years to attend college, her roommate, an evangelical Christian, began to talk to her about Jesus Christ, who died for her sins. Sandy's roommate explained to her what the Bible taught about Satan, demons, witchcraft, and astrology. At first, Sandy was hostile, but during the semester she accepted the challenge to read the Bible for herself. Under the guidance of her roommate, she came to see that what she knew as religion would never provide eternal life and that she must trust in Jesus Christ alone for her salvation.

After Sandy was saved, she began attending a large church in town. Because of her background, she still had many questions about her new faith and the witchcraft that she had left behind. Her roommate suggested that she go to one of the counselors in the church for answers. The counselor told her that trusting in Christ alone as her Savior was not enough. Because Sandy had come from such an occultic background, she needed to renounce all of these practices and very possibly needed deliverance from the demons that she inherited through her family.

Does the Bible teach that a person who is saved from an occultic background can have a demon that was passed on from one generation to another? Must such a person not only turn completely to Christ but also be delivered from these inherited demons as a separate step?

You Are at War

Each of the stories that you have just read is based on a true incident, and each represents a cross section of what is happening in the lives of many people today. Each of these Christians wants to live a life that is pleasing to God, yet each faces daily struggles and opposition in his or her walk with the Lord. The Bible teaches that life has a dimension that goes beyond the material, physical environment. This arena centers on the immaterial part of your being—the real you—and your relationship to God. In opposition to God is Satan and a vast army of immaterial, rational creatures that are subservient to him. They have all been sentenced to eternal condemnation in the lake of fire (Matt. 25:41). Yet, that sentence has been postponed until the end of human history. Between the pronouncement of that verdict and the execution of the sentence lies the entire panorama of human history. Man was created to play a vital role in the resolution of this angelic rebellion. Man is the focal point. This is the essence of spiritual warfare.

If you are a believer in the Lord Jesus Christ as your Savior, then you, too, have declared yourself to be a warrior in this cosmic conflict. Perhaps you did not realize this; maybe you are not aware that the Bible teaches that Satan is the prince of the power of the air (Eph. 2:2) and the god of this age (2 Cor. 4:4) and that before you were saved, Satan was at work in you as one of the sons of disobedience (Eph. 2:2). Once you were saved, you became a significant soldier in the greatest war ever fought, a spiritual war fought between the power of God (light) and the forces of Satan (darkness). As we will discover in the following pages, the Bible clearly teaches all of these truths. In addition, the Bible teaches that each believer must learn how to fight in the battle. The Bible is our combat manual, and in it we find the vital instructions we need to combat Satan and his two great allies, the world system and the sin nature.

We are called not simply to be in the army but to be champions in Christ. At the moment of salvation, God graciously bestowed on us every spiritual blessing and asset we would ever need to be victorious in the conflict (Eph. 1:3). This is our positional strength, "in Christ." We have the completed revelation of God, which supplies all of the information that we need, and the Spirit of God indwells, teaches, guides, fills, and illumines our thinking to the truth of God's Word. In the power of Christ we stand. Just as the young David, untrained in the world's methods of warfare, became a champion for Israel against the mighty giant Goliath, so, too, must the believer today be a champion in Christ. David chose to enter the battle on the basis of divine resources, not human ability or technique. He is our model. To be victorious in spiritual warfare, we must not be seduced into using thinking or strategies that are influenced by nonbiblical thinking. We most hold our ground on the provisions, promises, and power of God. The battle is the Lord's.

In the coming pages, we will examine each of these three enemies: the world, the flesh, and the Devil. We will discover the fantastic principles that God has freely given us in the Scriptures to defeat these enemies in our personal lives. We will see more clearly the role that Christians are to play in this cosmic spiritual drama. And we will come to understand that our knowledge of these teachings comprises the basics of the Christian life.

Watching the Game Films

Unfortunately, contemporary teaching on the crucial doctrine of spiritual warfare has caused Christians to focus almost exclusively on battles with Satan and demons. If this were truly the emphasis of Scripture, then there would be no problem. However, because this is *not* the primary focus of Scripture but only one aspect of the teaching, then this overemphasis is misleading and even dangerous. It becomes dangerous when it causes Christians to focus on attacks and solutions in only one realm of spiritual warfare, leaving them vulnerable to attacks from the other two realms. The Bible clearly addresses spiritual warfare as taking place simultaneously on three battlefronts: the world; the flesh; and the Devil. So must we.

Just as a football coach studies the game films of his opponent before the big game to discover his strategies and tactics, so Christians must know the strategies, tactics, and abilities of their enemies before they can effectively defeat them. In other words, we must understand the nature of the warfare and who attacks us before we can accurately understand what we should be doing. By examining the lives of the great saints and the great spiritual battles of Scripture, we can see the strategies of the enemy and learn principles for avoiding the snares and assaults of the Devil, the traps of worldliness, and the drive of our own sinful nature.

Once we understand the spiritual war of which we are a part, then we must decide what we are to do. How can we live in the world and not be worldly? How can we have victory over the lusts of the flesh? And what does it mean to resist the Devil? We need biblical insight into how we will be attacked so that we will know what God has supplied for our protection.

The Highest Authority

Many Christians today are losing the battle in spiritual warfare because they lack an adequate knowledge of God's Word. This ignorance has led some people into occult practices that are cleverly disguised as "neutral" self-help techniques. Others have one foot in the world and the other foot in the Bible; thus compromised, they cannot understand why biblical principles never seem to work for them. Defeat is commonplace because their lives are not established on truly biblical principles but rather on the shifting foundation of human experience.

As we have surveyed much of the contemporary literature written for Christians, we have discovered an extremely wide range of ideas, many of which are mutually contradictory. Both the issues and the solutions differ widely. We have read many fine-sounding discussions on spiritual warfare that did not have a biblical basis. Some people teach that Christians can be demon possessed whereas others teach that they cannot. On the other hand, if one view is true, then Christians must live one way and the solutions to the problem must lie in one direction. If the other view is true, then the problems and solutions offered by the first view are irrelevant. How can we find our way out of this maze and find timeless truth on which we can base our lives?

We believe that the Bible is our highest authority, and only God has sufficient, infinite knowledge and understanding of both our enemies and our human nature to inform us accurately about spiritual conflict and what to do about it. The Christian must always be like the men and women of Berea who received the highest praise from the apostle Paul because they did not simply take his word but searched the Scriptures daily to verify his teaching (Acts 17:11).

The Real Source of Truth

Many of the errors that have crept into the church, some of which have become very popular, are based on misunderstandings and misinterpretations of Scripture. Sometimes this happens because the writers have not taken into account the original languages of the Bible or have misused them. Therefore, it is important that we occasionally refer to the original Greek and Hebrew wording of Scripture to interpret more accurately God's Word.

At other times, error creeps in because we rely upon interpretations of experiences or personal testimony that might not be consistent with Scripture, especially in the area of Satan and demons and what they can do to Christians. Testimonies of missionaries working among pagan tribes where demonic activity abounds are used to support a particular line of teaching. How should these stories be evaluated, especially since some of these occurrences are used to support one position and others are used to support a contradictory position? Is appealing to these types of experiences a valid means to find truth?

Before we can ever hope to have victory over the sin and evil that are part of our universe, we must first understand the role of God's Word. Much of what is taught today contains testimonies of personal experience or the experiences of other people. We must find out how we are to regard such testimony, and we must continually seek to determine a true, biblical approach to spiritual warfare. Failure to do so is one reason that so many believers are impotent in the warfare. They have either lost the sure foundation of the Word of God or severely weakened it by relying upon interpretations of experiences that run contrary to what the Bible clearly teaches.

When you have finished reading this book, we hope that you will understand the difference between the worldly, almost superstitious views of Satan that have invaded many of our churches and a truly biblical perspective of evil and our calling to spiritual warfare. We pray that you will be armed with the truth of the Scriptures and will stand firm against the schemes of the Devil and his terrible deception.

2

ULTIMATE INTELLIGENCE

*The unfolding of Thy words gives light; it gives under-
standing to the simple.*

—*Psalm 119:130*

During the Second World War, one of the most critical elements
of the Allied victory was provided by the underground forces
in the German-occupied countries. These groups kept tabs on the
German units in their vicinity and relayed this information to Allied
headquarters in London. In London, General Eisenhower's military
intelligence staff collated the information, which was then used to
formulate strategy and tactics. Rarely did more than a handful of
people have access to all of this information. Lower-level command-
ers and soldiers were told only what they needed to know to carry out
their specific responsibilities. No soldier would ever have thought to
ask for all of the information available to Eisenhower so that he could
verify the validity of his own orders or even understand why he was
being ordered to carry out a particular mission.

Only God Knows

In the same way, only God has a complete picture and full understanding of the warfare that takes place in the heavenlies. Christians
are analogous to His foot soldiers. Our operations orders are outlined
in the Scriptures, which tell us everything we need to know to carry

out successfully our specific mission. That mission is to pursue maturity in the spiritual life, holiness, or Christlikeness.

Unlike human armies, which face physical opponents, Christians face intangible and invisible opponents. Under normal conditions, the enemy against which we wage war cannot be perceived by human senses. The danger we face is attempting to rely upon our own reason and experience to develop strategies for warfare. Because we know very little about the strengths, capabilities, and strategies of our opponents, and because we cannot see into that realm, we must rely exclusively upon the combat information revealed to us in the Scriptures. Like the soldiers in physical military conflict, God has not told us everything that is going on in these realms, but He has told us *all* that we need to know to protect ourselves and carry out our mission successfully. When we begin to rely on information based on sources other than the Bible, we may render ourselves vulnerable to defeat because we have unknowingly overstepped our bounds.

The apostle Paul wrote in Ephesians 6:12, "Our struggle is not against flesh and blood, but against the rulers, against the powers, against the world forces of this darkness, against the spiritual forces of wickedness in the heavenly places." The struggle in which Christians are engaged is not a *physical* struggle but a *spiritual* struggle. It is a struggle that ultimately is not against other human beings but against the powers of darkness. Left to our own resources, we are totally blind and ignorant when it comes to knowing what the enemy is doing. How can we know what is happening when we are operating in the dark?

Not in the Dark

We operate in an arena in which we are virtually blind to all that is taking place around us, especially when it involves the unseen spiritual forces of the demonic realm. However, God is a loving God, and He has not left us in the dark to attempt to figure things out on our own. Just as God told Adam and Eve all that they *needed to know* (but not all that they *could have known*) for them to live for Him in the garden, so He has informed us in the Bible of everything that we need to know about the powers of darkness. Not only does the Bible tell us about the struggle in which we are involved but also, if it were not for the Scriptures, we would be only vaguely aware that we were in a struggle in the first place. We would be severely limited by our finite experience and knowledge. God has not only given Christians the Bible but also supplied the Holy Spirit, who enlightens our minds so that we can understand the Bible and, on the basis of this knowledge, exercise discernment in the decisions we make.

Scripture is clear that Christians are engaged in a struggle with unseen forces. This knowledge should cause several important questions to come to our minds: Who are these forces, these rulers, these powers, these world forces of darkness? What is their objective, and how do they operate? How can we identify them, how can we fight against them, and how can we be protected from them?

Today, we are faced with much teaching about these demonic forces that cannot be derived from Scripture; instead, it derives from the personal experiences of Christians. Is such experience a valid source, or is Scripture all that we need to resist Satan successfully?

The One True Source

The Bible itself claims to be our only source of certain knowledge about these forces against which we are struggling. It claims not only to be the sole source of knowledge about this angelic rebellion but also to give us all of the information that we need to be equipped completely for this struggle.

Second Timothy 3:16–17 tells us that "all Scripture is inspired by God and profitable for teaching, for reproof, for correction, for training in righteousness, that the man of God may be adequate, equipped for every good work." This passage provides valuable information about the Scriptures. First, the source of the Bible is God. This is not a book written by men who are relating their religious experiences with God but a book written *by God through men* to inform us about every area of life.

The apostle Peter makes this fact clear in 2 Peter 1:20: "Know this first of all, that no prophecy of Scripture is a matter of one's own interpretation." The human authors of Scripture did not merely reflect on their experiences of life, write them down, and call this the

Word of God. That is the approach of men without revelation from God. Instead, Peter insists, the divine Author initiated and produced God's Word: "No prophecy was ever made by an act of human will, but men moved by the Holy Spirit spoke from God" (2 Peter 1:21). The word usually translated "inspired" in 2 Timothy 3:16 is from the Greek word *theopneustos*, meaning "God breathed." The source of the Scriptures is the true God, who is not a liar; therefore, the Bible is absolutely true in everything it affirms.

Second, because the Bible is absolute truth, it is profitable to teach us, to correct our thinking, to reprove or reprimand us for wrong thinking and living, and to instruct us. Our Lord said in His prayer for the disciples the night before He was crucified, "Sanctify them in the truth; Thy word is truth" (John 17:17). It is the Word of God *alone* that gives us the truth we need to live for Him.

The third point we want to emphasize from 2 Timothy 3:16-17 is the purpose of the Word of God: to make the believer, the man or woman of God, completely equipped for every good work by communicating information that he can acquire from no other source. The word translated "adequate" is the Greek word *artios*, which means "fit, complete, capable, sufficient." It means that the Word of God gives us the information or guidelines necessary to meet every situation that we face in life.

This point is further emphasized by the word translated "fully equipped," which has the idea of being completely outfitted and prepared for every contingency. In the ancient world, this word was used to describe a ship that was fully loaded for a voyage or a rescue boat that was completely outfitted and prepared for any emergency. The Bible claims not only to give us true and accurate information but also *all* of the information we need to handle *any and every* situation that might arise in our lives.

Enough for Every Need

This passage is not the only passage of Scripture that teaches this foundational doctrine that Scripture is completely and totally sufficient for every need in the Christian's life. Second Peter 1:3-4 says,

His divine power has granted to us *everything* pertaining to life and godliness, through the true knowledge of Him who called us by His own glory and excellence. For by these He has granted to us His precious and magnificent promises, in order that *by them* you might become partakers of the divine nature, having escaped the corruption that is in the world by lust. (emphasis added)

As we will describe in the next chapter, the corruption that is in the world by lust came into the world as a result of the fall of the angel Lucifer, and the consequent fall of the human race was a result of the sin of Adam in the Garden of Eden (Gen. 3:1–7). This passage teaches us that the only way to escape this corruption is by means of God's "precious and magnificent promises," and that through these promises God has given us everything that we need to know pertaining to life and godliness.

The importance of the all-sufficiency of Scripture can hardly be overemphasized. In some segments of Christianity today, the inerrancy and infallibility of Scripture is being questioned. But we believe that even among those who affirm the inerrancy and infallibility of Scripture, many Christians deny this authority of Scripture in the way they apply (or fail to apply) Scripture to their daily lives. Many Christians do not seem to view the Bible as sufficient for every good work when we look at certain practices that they have adopted that are built upon viewpoints found outside of the Bible. This is especially true in the arena of spiritual warfare.

In recent years, much sensationalist teaching on demons and exorcism has abounded. It has been popular to teach people to "bind" the demons, to "take dominion" over Satan, or to give people special instructions for dealing with so-called "territorial spirits." We should ask if these are scriptural concepts to begin with and, if so, what they mean. We must also search the Scriptures to see exactly what form spiritual warfare takes and what Christians are to do when they encounter demonic forces.

The two passages mentioned earlier, 2 Timothy 3:16 and 2 Peter 1:3–4, teach clearly that in the Bible God has given us everything we need to know to handle any situation that might arise in our lives. At the very least, this teaching includes every aspect of spiritual warfare.

Why Go to School?

Whenever we have taught this principle that the Scriptures are totally sufficient for every need and situation in the believer's life, someone inevitably asks why, if this is true, we should even go to school or pursue studies in any other area. If this were true, their reasoning goes, then civilization would be set back hundreds of years and none of the technical advances made in the history of civilization would have taken place because all that people would have done was study the Bible.

This question arises because people do not realize how the truth of God's Word affects all of the different realms of life. In this book we are talking about the sufficiency of God's Word in enabling us to live a life that is pleasing to God. God's Word does not claim to be a textbook about oceanography or accounting or engineering, although it does contain some broad but completely accurate information about these areas of study.

What the Bible claims to provide is *absolute truth in all areas of Christian life and spirituality.* At the very least, this truth must include information about the spiritual realm and how it affects Christians. The Bible claims to tell us the truth about life, our purpose for existence, and how we can lay hold of our eternal destiny. All of these truths are issues in spiritual warfare; therefore, spiritual warfare and the world of the demonic are areas in which Christians should acknowledge the exclusive authority of the Bible.

This book will not be dealing with how a biblical philosophy of life (a "worldview") is derived from the Bible and applied to broader, extrabiblical areas of learning found in God's creation. In a nutshell, the Bible deals with every area of life indirectly through the grid or framework that is taken directly from the Bible. Within this biblical framework or mindset, we can examine the underlying principles of science, art, literature, politics, and recreation and evaluate them in the light of God's standards.

The Bible does not tell us exactly how to pass a test for our driver's license, but it *does* tell us that we should obey the government by having a driver's license if we drive a car. Also, it tells us that we should glorify God in everything we do, including the way in which we take the test for the driver's license. Therefore, the Bible *does* speak to every area of life in God's world, either directly (as in the case of spiritual warfare) or indirectly (as in the case of getting a driver's license).

Reliance upon experience and reason when dealing with principles of spiritual warfare is so common today that we must evaluate the role that experience and reason should play in finding the truth about spiritual warfare. We must ask the same question that Pontius Pilate asked Jesus: "What is truth?" (John 18:38). The answer to this question will enable us to learn God's principles about spiritual warfare.

What Is Truth?

Simply put, truth is what God says it is. People can find truth in God's Word. Something is true or false in terms of how it squares with what God says about it, no matter what the majority of people think on a given Gallup Poll. Truth is not a relative concept; it is absolute and universal. There is not one truth that applies to one person and an opposite truth that applies to someone else. If truth were relative, situations would exist in which principles would apply randomly to various people. For example, if two people jumped off a tall building, then one might go up toward the sky while the other one would plunge down to the pavement. Instead, all people fall down because truth is true for all people. You cannot beat Christ's clear and simple statement on this subject: "Thy word is truth" (John 17:17b).

Psalm 36:9 proclaims, "With Thee is the fountain of life; in Thy light we see light." Psalm 119:130 declares, "The unfolding of Thy words gives light; it gives understanding to the simple." The Bible tells us that we come to know truth by God's gracious revelation of Himself. We can respond to His Word either by submitting to it and thinking God's own thoughts or by rebelling against His light and thinking our own thoughts. Therefore, two basic approaches to our search for truth and knowledge exist. Either we are *dependent* upon

God and the light of His revelation or we are *independent* of God and attempt to discover truth by our own fallible thinking.

Finding the Truth

There might be two ways to *search* for truth, but there is only one way to *find* truth, and that is by taking God's word for it. In fact, because "the sum of Thy word is truth" (Ps. 119:160), to look for spiritual truth in any place other than God's Word is to guarantee that we will not find it. This point is driven home by Christ in His comments about the two ways to search for truth: "Everyone who comes to Me, and hears My words, and acts upon them . . . is like a man building a house, who dug deep and laid a foundation upon the rock" (Luke 6:47–48).

Christ is saying that stability in life starts with trust in His Word, and we must dig deep to lay a sure foundation upon the rock of God's Word. Many Christians are convinced that God's Word is true, but they do not dig deep into God's Word to build their lives upon God's bedrock of truth. The benefit of laying our foundation for life upon the rock is that "when a flood arose, the river burst against that house and could not shake it, because it had been well built" (v. 48b).

The believer who is truly grounded upon God's Word will not be wiped out by the flood of problems that we all face in life. Those who do not have confidence that God's Word is the rock will fail, along with those who have not taken the time or made the effort to dig down to the bedrock. Christ depicts "the one who has heard, and has not acted accordingly" to someone who "built a house upon the ground without any foundation; and the river burst against it and immediately it collapsed, and the ruin of that house was great" (v. 49).

The emphasis of Christ's contrast is between the one who dug down to the rock and built a proper foundation and the one who did not extend the effort to dig, but just built upon the ground without adequate preparation. Those who are not grounded upon the foundation of God's Word are not able to withstand the storms of life without suffering severe damage. When the spiritual battle heats up in their lives, they fall apart and end up living as if they were still under Satan's control. Those who are founded upon the truth find God and His Word to be more than sufficient in handling the adversities of life. When the battle comes to them, they are able to stand firm and are not tossed about by the winds of false doctrine (Eph. 4:11–14).

Which Viewpoint?

There are only two basic ways of looking at things: God's way, which we will call divine viewpoint, or man's way, which we will call human viewpoint. From beginning to end, the Bible expresses one consistent view of life and addresses every issue of life from that viewpoint—God's viewpoint on life. Understanding and applying God's viewpoint leads to capacity for life, love, and happiness, but living according to human viewpoint leads to death: "There is a way which seems right to a man, but its end is the way of death" (Prov. 14:12; 16:25).

Divine viewpoint and human viewpoint can be illustrated by the two basic approaches that a parent can use when assembling a new toy for his child's Christmas present. One approach is to read the instructions and follow the steps provided by the manufacturer who made the toy. If the instructions are clear, and if the parent has read and understood the directions, then the parent can produce a toy that is properly assembled and ready for the child to play with it. The person operating from divine viewpoint studies God's Word diligently so he can look at life through God's eyes—His Word—and apply it to his own life. What satisfying results when one follows the directions carefully!

The other approach is used when the parent either does not want to bother to read the instructions or does not want to acknowledge that he is dependent upon something or someone other than himself to do the project right. Sometimes we think that we are familiar enough with a particular kind of toy that we can rely solely on our intuition or experience to assemble it. This assumption is similar to our living on the basis of human viewpoint about life and spiritual matters. No matter the cost, we think that we must do it ourselves, without reading, understanding, and following the manufacturer's instructions. More often than not, this approach results in a toy that fails to work properly or a frustrated parent who cannot understand why the manufacturer included all of those extra parts!

Independence and Idolatry

Independence and *idolatry* are the two main reasons for adopting the human viewpoint in our search for truth. Independence—characterized by self-assertion, self-rule, or self law—forms the foundation of idolatry. In the arena of knowledge, the independent person constructs a worldview based on his own limited experience and reason. This is what Adam and Eve did, and it resulted in their tragic sin. An independent or autonomous person has an attitude of inner hostility toward God's revelation and creation (Rom. 3:10–12; 8:5–11). Because God has left His fingerprints upon virtually everything, it is not surprising to see rebellious humanity attempting to wipe off God's set of fingerprints and replace them with their own. This fact explains why unbelievers often are not even aware that they are rebelling against certain things.

Although it is true that the person who is operating on human viewpoint may include certain ideas from God's Word that are true (just as Satan did in the Garden), these ideas are always modified or interpreted to fit the person's self-determined framework. This tendency can be compared to one's taking pieces from one jigsaw puzzle to fill the gaps left by missing pieces in another puzzle. The pieces may or may not fit exactly, but in their new place they have a different meaning because they are in a different context. As Paul said in Romans 1:25, the way of the human viewpoint is to exchange "the truth of God for a lie." Never will an independent thinker bow his knee to the full authority of God's Word.

Whenever the God of the Bible is removed from the picture, something else takes His place. This is what the Bible calls idolatry. As Romans 1:18–25 makes clear, when the Creator is not the object of worship, the only candidates remaining are found in the creation. Whether the object of worship is a physical idol, an idea, or a lifestyle, ultimately it is *man* that is being worshiped because man is the one who attempts to control the situation by determining what will be worshiped. *Idolatry is the worship of anything in place of the God of the Bible.* All gods other than the God of the Bible are simply projections of man's own self. The narcissism of contemporary America is a classic example of this self-worship.

Two Pursuits of Truth

Within the realm of human viewpoint, people usually attempt to establish truth in two general ways. The first approach in attempting to find truth independent of God and His Word is often called *reason* or rationalism. In its pure form, rationalism is the belief that each person is born with certain innate ideas. The rationalist claims that, on the basis of these innate ideas, man can use reason and logic alone to discover ultimate truth. The rationalist does not believe that he must be dependent upon God's Word to think true thoughts about reality. Because rationalists do not think that they need God's Word to think accurately, they replace God's Word as the starting point with the arrogant assumption that their own logic and reason alone is sufficient for arriving at truth. What idolatry! However, because the rationalist cannot prove those innate ideas, he is left with an uncertain foundation.

Divine viewpoint does not reject the use of reason or logic—after all, God gave us a logical mind to use—but it rejects the *independent* or autonomous use of reason and logic. The divine viewpoint uses reason and logic *dependently*, starting with God's revelation as a basis for thinking God's thoughts after Him. This use is called *the dependent use of logic:* logic used under the authority of God's Word to maintain consistency of thought in accordance with God's Word. The all-knowing God has already told us through revelation what is true, and dependent logic seeks to apply this truth to every issue in life to see how it does or does not correspond with God's revelation. A person would be illogical to start with error, or a mixture of truth and error, to try to end up with truth. Only when you start with *pure truth* as a foundation can you arrive at the full truth in all of its ramifications. The psalmist declared, "In Thy light we see light" (Ps. 36:9).

The Misuse of Logic

Human viewpoint, on the other hand, uses reason and logic as the ultimate authority to determine what is possible and what is not possible. Reason is used to determine what can and cannot be, and then these conclusions are imposed on the Bible. This process is evident in the thinking of those who reject the Bible's accounts of the miraculous. Because they cannot explain miracles on the basis of their own reason, they, when reading miraculous accounts in the Bible, reject these accounts as superstitious explanations. A rationalist denies the possibility that demons could possess and influence people—if he accepts the existence of demons at all. Because he cannot arrive at the existence of demons on the basis of his own reason and logic, he rejects the unseen world entirely. Instead, he seeks to explain it in terms of some naturalistic, cause-effect theory because this is the only world he personally knows; he has rejected the witness of God's Word. This attitude elevates human reason to the position of ultimate authority: human reason determines what is and is not true in God's Word. By putting reason at a higher level than the Bible, reason replaces God and so becomes an idol.

The real conflict is not between using reason at all and not using reason at all, but between *using reason under the authority of God* and *using reason independently of God.* The true issue is *the proper place and use of logic.* Human viewpoint uses logic idolatrously, placing it in the arena reserved exclusively for God's Word.

The fatal flaw in this use of reason is that it provides *no external, objective criterion* for evaluating its conclusions (because it rejects the Bible as a valid criterion). Ultimately, this position must lapse into some form of subjectivity such as mysticism or emotionalism because reason alone can never establish an objective criterion upon which to determine why one thing is true and another thing is not true.

The rationalist rejects the resurrection of Christ as irrational by asserting that his reason is so great and his knowledge is so extensive that he knows for a fact that such a thing as resurrection could never have happened. This attitude is not only arrogant but also extremely subjective. God never intended people to use reason as a tool to establish what is ultimately true; this is the role of God's Word alone. Reason and logic were given as tools *to enable us to study God's Word and to help us think consistently in terms of it* so we may faithfully apply it in every area of our lives. We are stressing this point because it is crucial to recognize that reason and experience are miserable failures when it comes to providing sure knowledge about God, angels, the nature of man, the need for salvation, and the meaning of life. *Only the Bible provides the basis for such knowledge.* Ultimately, the consistent rationalist must reject the existence of God, angels, and demons because he has no way of verifying their existence.

Misusing Experience

Because independent reason cannot serve as a basis for arriving at the truth about God, angels, man, salvation, and the meaning of life, philosophers have searched elsewhere for a solid rock on which to build their views. This second human-viewpoint approach to truth is often called *experience* or *empiricism*, and it is the backbone of the scientific method. Empiricists believe that one can attain knowledge of ultimate truth on the basis of sense perceptions. They claim that by observing, collecting facts, forming hypotheses, testing hypotheses, and further testing of sense data man can ultimately arrive at true knowledge about the existence of God, angels, the nature of man, salvation, and the meaning of life.

Although the empirical approach—when used correctly—does have a place within the plan of God, human viewpoint once again misuses God's intended purpose for this ability. Through the use of empiricism in science people can make many important observations about God's creation. Empirical observations have helped propel great advances in industry and technology in the last two centuries. Yet, without a framework that consistently interprets and applies the results of empirical observations, competing and contradictory systems of thought develop. Furthermore, man's experience, even when it is extended through historical witness and instruments to observe the microscopic, is still limited. Only the Word of God provides an adequate basis for consistently evaluating and applying the results of empiricism.

Ants and Angels

If we rely solely on empiricism apart from biblical revelation, we will not always draw accurate conclusions. A look at the work habits and social behavior of ants provides an interesting illustration. One observer would note that there are multiple mates for any one female. Another person might observe that the ants are industrious workers. Without the biblical framework, human-viewpoint thinkers could take both observations and apply them to human society. In fact, some modern sociologists have done just that by observing the rarity of monogamy in the animal kingdom and suggesting that multiple mates would be a better situation in human life, thereby rejecting the biblical idea of one mate until death. In contrast to the subjectivity of this approach, the Bible gives us the framework for rightly applying the data discovered through observation. We are to learn from the ants in their diligence, but not in their mating habits (Prov. 6:6–11).

This same principle applies in the area of the existence of angels and demons. The empiricist will gather all of the information he can from those who claim to have had some experience with an angel or a demon, or those who have helped deliver people from demonic influence. He will find out what they learned from these encounters and which methods, in their opinion, proved successful in delivering a person from the demonic oppression. He will collect these case studies and then draw conclusions about what we are to do when we encounter a demon. Even when he does consult the Bible in this process, no matter how high the empiricist's view of Scripture, in practice he treats the Bible as just another voice or witness to demonic activity. This assumption always results in his adjusting the biblical teaching on demons until it fits with the conclusions of various experiences.

Adding to Scripture

Numerous problems exist with the pure empirical method, but the fundamental problem is a rejection of the complete sufficiency of Scripture. Rather than believing that the Bible tells us everything we need to know about angels and demons, the empiricist seeks to find out more. Rather than being satisfied with what God has said on the subject, the empiricist bases his understanding of demons on experiences that he or other people have had. This insistence ultimately leads to much speculation about demons: what they do, what they look like, what their names are, how to perform exorcisms, and how to protect ourselves from demons. We should remember that the Bible expressly forbids such speculation because it goes beyond the information contained in the Scriptures (1 Cor. 4:6; 1 Tim. 1:4; 2 Tim. 2:23).

One writer demonstrates this contemporary use of experience over Scripture in his treatment of spiritual warfare with territorial spirits. He suggests that even as it is a common practice to discover the names of specific demons to deliver an afflicted individual, "it might be reasonable to postulate that it could also be done with territorial spirits."[1] Experience is then relied upon to determine the names of territorial spirits.

Latin American Rita Cabezas has done considerable research on the names of the highest levels of the hierarchy of Satan. I will not at this point describe her research methodology except to mention that the beginning stages were associated with her extensive psychological/deliverance practice and that it later evolved into receiving revelatory words of knowledge. She has discovered that directly under Satan are six worldwide principalities that are named (allowing that this was done in Spanish) Damian, Asmodeo, Menguelesh, Arios, Beelzebub, and Nosferasteus. Under each principality, she reports, are six governors over each nation. For example, those over Costa Rica are Shiebo, Quiebo, Ameneo, Mephistopheles, Nostradamus, and Azazel. Those over the United States are Ralphes, Anoritho, Manchester, Apolion, Deviltook, and one unnamed governor.[2]

Like any good empiricist, this writer does not fully rely upon this information alone but seeks verification. But verification is found only circumstantially in the Bible. Considered as having equal validity with the Bible are the *Dictionary of Gods and Goddesses, Devils, and Demons*, the Apocrypha, *Paradise Lost*, and *The Pilgrim's Progress* (which are the other sources used to validate the preceding statement). The whole statement is treated as having credibility simply because two of the names happen to have been mentioned in the Bible.

Borderline Spiritism

This type of activity comes dangerously close to spiritism, in which information gained either directly or indirectly from demonic encounters is made a part of teaching on demons. In the same paper on territorial spirits, the author accepts as valid the information received from a former occult leader regarding the number of demons and their operations in Nigeria.[3] This information was acquired while he was an occult leader, and so its source is demonic. We must remember that Satan is a liar and a deceiver. Methods that he and the demons use are often designed to confuse and distract Christians by getting them involved in illegitimate areas, with the result that they unwittingly end up serving Satan's ends rather than God's ends. An extreme example of this situation occurred in the mid-1970s. A man named John found wide acceptance in certain Christian circles by giving people "inside information" about Satan and his current schemes (to which he had had access as a former Satanist). His teachings included such information as the proper names of some of the demons, how they are organized, and certain of their strategies and tactics. None of this information was gleaned from the Bible; rather, it was gained from the time the man spent as a Satanist (upon which time he relied even as a believer). Many people within Christian circles were eager to listen to this information gleaned from demons until they learned that the occult expert had fabricated much of what he was saying while simultaneously seducing young Christian girls.

Deceptions and Discrepancies

We are so limited in our ability truly to discern what is taking place in the spirit realm that we are often completely distracted and in some cases downright duped. Several years ago, an associate of ours whom we will call Bill was involved in counseling a woman whose background was marked by years of sexual abuse. From early childhood she had been raped and sexually abused by her father. When she was in her twenties, she heard the gospel and put her faith in Jesus Christ as her Savior. Although saved, she still struggled with many issues rooted in her past. During the time that Bill was counseling her, he discussed her case with a pastor from Fort Worth, who suggested that the reason this girl had never had victory over these past problems was demonic influence or possession. He believed that demons were involved in every case of sexual abuse and suggested an exorcism.

One night, Bill and the woman met with three pastors in Fort Worth for an exorcism. They apparently contacted seven different demons, which they then cast out of her. The woman went home much relieved; however, her "healing" had only short-term results because she still had problems.

Several months later, Bill discovered a series of discrepancies in the woman's account of her life, and he began to question if any sexual abuse had ever occurred in the first place. He and another man who had also counseled her then confronted her with the evidence, and she admitted that most of what she had said and done was made up. When they asked her about the exorcism episode, she finally admitted that it had all been an act motivated by her confusion and what she perceived to be the expectations of her counselors.

Since then, we have discovered that this woman has had a long history of using her problems as a means of gaining attention and care from other Christians. Over a period of several years, she has gone from church to church and from group to group with the sad story of her life. Each time, some concerned and caring Christians have taken her in to help her. However, each time they discovered her deception, and then she would drop out of sight temporarily only to surface again at another church. She is now under the care of a nationally known biblical counselor. According to him, she was never demon possessed or demon influenced in the first place, and the whole episode only served to complicate an already-complex spiritual problem.

The Failure of Secular Systems

The point of this story is to show that two groups of people, both of whom claim to be biblical, attempted to help an unfortunate woman. In one case, the solution was sought through a demonic deliverance; in the other case, the solution was sought through the use of Scripture in counseling. We are not attempting here to decide whether this girl was ever demonized; the point we are making is that one particular group of pastors, who had had years of experience in a deliverance ministry and had developed a technique of dealing with demonized people based on experience, were apparently fooled.

(If they were not, then their empirically developed deliverance techniques were a failure.) Anytime we base a technique for dealing with demonized people on anything other than the clear teaching of the Word of God, we are doomed to failure. In fact, using any approach based on information not directly derived from the Scriptures is, in practice, a denial of the authority and sufficiency of the Bible. These examples simply show the inadequacy of personal experience in validating demon possession.

In the last two centuries, many philosophical systems have sought to combine rationalism and empiricism. However, if neither of these two methods can arrive at certainty about God and the spiritual realm on their own, combining them will not solve the problem either. Rationalism and empiricism both fail to provide an adequate basis for objectively verifying knowledge about the spiritual realm. How then *can* we know about the existence of God and angels and about the nature of man, salvation, and the meaning of life?

The Only True Basis

The only trustworthy basis for knowledge about the supernatural is God's revelation. Because man is incapable of arriving at ultimate truth through his own resources, whether through reason or sense data, he must rely upon God's revelation. In Romans 1, Paul tells us that although human beings have a clear testimony of God in the creation all around them, they reject that evidence because they are sinners: "That which is known about God is evident within them; for God made it evident to them. For since the creation of the world His invisible attributes, His eternal power and divine nature, have been clearly seen, being understood through what has been made, so that they are without excuse. For even though they knew God, they did not honor Him as God, or give thanks; but they became futile in their speculations, and their foolish heart was darkened" (Rom. 1:19-21).

The effect of Adam's sin on the abilities of the human mind is extensive and must never be underestimated when one is discussing the issue of knowing truth. The preceding passage from Roman 1 tells us that man's heart is darkened. Romans 3:11-12 says, "There is none who understands, there is none who seeks for God; All have turned aside, together they have become useless; there is none who does good, there is not even one." Paul again stresses the effects of sin in Romans 8:7–8: "The mind set on the flesh is hostile toward God; for it does not subject itself to the law of God, for it is not even able to do so; and those who are in the flesh cannot please God."

God describes the effect of sin on man in a number of different ways: He says that the unsaved are in darkness, that Satan works within them, that they are blind and ignorant, that they willfully suppress the truth, and that they are enslaved to sin and unrighteousness. The only path out of this predicament is the lucid Word of God.

The Only Deliverer

The eighth chapter of the Gospel of John tells us of a very important dialogue between Jesus and some of the Jewish leaders. In that exchange, He said, "You shall know the truth, and the truth shall make you free" (v. 32). It is *the Word of God* that brings light into darkness and tells us everything we need to know about sin and Satan and how to be set free from them. Remember Psalm 119:130, which we noted earlier: "The unfolding of Thy words gives light; it gives understanding to the simple."

Some Pharisees who were in the crowd objected to Christ's statement, claiming that because they were Abraham's offspring they did not need to be liberated. In fact, however, they were enslaved in at least four ways: They were in bondage to the Roman Empire, they were in bondage to the religious traditions of the Pharisees, they were in bondage to Satan, and they were in bondage to sin. Jesus stated that the only means of freedom was through Him: "If therefore the Son shall make you free, you shall be free indeed" (John 8:36).

The only source of deliverance from bondage is Jesus Christ. According to Colossians 1:13, all people are born in the domain of darkness. But through faith in Jesus Christ we are delivered from the domain of darkness and transferred to the kingdom of Jesus Christ. If you have never taken the opportunity to put your faith alone in Christ alone, you, too, are enslaved to sin and Satan, and the only way you can be free is to trust in Jesus Christ as your Savior.

The Equipment You Need

We hope that you have seen in this chapter that as God's creatures we are dependent upon His Word alone as the sole basis for evaluating our thoughts and experiences in relationship to everything, but especially those things with which He has dealt specifically, such as God, angels, demons, the nature of man, the need for salvation, and the meaning of life. Although most Christians agree in theory that God's Word is sufficient to deal with the issues of Christian living, more and more Christians are denying the sufficiency of God's Word in daily practice. Rather than relying on the Bible alone, they seek more information about Satan and demons and end up relying upon information gained from former occult leaders and from various experiences with demons. This information is then taught to Christians as biblical doctrine when, in fact, its source is demonic (read 1 Tim. 4:1).

In subsequent chapters, we will show that God's Word alone is sufficient to equip you to be a winner in your struggle against the world, the flesh, and the Devil.

3

ORIGINS OF CONFLICT

*You said in your heart, "I will ascend to heaven; I will
raise my throne above the stars of God, and I will sit on the
mount of assembly in the recesses of the north. I will ascend
above the heights of the clouds; I will make myself like the
Most High."*

—Isaiah 14:13–14

A glimpse of the evening news or the daily newspaper reminds us
that evil is a very real problem in this world. War, rape, murder,
famine, terrorism, and child abuse all reveal to us that life is not what
it ought to be or what we expect it to be. All people seem to have this
awareness. Not only is life different from what it ought to be in the
hopes and dreams of humanity but also natural disasters such as
floods, hurricanes, tornadoes, and earthquakes all testify that even
in the realm of nature things are not what they ought to be. How did
things get so messed up? Is this just the way it happens to be, simply
the product of our naturally evolving impersonal universe, or is there
something more to it?

Four Explanations

When we are confronted with the existence of evil, only four possible explanations can be offered. The first three explanations resolve
the problem of evil on the basis of finite human rationalism, empiri-

cism, or a combination of the two apart from the Scriptures. The first explanation denies the ultimate reality of evil; present suffering is merely an illusion. This view is reflected in the thinking of the Greek philosophy of Platonism, some Eastern religions, and most mind-science religions (such as Christian Science).[1] Sometimes these systems of thought claim to be dualistic, recognizing some form of evil. At best, they only give evil lip service. Because ultimate reality in those systems is "one," they must—to be consistent—deny the ultimate existence of real evil. According to this first answer, the suffering and misery that we encounter in everyday life is simply an illusion; it is not reality. Pain and suffering are merely delusions because we fail to have the right knowledge; true reality exists on some higher plane.

A second way to resolve the problem of evil denies the existence of morality. This view rejects the sense of a moral "ought." Evil, suffering, and misery are simply natural parts of the natural universe, and all that *is* must be good. Darwinian evolution asserts the survival of the fittest, a principle that necessitates that struggle and death are the normal realities of the universe; therefore, there is no good or bad, just relative differences. Some states are better than others. Because everything is relative, no basis exists for morality, for distinguishing between good and evil. T. H. Huxley, noted evolutionist and "Darwin's bulldog," clearly recognized this principle:

> The thief and murderer follow nature just as much as the philanthropist. Cosmic evolution may teach us how the good and evil tendencies of man may have come about: but, in itself, it is incompetent to furnish any better reason why what we call good is preferable to what we call evil than we had before.[2]

Huxley was consistent with his naturalistic assumptions.

A third way by which people have sought to resolve the problem of evil is simply to resign themselves to accept this tension as part of the absurdity of life. This is the answer of modern existentialism, which says that there are no rational explanations for life, so just enjoy your life despite its irrationality. Frank Sinatra's popular song "That's Life" embodies this approach. He sings, "You're riding high in April, shot down in May." The rest of the song conveys the idea that you just have to learn to roll with the punches because that is simply the nature of life, so you just roll with the punches.

In contrast to these attempts to resolve the problem of evil on the basis of the independent use of human reason and experience, the Bible clearly teaches that evil is neither an illusion nor natural. God's original creation was holy and perfect and devoid of evil. Perfect God can create only perfection. Evil in the universe is the direct consequence of the sin of the angelic creature Lucifer; thus, evil and suffering are not normal but abnormal, introduced by the rebellious decision of the creature. This sin, this act of rebellion on the part of the creature, introduced discord into the universe and initiated the angelic rebellion against God, the invisible war in the heavenly realm. It is in this cosmic conflict that the human race is enmeshed. Autonomous human reason and experience cannot reveal this to us, only the infallible revelation of God in the Bible can do that.

How the War Began

Before we can begin to understand our role in this war, why we are involved, and what we should do about it, we must first understand how the war began. The Bible clearly reveals Lucifer's attempt to establish his own rebel kingdom in defiance of God. From the biblical account of this takeover plot we learn of Lucifer's goals and strategies, his abilities, how he subverted the human race and brought them under his authority and kingdom, and how God provided a way for the human race to renounce their allegiance to this evil ruler. By turning to God when we accept His free offer of salvation in Jesus Christ we are rebelling against the unholiness and evil of Satan and his kingdom. At that instant, we are transferred from the dominion of Satan to the kingdom of God (Acts 26:18).

The Bible tells us that Satan is the prince of darkness, the "ruler of this world" (John 12:31; 16:11) and the "god of this world" (2 Cor. 4:4). During this present time, God has allowed Satan to have his own realm, domain, or kingdom, and Satan's kingdom of darkness wages intense war against God's kingdom of light. *Light* and *dark-*

ness are often used in the Bible as figures of speech for God's kingdom (*light* in 1 Tim. 6:16; 1 John 1:5, 7) and Satan's kingdom, respectively (*darkness* in Luke 22:53; Eph. 5:8; 6:12; 1 Peter 2:9). Satan is the archenemy of every believer. Scripture clearly teaches that everyone is originally born in Satan's "domain of darkness" (Col. 1:13; cf. Acts 26:18). The original Greek word for *domain (exousia)* means "authority." When we are born, we are under the authority of Satan, who is the god of this world (2 Cor. 4:4); yet, when we turn to God at the point of salvation by trusting in Jesus Christ as our Savior, this same verse says that we are transferred to the kingdom of His beloved Son. The allegiance of the Christian is now given to God rather than to Satan. Christians have become holy rebels against the god of this age. If we are going to be champions for God in this spiritual warfare, we must understand exactly what the Bible teaches about Satan, how he became Satan, and his goal for planet Earth.

The Sons of God

The first creatures that God created to inhabit His kingdom were an order of rational, spirit beings called angels. Both the Greek *angelos* and the Hebrew *mal'ak* mean "messenger," indicating one of the roles of these remarkable creatures. One of the oldest books of the Bible tells us of Job, who faced an incredible number of personal tragedies. After resisting the bad advice of friends and family to blame his suffering on his own failures or to "curse God and die," Job finally succumbed and began to question the goodness and judgment of God. When God replied to Job, He never explained to Job the reason for the adversity, but, through a series of questions, God focused Job's attention on his own limitations in contrast to the Lord's essence and right to rule creation according to His perfect knowledge. Hidden in these questions are insights into the original creation of the universe:

> Where were you when I laid the foundation of the earth!
> Tell Me, if you have understanding,
> Who set its measurements, since you know?
> Or who stretched the line on it?
> On what were its bases sunk?
> Or who laid its cornerstone,

> When the morning stars sang together,
> And all the sons of God shouted for joy?[3]

At the time of the creation of the earth, all of the angels were still unified. The term "sons of God" is an expression used in the Old Testament to refer to angels.[4] There was no hint of division or rebellion, no pride, no one trying to outdo anyone else. They *all* rejoiced together over God's new creation!

The Highest of the Angels

This unity soon dissolved. At some point, a tragic split occurred among the angelic host. The highest of all of the angels, Lucifer, decided that he wanted to be like God. When God removed this rebellious angel from his position of authority, Lucifer gathered a group of other angels and led a revolt against God. Two passages in Scripture describe these events, revealing critical information about Lucifer/Satan (Ezek. 28:11–19; Isa. 14:12–15). Understanding the principles that are revealed in these passages will help us know our enemy and avoid falling into his traps. Nowhere in the Scripture is any indication that he has changed since that day of rebellion.

The prophet Ezekiel describes this calamitous event (Ezek. 28:11–19). At the beginning of this chapter, Ezekiel is instructed to take up a lament against the prince or leader of the city of Tyre (vv. 1–10). In this funeral dirge, Ezekiel pronounces judgment upon the prince of Tyre because he has said in his heart that he is a god. In verses 11–19, a second lament is taken up, but here it is directed not to the *prince* of Tyre but to the *king* of Tyre, clearly a different personage. The things said of this king of Tyre could not possibly apply to a human leader of Tyre. For example, he is said to have existed in Eden, the garden of God (v. 13) and to have been created blameless (v. 15). The individual addressed in this section is the real power behind the human king of Tyre: Satan or Lucifer. Often in Scripture Satan is addressed through the creature that he influences. For example, when Jesus foretold His crucifixion, Peter began to rebuke Him. But Jesus rebuked Peter and said, "Get behind Me, Satan!" (Matt. 16:23). Peter was not possessed by Satan at that point; nothing in the language of the text would suggest that. Peter voiced an objection that represented the agenda of Satan to forestall the saving work of Christ on the cross. Because he represented Satan's agenda, Christ addressed the ultimate problem behind the objection, Satan. A second example is when God pronounced a curse on Satan in Genesis 3:14–15. There, God addressed Satan indirectly through the serpent. So the "king of Tyre" mentioned here is none other than Satan himself.

Here is how Ezekiel describes Lucifer in 28:12–16:

> Take up a lamentation over the king of Tyre, and say to him, "Thus says the Lord God, 'You had the seal of perfection, full of wisdom and perfect in beauty. You were in Eden, the garden of God; every precious stone was your covering: the ruby, the topaz, and the diamond; the beryl, the onyx, and the jasper; the lapis lazuli, the turquoise, and the emerald; and the gold, the workmanship of your settings and sockets, was in you. On the day that you were created they were prepared. You were the anointed cherub who covers, and I placed you there. You were on the holy mountain of God; you walked in the midst of the stones of fire. You were blameless in your ways from the day you were created, until unrighteousness was found in you. By the abundance of your trade you were internally filled with violence, and you sinned; therefore I have cast you as profane from the mountain of God. And I have destroyed you, O covering cherub, from the midst of the stones of fire.'

Before his fall, Lucifer was a magnificent creature, the most incredible of all God's handiwork.

Model of Perfection

This awesome creature is *the model* or *prototype of perfection*. He is described as "having the seal of perfection," which in the Hebrew has the idea of one who sets the standard. Just as the national standard for all measurement is in the National Bureau of Standards, so Lucifer was the ultimate standard of perfection. This quality highlights his superiority over all other creatures. Later, in verse 15, we are told that he was blameless, or perfect, in all his ways.

As the prototype or pattern of perfection, he was also the most beautiful and glorious of the angels; he was "full of beauty." His appearance was nothing less than magnificent, and this was further enhanced by his dress. His splendid personal adornment indicated the most elevated of creaturely positions. His raiment was adorned with a brilliant collection of precious stones. Whenever these jewels are mentioned together in Scripture, they have something to do with the very presence of God. If you were a Jew at that time, this description would instantly remind you of the uniform of the High Priest of Israel. Eight of the nine jewels were in the breastplate worn by the High Priest of Israel (Exod. 28:17–20) and six are also found in the foundation stones of the wall of the New Jerusalem (Rev. 21:19–20).

Another way that Lucifer exemplified perfection was in his intelligence, for he was "full of wisdom." Wisdom in the Bible is not simply vast academic knowledge but the ability to apply that information skillfully to produce incomparable art that glorifies God. No other of God's creatures has matched his intelligence, understanding, and skill.

Not only did he have looks and brains but he also possessed the power and authority to go with these qualities. He was "the anointed cherub." The word *anointed* means "one who is set apart to God for a special task." This is the same word that is transliterated *Messiah* and is rendered in English by the word *Christ* in the New Testament. Lucifer is the first creature ever designated as "the anointed one." In Scripture, three groups of people were anointed: prophets, priests, and kings. Prophets speak God's word to people, priests carry the worship of the people to God, and kings rule over subjects. Before he sinned, Lucifer functioned as a prophet, a priest, and a king. He was the ruler of the angels and led them in their worship and praise of God.

An Anointed Cherub

Lucifer was a cherub, one of the highest ranks of angels associated with the glory and presence of God. When God instructed Moses to build the ark of the covenant, He told him to place on top of it two cherubs looking down upon the mercy seat (Exod. 37:9). Their wings were to *cover* the mercy seat, and this is the same word for covering that is used here in Ezekiel 28:13–14. Typically, the image that comes to mind when people hear cherubs mentioned is that of a baby with wings. This absurd notion has no basis at all in Scripture but was the innovation of medieval artists. Scripture has a completely different description of cherubs:

> This was their appearance: they had human form. Each of them had four faces and four wings. And their legs were straight and their feet were like a calf's hoof, and they gleamed like burnished bronze. Under their wings on their four sides were human hands. As for the faces and wings of the four of them, their wings touched one another. Their faces did not turn when they moved; each went straight forward. As for the form of their faces, each had the face of a man, all four had the face of a lion on the right and the face of a bull on the left, and all four had the face of an eagle. (Ezekiel 1:5–10)

Images of cherubs were also embroidered on the veil or screen which separated the innermost room of the tabernacle, the Holy of Holies, from the outer room, the Holy Place. They were earthly symbols of God's heavenly throne room. The word for "veil" is the same word that is translated "covering." Apparently, Lucifer's position in the throne room of God involved personally covering the throne of God with his wings. He held a very exalted position indeed!

That Lucifer operated in the very presence of God is further emphasized by the statements that he was in "Eden, the garden of God." *Eden* could refer to the earthly Garden of Eden, but the context here indicates the heavenly throne of God because he was "on the holy mountain of God" and "walked in the midst of the stones of fire" (a phrase used of God's presence).

As far as a creature can be said to be perfect, this one was. His appearance was so impressive and brilliant that Isaiah referred to him as "Lucifer" (14:12 KJV), which means "lightbearer" and was a reference to the morning star, the planet Venus. This luminary announces the coming of the sun by its reflection of the sun's light. In the same way, Satan appears to have been the herald of God through his reflections of God's glory.

Turning Point

Perfect God can create nothing less than perfection. God did not originate evil; evil originated from the disobedient choice of the creature. The reason is given in the next verse (Ezek. 28:16): "By the abundance of your trade you were internally filled with violence, and you sinned." If we read between the lines a little, we see Ezekiel's analogy with the culture of Tyre—a maritime power whose economy was built upon trade. Because the people of Tyre excelled as merchants and had a positive trade balance that elevated them above other nations, they sought to take advantage of this fact to build their own kingdom. Apparently, part of Lucifer's responsibility was to carry the worship of the angelic hosts to God in his priestly function, and in so doing he began to trade on his influence to build his own kingdom. When Lucifer sinned, Satan's career began. The exact nature of this sin is further described by the prophet Isaiah.

The Lord commanded Isaiah to "take up this taunt against the king of Babylon" (Isa. 14:4). A "taunt" was a discourse designed to humble those who have rebelled against God. As in the Ezekiel passage, the taunt is directed against a human king, but the statements go far beyond the sin of any human king.

> How you have fallen from heaven, O star of the morning, son of the dawn! You have been cut down to the earth, you who have weakened the nations! But you said in your heart, "I will ascend to heaven; I will raise my throne above the stars of God, and I will sit on the mount of assembly in the recesses of the north. I will ascend above the heights of the clouds; I will make myself like the Most High." Nevertheless you will be thrust down to Sheol, to the recesses of the pit. (Isaiah 14:12–15)

Sin began not with an external act but with the internal decision of his soul. Five times Satan said, "I will. . . ." These statements reveal the essence of sin: the assertion of the creature's right to self-determination, independence from God, or personal autonomy. This fact explains why the autonomous or independent use of reason, experience, or anything else is an expression of rebellion against God.

The Ultimate in Self-Esteem

Lucifer became so impressed with his own beauty, brilliance, intelligence, power, and position that he began to desire for himself the honor and glory that belonged to God alone. No creature ever felt better about himself or had a better self-image than Satan. He was no longer satisfied with obeying God; instead, he wanted to overthrow God and be God himself. Filled with the violence of rebellion, he rejected the authority of God in his life, ignored the fact that he was who he was only because God had made him that way, and led a revolt against God. The result was judgment. He was cast away as profane (Ezek. 28:16). Profane is the opposite of holy; Lucifer became unholy because of his rebellion.

Lucifer's fall was the result of his decision to strive after self-exaltation, to assert his own position rather than to remain in a position of service to God. In other words, he gave in to arrogance and pride. (The New Testament constantly reminds Christians to avoid arrogance as the sin of the Devil [1 Tim. 3:6] and that God is against the arrogant [1 Peter 5:5]).

When Lucifer sinned, he did not sin alone but led a massive angelic revolt against God. As he carried out his commerce among the angels, he began to entice and seduce a number of them to serve him rather than God. When he sinned and was judged by God, these angels followed him, and the insurrection mushroomed. Scripture indicates that about a third of the angels followed him in his rebellion (Rev. 12:4). These fallen or unholy angels are referred to in the Scripture as demons, evil spirits, or unclean spirits.[5]

What's in a Name?

Throughout the Scriptures, we find that names and titles indicate something about a person's character. For example, Isaiah 9:6 records a prophecy about Jesus Christ that gives us four titles that describe

His character: "His name will be called Wonderful Counselor, Mighty God, Eternal Father, Prince of Peace." These names tell us about the character of the Messiah. *Wonderful Counselor* refers to the Messiah, who will bring counsel for eternal life and will rule with perfect wisdom (Isa. 11:2). *Mighty God* identifies Him with the power of God, which will ultimately be victorious over evil. *Eternal Father* is a poor translation, for the Messiah is not God the Father. A better translation is "father of eternity," a Hebrew idiom indicating that this personage would possess the attribute of eternality, an attribute unique to deity. *Prince of Peace* indicates that He is the one who brings peace, both personal and, eventually, when He inaugurates the Davidic kingdom at the Second Coming, worldwide.

Just as we learn many important things about the Lord Jesus Christ from the titles and names given to Him, so we also learn much about Satan from the titles and names given to him. It is important for us to examine these so we can accurately understand what he can do and his role in this age.

Serpent, dragon. In the Garden of Eden, a serpent appeared to Eve and tempted her to disobey the command of God. Genesis 3:1 tells us that "the serpent was more crafty than any beast of the field which the Lord God had made." The identity of this serpent is made clear in Revelation 12:9: "The great dragon was thrown down, the serpent of old who is called the devil and Satan, who deceives the whole world. . . ." This passage certainly tells us something about his character. In the creation account of man in Genesis 1:26, God made man to rule *over* the birds and *over* the cattle and *over* all the earth and *over* every creeping thing. Man was to rule *over* the serpent; yet, the serpent was crafty enough to subvert this authority by getting man to listen and submit to him. We must remember that Satan was created full of wisdom. His guile and cunning is so great that he is able to confuse and deceive man to do his bidding if man does not trust exclusively in God's Word.

Satan, Devil, accuser of the brethren. Our word *devil* derives from the Greek word *diabolos*, which means "slanderer" or "accuser." In Revelation 12:10, Satan is called "the accuser of our brethren." A slanderer is one who makes false charges or tells lies that are intended to defame and to damage someone's reputation. *Satan* translates the Hebrew *shatan*, which means "adversary" or "opponent." Satan opposes God's people in two ways. First, he brings charges against believers before God (Zech. 3:1; Rom. 8:33). Second, Satan accuses believers to their own conscience. His goal is to make us focus on our sin and failures and to get us wrapped up in our attempts to deal with it on our own. Self-absorption is the first step on the slippery slope of arrogance. By focusing on our failures, we forget that sin is no longer the issue for the believer.

Every sin was paid for by Jesus Christ on the cross. His substitutionary death on the cross is the basis for our continual cleansing for all sins committed after salvation (1 John 1:7). Post-salvation sins do not cause us to lose salvation but merely disrupt our fellowship with a holy, righteous God. The prescription is clear: when we admit or acknowledge our sin to God the Father, then He instantly forgives us (1 John 1:9). The slate is wiped clean, God no longer remembers that sin. "I, even I, am the one who wipes out your transgressions for My own sake, and I will not remember your sins" (Isa. 43:25; cf. Ps. 103:12).

When we become absorbed with past failures in guilt and remorse, we are rejecting the grace of God and His promised forgiveness. By focusing on self, we follow Satan in his sin. Such self-absorption is the starting point for arrogance. We forget that for the Christian sin is no longer the issue; it is paid for by Christ. The issue is spiritual growth, advancing toward spiritual maturity, not self-flagellation over past failures (Phil. 3:13). No matter how heinous our offense, we still possess the imputed, perfect righteousness of Christ. God looks upon us as righteous because of the righteousness of Christ that has been given to us. To realize our forgiveness sets us free from debilitating guilt feelings and frees us to advance in our spiritual life.

Accused but Forgiven

A beautiful illustration of how God responds to Satan's accusations is found in Zechariah 3:1–5, where Zechariah had a vision of the heavenly courtroom. God is the Supreme Judge of heaven and earth, and Joshua the High Priest of Israel stands before God. Satan stands as

the accuser, the witness for the prosecution. The response of the Lord
is to rebuke Satan as he indicts Joshua. The Lord reminds the court
that Joshua has been "plucked from the fire," that is, saved from
eternal condemnation in the lake of fire. Joshua, like all sinners,
stands before God dressed in the filthy clothes of his sin. But God in
His grace has clothed Joshua with clean garments of perfect, divine
righteousness and a clean turban about his head. As a recipient of
God's grace, he is free from guilt and should no longer be troubled by
Satan's accusations.

What a marvelous picture of what God does for every believer in
the Lord Jesus Christ! Satan stands as our accuser. From one perspective, he has every right to do this for, like Joshua, we once stood
before God dressed in the filthy garments of our sin. Isaiah 64:6 says
that "all our righteous deeds are like a filthy garment." However, the
instant that we trust in Jesus Christ, God graciously dresses us in His
righteousness, so that we are no longer guilty and Satan has no ground
to accuse us (Rom. 4:3-4; 2 Cor. 5:21). This is the message of 1 John
1:1-2:2, which tells us that the substitutionary death of Christ on the
cross is the basis for our forgiveness of sin in time and eternity and
that as believers we have a defense attorney before the bar of divine
justice to defend us against the charges of the accuser—Satan.

If you are not a Christian, this passage means that no matter what
you have done you can obtain complete forgiveness of sin by trusting
in Jesus Christ alone. If you are a Christian, this passage means that
when Satan seeks to accuse you, planting doubts in your mind because you have sinned or rebelled against God, you can stand firm on
God's promise that you have been clothed with the righteousness of
Christ and that for His sake God has forgiven you. There is then no
need to cave in to guilt or to a defeatist mentality; to do so is a denial of
God's promise that He cleanses us and forgives us of all unrighteousness
(1 John 1:9).

More Sinister Names

The ruler of this world. Twice the Lord Jesus Christ refers to Satan
thus (John 12:31; 14:30). The word *world* here is translated from the
Greek word *kosmos,* which encompasses the entire world system, in-

cluding all of the ideas and philosophies that Satan promotes among people to establish his kingdom on the earth. Some of the more popular of these ideas today are evolution, psychology, materialism, Marxism, pragmatism, secular humanism, moral relativism, and New Age mysticism.

More will be said in the next chapter, but here we want to remind every Christian that Satan is the ruler of this world system, that we were born under his authority (cf. Acts 26:18 with Col. 1:13), and that when we believed in Jesus Christ as our Savior and Redeemer we committed the unforgivable sin as far as Satan is concerned. We declared our allegiance to the King of Kings and Lord of Lords and became rebels against Satan's illegitimate authority on this earth. He is now out to get us, and the only way we can successfully survive is by following the explicit instructions of Scripture.

Prince of the power of the air. This title is given to Satan in Ephesians 2:2. It is related to the title "ruler of this world" and refers to the atmosphere. Within God's permission, Satan has control of man's environment; he is still in operational control of planet Earth. This verse also points out that he is the spirit who is now working in the "sons of disobedience," the unbelievers. Every person, every unbeliever is born under the authority of Satan as the ruler of this world, is influenced by him because he is the controller of the environment, and has Satan working in and through him. Because unbelievers are subjects in his domain, they may still be used by him to gain his nefarious ends.

God of this age. This title is closely tied to the two previous titles and is found in 2 Corinthians 4:4. It is during this age, between the fall of Adam and Eve and the coming of Christ, that God has given Satan the freedom to propagate his worldly system. This verse goes on to say that he is blinding the unsaved to the truth. One reason unbelievers do not understand the truth of the gospel message is that they are being blinded by Satan. The only way to overcome this tactic is through the teaching ministry of God the Holy Spirit, who enlightens people to the truth of the Word of God.

Evil one. Several passages (Matt. 6:13; John 17:15; 2 Thess. 3:3; 1 John 5:19) refer to Satan by this title. In these verses, we learn that in spite of his beauty, intelligence, and power, Satan is evil. Often his evil is a beautiful evil, attractive to mankind, and not merely an ugly evil, as is often thought. His evil pervades the whole world because it all lies in his power. Yet, as rebels against this incredibly evil personage, we have the protection of the Lord Jesus Christ. In His present role as our intercessor, Christ prays that we be kept from the evil one. We are also promised that because of His faithfulness we will be strengthened and protected from the evil one (2 Thess. 3:3).

Tempter. Matthew 4:3 gives this title to Satan when it tells how the Holy Spirit led our Lord Jesus into the wilderness to be tempted by the Devil. This is what is called *objective* temptation. Satan entices and lures people to do his will. He sets the trap and baits it well, but he does not have the power to make anyone step into it. We can fall prey to his temptation only when we *choose* to do so. The reason we so choose and Jesus did not is that we allow our sin nature to control us and willingly fall into Satan's trap. The internal or *subjective* side of temptation is described in James 1:14: "Each one is tempted when he is carried away and enticed by his own lust." If we are to avoid the traps and spot the bait, we must do what Scripture says to control our sinful nature. (We will discuss this issue in a later chapter.)

Roaring lion. First Peter 5:8 warns every Christian to be of sober spirit, which means to have the right mind set, objective thinking based on God's Word; not to be distracted but to be constantly alert because "your adversary, the devil, prowls about like a roaring lion, seeking someone to devour." This passage also gives us the advice that we need to avoid these attacks. (We will also discuss this in a later chapter.)

Deceiver. Paul referred to the deceptiveness of Satan and warned the Corinthians about it in 2 Corinthians 11:3. If Eve, who did not have a sin nature, was deceived by the craftiness of Satan, how much easier it is for believers who *do* possess a sin nature to be deceived! This deception may take any number of forms, but one form to which Paul refers in this chapter is *religious deception.* He warns us that, in his role as deceiver, Satan disguises himself as an "angel of light" and as a "servant of righteousness" (2 Cor. 11:14–15). Satan has the power to deceive even through miracles and signs and wonders. In fact, this is the very tool that he will use to deceive many people into following the coming Antichrist (2 Thess. 2:9–12). Jesus also warned that many who appear to be Christians and who even healed people, cast out demons, and performed many miracles *in His name* will be told by Him at the last judgment to depart because He never knew them (Matt. 7:21–23). The only way by which Christians can avoid the subtle deception of Satan is through a detailed knowledge of God's Word.

This picture of Satan that Scripture paints should cause each of us to recognize the incredible danger that Satan presents to every human being. We must not forget who he is or how much power and intelligence he has. It is a serious mistake to become arrogant toward Satan and ridicule him, an attitude that is never reflected in the Scriptures. This type of mentality among Christians was reflected in the message seen recently on a signboard outside a church in the Midwest: "Jesus is Hefty, Hefty, Hefty; Satan is Wimpy, Wimpy, Wimpy."

Subversion of the Race

Satan's genius in tailoring a temptation to appeal to each individual's lust patterns and areas of weakness is first seen in his attack on man in the Garden of Eden. Now that Satan had instigated his rebellious kingdom, he lusted to extend its influence. In the Garden of Eden, he was able to subvert mankind and bring them under his authority and dominion. As we look at how he did this, we see a basic pattern of attack that he commonly uses even today.

The crowning achievement of God's creation was mankind. This creative act took place on the sixth day, as recorded in Genesis 1:26–27:

> God said, "Let Us make man in Our image, according to Our likeness; and let them rule over the fish of the sea and over the birds of the sky and over the cattle and over all the earth, and over every creeping thing that creeps on the earth." And God created man in His own image, in the image of God He created him; male and female He created them.

God created the human race, one man and one woman, and placed them over the earth to rule it as His representatives.

As God's vicegerents over the planet, Adam and Eve were given everything they would need to carry out their responsibilities. (This provision is always true of God's grace toward His people.) God created the world and its environment in a perfect condition for man, then He filled it with both animals and plants. He provided abundantly for the sustenance of man, and then He instructed him about this provision (Gen. 1:29–30). And His continued presence gave Adam and Eve the opportunity to get answers to any problem they might have faced. God always provides everything that man needs to fulfill his obligations to Him.

Although God had provided everything for them, He also established one simple test by which Adam and Eve could demonstrate their love and devotion to Him: they were forbidden to eat of the fruit of one particular tree in the Garden. This tree was called the "tree of the knowledge of good and evil" (2:17). The Hebrew word used for *knowledge* here suggests *experiential knowledge* rather than academic knowledge. We have no idea what kind of tree this was or what kind of fruit it bore. But the issue was clarified to both Adam and Eve: "From any tree of the garden you may eat freely; but from the tree of the knowledge of good and evil you shall not eat, for in the day that you eat from it you shall surely die" (vv. 16–17). The test was simple: if they loved and trusted God, they would obey Him; if they did not love and trust Him, they would disobey Him, and the result would be death.

Satan's Age-Old Strategy

After observing Adam and Eve, Satan apparently decided that if he could win Eve to his side winning Adam would be easier. A careful analysis of Satan's approach to Eve reveals much that is characteristic of Satan's strategy even today. He began by disguising himself (in this case as a serpent). Genesis 3:1 states, "The serpent was more crafty than any beast of the field which the Lord God had made." The Hebrew *arum*, translated "crafty" here, carries the idea of being wary of the traps and knowing the dangers and pitfalls into which one can fall.[6] Satan is in the business of deception. He does not appear openly, nor does he make his desires plain. Instead, he wraps them in the cloak of apparent good (2 Cor. 11:14). Satan does not normally come up to people and say, "Do you want to sin?" Instead, his temptation usually takes the form of doing good. Satan began to work on Eve by first questioning what God had said (Gen. 3:1). Satan's usual technique is to cause people first to question the sufficiency of God and His Word and then to question the truth of what God has revealed. God revealed to Adam and Eve that they were not to eat of the fruit from the Tree of the Knowledge of Good and Evil. He did not go into detail; He did not enlighten them about His reasons for the command, neither did He explain every facet of the ways by which they could be tricked into eating the fruit. That was not necessary because all they needed to know was that they were not to eat from that particular tree.

The thrust of Satan's first statement was "Indeed, has God [*really*] said, 'You shall not eat from any tree of the garden'?" (Gen. 3:1). Through the use of innuendo, the shrewd Serpent planted doubt in Eve's mind, doubt that God really had their best interest in mind. He suggested that God was holding back something good and desirable. He was also probing to determine how well the woman knew God's instructions and to what degree she was committed to obeying Him. Satan uses these same strategies today. He first gets people to think that God's Word isn't true, that the Bible contains errors, and that the Bible is simply a record of the religious experiences of different people, primarily the Jews. Then they, like Eve, dismiss the revelation of God as irrelevant.

Satan's arguments can be very subtle. For example, many people today believe that the Bible is true and without error in all matters of "faith and practice." That statement is true as far as it goes, but in many cases it masks a subtle disregard for the actual inerrancy of Scripture. The thinking Christian ought to ask certain questions. Is the Bible true when it mentions historical events? Is the Bible true when it makes observations about nature and the creation? Often the critic of the Bible will say that it has mistakes in matters of history, geography, and science, but that we can believe the Bible when it discusses spiritual matters. Unfortunately for the critic, when the Bible discusses spiritual issues, they are not separated from history or creation. The spiritual issues are intimately interwoven with the historical statements, and the truth of the spiritual matter depends on the reliability of the historical or creation issue. Jesus and the apostles clearly believed that Adam and Eve were real, historical people and that they sinned (Matt. 19:4; 1 Tim. 2:13-14). The Fall was a literal event in history that changed history and had disastrous consequences on the human race. Because of their sin, Jesus, the second person of the Trinity, had to come to earth to die for man's sin. If Adam had not sinned as a historical act, no need would have existed for the Incarnation or the Crucifixion.

Spiritual and Physical Truth

In John chapter 3, we have the record of Jesus' conversation with one of the most prominent religious leaders of His day, a man named Nicodemus. In the course of their conversation, Jesus explained to Nicodemus that a person must be born a second time before he can see the kingdom of God. This statement stunned Nicodemus. In all of his years of study, he never had heard this statement, and he was confused by it. Jesus went on to explain that people are born once of their mother, but they are born sinners and spiritually dead: "What is born of flesh is flesh." When Adam sinned, he died spiritually, that is, he lost the ability to have a relationship with God and to understand divine truth (1 Cor. 2:14). Man's problem is spiritual death, and he needs to be reborn spiritually.

When Nicodemus asked how this spiritual rebirth could take place, Jesus responded, "If I told you earthly things and you do not believe, how shall you believe if I tell you heavenly things?" (John 3:12). The point is that *spiritual truth cannot be separated from physical truth.* If we do not believe the Word of God when it speaks about history, geography, nature, and creation—things we can see and about which we can read—how can we trust it when it talks about things in the spiritual realm? The Bible is not true just when it speaks about matters of faith and practice, but it is true in *everything it says.* We must be careful not to fall into Satan's trap of believing that God's Word is only partially true.

Eve's response shows that Satan's strategy was already working. Her answer reveals that she had already begun to drift from God's command and to add to it: "The woman said to the serpent, 'From the fruit of the trees of the garden we may eat; but from the fruit of the tree which is in the middle of the garden, God has said "You shall not eat from it *or touch it*, lest you die" (Gen. 3:2–3, emphasis added). Eve was already accepting the idea that God was being too restrictive, and she revealed her inadequate knowledge of God's Word.

In contrast, when Jesus was tempted by Satan, He used the Word accurately (Matt. 4:1–10). Satan used the same technique of misapplying the Word of God and twisting it to bring about confusion. But Jesus relied solely on the Word. He did not oblige Satan by entering a dialogue about theoretical possibilities. He just stuck to the Word and used it correctly. The result was that He withstood the temptation.

Has God Told Us Enough?

Another strategy of Satan is to cast doubt upon the sufficiency of God's revelation: Has God really told us enough? While there certainly is a lot more that God could have told us about a great many things, the issue is whether God has in fact told us everything we need to know. As we demonstrated in the second chapter of this book, the Bible claims to tell us *everything* we need to know for life and godliness (2 Peter 1:3–4). Satan's question to Eve was designed to make her doubt God's instructions and to wonder why God said what He said.

Satan's question also implied that he could supply her with more information about the matter, supposedly so she could make a better, more informed decision. This is still one of Satan's lures today—the idea that he has additional information which God is withholding from us, information that we need to deal with various situations that are not covered in the Bible. Such a pursuit of extrabiblical knowledge is really a criticism of God and His character. Too often, the motive for "needing" more inside information is that we can check up on God to see if He has really made a wise decision for us. Once we start this line of thinking, we open ourselves to Satan's distorted perspective on a situation, which, in effect, is trusting Satan's word instead of God's Word. Eve should have trusted God and obeyed His simple command not to eat of the forbidden fruit, without having to know more about why God gave such a command.

The Bold Lie

Once Satan had put this suggestion in her mind and initiated the doubting process, he then openly stated that what God had said was not true: "The serpent said to the woman, 'You surely shall not die! For God knows that in the day you eat from it your eyes will be opened, and you will be like God, knowing good and evil'" (Gen. 3:4–5). God said that they would die, but Satan said that they would not, that they had no reason to fear any harsh consequences for their actions.

The second part of this statement impugned the character of God. Satan stated that the real reason God did not want them to eat of the fruit was because they would become like God. In other words, God was holding back from them. God didn't really have their best interests in mind but was simply trying to keep them from having everything they could have, trying to impede them from realizing their full potential. Now that Satan had her attention, Eve probably started wondering why God didn't want her to eat from the tree. And Satan came along with just the right answer: God doesn't want you to know everything He does because He's jealous. If you eat the fruit, you will be just like Him.

This lie of Satan is still prevalent today and is found increasingly even within the church. Some men who claim to be preachers of the Christian gospel actually teach that people are gods—a heresy prevalent in many false religions.

The Cyanide Principle

Throughout the temptation of Eve, Satan mixed a relatively small part of a lie with a fairly substantial amount of truth. But remember that a glass of water with just one drop of cyanide in it is lethal. It is not the water that is harmful but the small amount of cyanide. The first part of Satan's statement was a lie: God had said that they would die, and Satan said that they would not. But the second part of his statement was true: when Adam and Eve ate of the fruit, their eyes would be opened, and they would become like God in the sense of knowing good and evil. In Genesis 3:22–24, after Adam and Eve had sinned and God had told them the consequences of this sin, God closed off the Garden of Eden to them. In verse 22 God said, "Behold, the man has become like one of Us, knowing good and evil." God did not say that they had *become a god* but that in one particular and important way they had become *like God*, knowing, in the sense of "determining," what was good and evil. Adam and Eve had set themselves up as the final arbiter of God's prohibition.

The point of the original test in the Garden was to demonstrate whether Adam and Eve would submit to God and do what He told them and believe what He said. But Adam and Eve were not content with that; they wanted to make up their own minds as to what was good and what was evil. By so doing, they acted as if they were gods because only God has the right to determine what is good and evil. When Adam and Eve attempted to use their own experience and reason without orienting it to God's Word, they were acting as if they were gods, and the result was catastrophic for the human race.

Satan was successful in his strategy, for he cast doubt on the truthfulness of God's Word, then on the sufficiency of God's Word, and then on the personal integrity of God. Thus confused, Eve allowed herself to get in the position of trusting her own experience and reason to make the decision instead of simply obeying God's Word. This is the danger point. Once we begin to doubt either the truthfulness of God's Word or its sufficiency, we begin to rely instead on our own experience and reason. But our experience (even after all of these years) and our reason (despite our IQ and advanced education) are too limited and too affected by sin ever to be able adequately to handle Satan's shrewd strategies. Once we get to this point, Satan can twist us around his little finger just as he did Eve.

Citizens of Satan's Kingdom

Once Eve began to look at the fruit the way Satan wanted her to, she began to desire it. She "saw that the tree was good for food, and that it was a delight to the eyes, and that the tree was desirable to make one wise" (Gen. 3:6). She then ate of the fruit. Apparently nothing happened instantly, and Eve began to think that the lie of the serpent was the truth. So she went to Adam and gave him some fruit, and he ate too. Then things changed immediately.

It was Adam's sin that was determinative. The Scriptures teach that Eve was deceived. She had been confused and duped into eating the fruit, but there was no excuse for Adam. Adam sinned knowingly: "It was not Adam who was deceived, but the woman being quite deceived, fell into transgression" (1 Tim. 2:14). Adam was the head of the race. He was the head of the family. His was the decision that made the difference. It was only after *he* ate that their eyes were opened. Would the entire race have fallen if Adam had not eaten? We can only guess at the possible outcome. The sobering fact remains that Adam *did* eat the fruit, and we have been living with the consequences ever since.

When Adam chose to eat the fruit, he was choosing to disobey God and to believe and obey the serpent. At that point, Adam rebelled against the authority of God and aligned himself with Satan. The result was that the human race came under the control and dominion of Satan. By declaring their independence against God, Adam and Eve became citizens of Satan's kingdom and cast all of humanity under his domain. Satan had won his victory and gained the prize. The world and the human race became legally under Satan's authority.

Satan had promised them that they could be like God, without anyone telling them what to think, believe, or do. But the horrible truth was that now they were slaves to Satan, under his rule and authority. Two key New Testament passages inform us that the unsaved person is under Satan's authority and dominion. In Acts 26:18 Jesus commissioned Paul to go to the Gentiles to preach the gospel "to open their eyes so that they may turn from darkness to light and from the dominion of Satan to God. . . ." Colossians 1:13 tells us that when a person is saved by trusting in Jesus Christ as his Savior, he is delivered "from the domain of darkness." In both of these verses, the literal meaning of the Greek word translated "domain" or "dominion" is *authority*. Because of Adam's choice against God, all of his descendants are born under the authority of Satan.

The Worst Kind of Death

The second thing that happened immediately after Adam and Eve ate the fruit was that they died. God had said, "In the day that you eat from it you shall surely die" (Gen. 2:17). Death in Scripture does not refer to cessation of existence but emphasizes the idea of *separation*. Physical death is a separation from the physical world, but the soul (the essence of each person) continues to exist. Spiritual death is the separation of a person's human spirit from God. The penalty for sin was not physical death, but spiritual death. Physical death is just one of numerous consequences of spiritual death. This was the result with Adam and Eve, as can be seen in what immediately took place after they ate the fruit. Ultimately, the unsaved soul spends eternity separated from God in hell, an eternal death.

As had been usual, God came to walk with Adam and Eve in the Garden. When Adam and Eve heard Him, rather than running joyfully to Him to spend time with Him, they hid themselves because they were afraid. They no longer enjoyed fellowship with God. Their sins had separated them from God.

The second result of their disobedience was that they acquired a sin nature. They became selfish and irresponsible; their previous relationship, which had been perfectly harmonious, became torn apart. When God asked them why they hid themselves and if they had eaten of the forbidden fruit, they responded by denying what they had done and by passing the buck. Such is the trend of the sin nature, to avoid personal responsibility for bad decisions and to blame others, human or demonic. Adam blamed Eve, and Eve blamed the serpent. They tried to avoid responsibility for their actions and sought to shift it to someone else. The result of their sin brought a horrible curse upon the human race, the curse of spiritual death.

The Fatal Blow

Although God justly pronounced this curse on them, in His grace He also provided a way out, a way of salvation. God addressed the serpent and told him He would "put enmity between you [the serpent/Satan] and the woman, and between your seed and her seed; he shall bruise you on the head, and you shall bruise him on the heel" (Gen. 3:15). This verse is the first mention of God's plan of salvation. The seed of the woman refers to Jesus Christ, the Savior whom God would provide, born of a woman. Although the serpent would bruise Jesus at the cross, Jesus would then deliver the fatal blow to Satan.

This is the good news: although man rebelled against God and is born under the authority of Satan, God in His great love has provided a way of escape. The penalty for sin is death, but God provided His own Son, who would pay that penalty for man by dying on the cross in payment for their sins. "The wages of sin is death, but the free gift of God is eternal life in Christ Jesus our Lord" (Rom. 6:23).

Two Vital Secrets

We must not overlook two critically important lessons. First, Satan's skill at deception was so clever that people with no sin nature and who enjoyed an incredibly close relationship with God were deceived. They were tricked because they allowed Satan to direct their thinking away from God's command and to entice them into dealing with him apart from the revealed Word of God. If we are to avoid the same snare, we who *do* have a sin nature must be even more armed with the Word of God and to ensure that we are using it accurately. Unfortunately, the superficial knowledge that most Christians have of God's Word makes them easy marks for Satan's deceptions.

Second, failure to rely solely on the sufficiency of God's Word will always lead to disaster in spiritual warfare. God is a jealous God; He wants to be trusted alone. To rely on anything alongside the Word of God is to destroy its power in our lives. That is one reason why so many Christians today lead such ineffective Christian lives and struggle so much with sin. They are merging biblical teaching with self-help techniques, psychology, drugs, unbiblical teaching about demons and sin, etc. Only by understanding what God has revealed in His Word about the enemies facing us can we erect the defenses necessary to guard effectively against them.

4

WORLDVIEW FOR CONQUEST

Do not love the world, nor the things in the world. If any one loves the world, the love of the Father is not in him. For all that is in the world, the lust of the flesh and the lust of the eyes and the boastful pride of life, is not from the Father, but is from the world. And the world is passing away, and also its lusts; but the one who does the will of God abides forever.

—1 John 2:15–17

Worldliness is one of the most difficult concepts for many Christians to understand; therefore, we continue to be vulnerable to it. Fundamentalists have frequently identified worldliness with certain activities. A Christian who smoked or drank alcoholic beverages or went to movies was often considered worldly. However, actions in themselves should not be classified as worldliness when viewed from the biblical perspective. When a person submits to lustful temptations and commits sinful acts such as sexual immorality, drunkenness, or gossip, these are *sins of the flesh* and not worldliness, per se.

The biblical concept of worldliness has more to do with a way of thinking, a mind set, or a worldview than with particular actions. From generation to generation, the dominant worldly ideas that influence people tend to change. Satan is constantly working behind the scenes, influencing the way people think—the attitudes and ideas that influence each generation. In one generation worldliness might involve a trend toward a relativistic morality whereas in another generation it might be expressed through an ultrarigid morality. Worldliness is best understood as an overall philosophy of life or way of thinking that stirs up the flesh to indulge in specific sins such as sexual immorality, drunkenness, gossip, or self-righteous arrogance. Worldliness is a way of thinking about life that is contrary to the biblical way or divine viewpoint. Worldliness may contain a large amount of truth, yet its overall makeup and foundation is divorced from Scriptural authority. As such, worldliness provides a rationale for sin, and it is often associated with false teachings that blind people to the truth and lead them away from God (2 Cor. 4:4).

The New Testament contains several passages that emphasize the distinction between the Christian and the world. This contrast is so marked that James warns us that friendship with the world is hostility toward God (James 4:4). There is no middle ground or place of neutrality. When what we think aligns with the world, we are hostile to God. And such worldly thinking will eventually trip us up in the sins of the flesh. Remember, believers are not to be conformed to the world (we must expunge from our thinking such worldly influences as pragmatism, mysticism, idealism, and relativism) but transformed by the renewing of our minds (Rom. 12:2). Therefore, it is critical that we understand what the Bible means by the world, how worldliness is manifested in our present generation, what the characteristics of worldliness are, and how God tells us we can avoid worldliness.

What It Means to Be Worldly

In the New Testament, the word *world* (from which we derive our English word *worldliness*, or "world-like-ness") is a translation of the Greek noun *kosmos*. It was used to signify the orderly arrangement of individual parts into an integrated whole, as of the orderly arrangement of soldiers in battle formation. A synonym we will use for this system of thinking is *cosmic* thinking.

In Greek thought, the concept of beauty and order were linked together. So *kosmos* often expressed the idea of a beautiful arrangement or an adornment or decoration. This word was appropriate for the Holy

Spirit to choose because Satan loves to decorate his ideas with the most beautiful attire. We should understand "world," "worldly," and "worldliness" as the external arrangement of nonbiblical thinking (or what we called *human viewpoint* in chapter 2). Worldliness is an organized and attractive system of ideas, concepts, attitudes, and methods that Satan uses to compete with God's concept of how people should live on planet Earth. Satan is the head and controller of this system of thinking. Whenever we think like the world, we are thinking exactly as Satan wants us to think. Lewis Sperry Chafer, an outstanding Bible teacher of a previous generation, described the world system as follows:

> The *cosmos* is a vast order or system that Satan has promoted which conforms to his ideals, aims, and methods. It is civilization now functioning apart from God—a civilization in which none of its promoters really expect God to share, who assign to God no consideration in respect to their projects. This system embraces its godless governments, conflicts, armaments, and jealousies, [as well as] its education, culture, religions of morality, and pride. It is that sphere in which man lives. It is what he sees, what he employs. To the uncounted multitude it is all they ever know so long as they live on this earth. It is properly styled *the satanic system,* which phrase is in many instances a justified interpretation of the so-meaningful word *cosmos.* It is literally a *cosmos diabolicus.*[1]

It is *cosmic* thinking that often shapes the themes of popular television shows and movies in which man is depicted exploring space to expand his empire, building his own world, searching for meaning to life. Yet the God of the Bible is nowhere to be found.

Worldliness is often presented as something beautiful, desirable, and enlightening. As Eve thought after agreeing with Satan's temptation, "it was a delight to the eyes and . . . desirable to make one wise" (Gen. 3:6). As this verse indicates, Eve was ready, willing, and able to sin when she starting looking at things from Satan's point of view rather than from God's point of view. The *cosmic* system is Satan's window dressing, presenting evil in a way which seems like the good, right, and proper thing to do. When a person is not trusting God's Word to direct him, it is very easy for him to be deceived into adopting worldly thinking. Because Satan is a beautiful creature of God, he is able to present evil as a beautiful thing. Thus, we see an affinity between human viewpoint, *cosmic* thinking, and Satanic philosophies.

Three Strong Desires

Many people today speak constantly about spiritual warfare. Often, their attention is focused exclusively on Satan and demons, even though spiritual warfare in the Bible is presented as a threefold operation against the world, the flesh, and the Devil. As a result of being so preoccupied with only one phase of the battle, many Christians have suffered profound infiltration on the fronts of the world and the flesh.

If we want to be successful as Christians in avoiding worldliness, we must first understand its basic characteristics. First John 2:16 and James 3:15 are two crucial New Testament passages that tell us about the nature of this *cosmic* system.

In 1 John 2:16, the apostle John describes the totality of the world system, "all that is in the world," as being composed of three parts: (1) "the lust of the flesh"; (2) "the lust of the eyes"; and (3) "the boastful pride of life."

The first component is "the lust of the flesh," which refers to our evil desire to satisfy the impulses that stem from our fallen nature called "the flesh." "If it feels good, do it," a popular slogan generated by the world a number of years ago, accurately captures the idea behind the lust of the flesh. The idea often used in commercial advertising that we deserve all of the fine things in life is a worldly idea that appeals to the lust of the flesh.

Then we come to a somewhat similar phrase, "the lust of the eyes." This has to do with desire for things that we see, things which catch our eye. The emphasis is on external attractiveness without examining the underlying values. "The lust of the eyes" is associated with greed, envy, and covetousness. This type of greed is one of the major controlling principles in the world system.

"The boastful pride of life" is cited as the third controlling principle of this world system. It is the arrogant attitude by which people think more highly of themselves than they ought to think. It is the ambition to center one's life on self rather than on God.

All three of these characteristics originated with Satan in his fall, were passed down to Adam and Eve, and are daily the most imitated philosophy of life on the globe today. The central idea of the world's approach to life is selfishness, summarized in three words: passion, greed, and pride. The world system favors "men who are alienated from God [who] have [as] their ambition in life the desire to please the longings of a nature corrupted by sin; to possess the things they see and can enjoy; to prevail over their fellow-men in power and prestige."[2] These are Satan's rules for the game of life in this present world system.

In contrast, the believer is called to live a life of love toward God that makes transforming his thinking the highest priority (Rom. 12:1–2; John 14:15). The *cosmic* system hates God and all who are aligned with Him (John 15:19) because the principles of the world are diametrically opposed to those of the Christian. Thus, the apostle John commands believers not to "love the world, nor the things in the world" (1 John 2:15).

The apostle James contrasts the wisdom of the world with the wisdom from above in James 3:15–17. Again we see only two ways of thinking, the *cosmic* thinking of human viewpoint versus God's way of thinking, or divine viewpoint. The three terms employed in this description—"earthly, natural, demonic" (James 3:15)—should shake us up about many of our deeply cherished opinions. Here James clearly delineates that human-viewpoint thinking is not merely neutral, or wrong, but is specifically defined as demonic.

Wisdom in the Bible means "skill in living." It includes not only intellectual insights but also the element of knowing how to put knowledge into practice skillfully and successfully. Worldly wisdom excels at instructing us on how to solve problems in life and gain happiness and stability in this life. Many of these systems work, for a time, and provide a measure of happiness. Yet, their viability is never the issue. Satan's systems are often quite successful, yet their end result is tragic:

"There is a way which seems right to a man, but its end is the way of death" (Prov. 14:12).

Earthly has to do with one's perspective. The wisdom of the world does not have a perspective beyond the horizon of this temporal environment. Neither a heavenly nor an eternal perspective is found. It is time-bound. *Natural* refers to the nature of fallen man. For something in the Bible to be natural means that it is still in the fallen, unregenerate state, not under the influence of the Spirit of God or the spiritual (1 Cor. 2:14). *Demonic* means just what it says, a wisdom consistent with Satan's program that attempts to control us by doctrines of demons. It is a wisdom that rejects God as the source for skill in living.

Let us bring the point home. What we have seen so far is that every human being is born a sinner, a citizen of Satan's domain, and is brainwashed to think according to Satan's cosmic system from birth. Despite the presence of many true and accurate concepts, the overall orientation of our thinking from birth is based on arrogance. Thus, the Bible classifies the thinking of every human being from birth as demonic—not a complementary picture. For this reason, a transformation of the believer's thinking on the basis of detailed and extensive Bible teaching is a high priority. We must completely scrap our old mind set and way of thinking, not just exchange a few pieces of wrong data for a few pieces of correct information. We must renovate our entire frame of reference according to God's revealed Word. Romans 12:2 is not calling for simply learning Bible stories and biblical standards; it is calling for a radical overhaul of *how* we think as well as *what* we think.

Worldliness Fleshed Out

Perhaps a clearer way to grasp the idea of worldliness is to see it fleshed out in the examples of the Old Testament. Because the Jews did not have a Greek word like *kosmos* of the New Testament, they developed the idea of worldliness by showing its characteristics through a nation. It is primarily through the intellectual, cultural, and spiritual heritage established in Babel that Satan molds the image of worldliness in the Old Testament. Throughout the Bible, *Babel* and *Babylon* epitomize worldliness.[3]

Nimrod was a grandson of Ham, one of Noah's three sons who came to the new world on the great ark. Noah and his three sons were responsible for founding society and its new culture after the Flood. Nimrod was somehow able to coerce many men of his time into forming a kingdom of his own making. Under Nimrod, sinful people quickly resumed the evil activities for which God had sent the Flood.

Babel was the birthplace and center from which Nimrod's activities and the kingdom of man went forth. Babylon was the first attempt of men down through history to unify people to solve their common problems. In essence, it was the first United Nations and the origin of the global-unity idea that is at the root of all such movements. This attempt to unite man apart from God brought down God's judgment. God confused the language of rebellious mankind and scattered them geographically across the globe to prevent this autonomous unification. God's confusion of language was intended to minimize the spread of worldliness by adversely affecting the communication of man's false ideas from one group of people to the next. This has served to slow down mankind's reunification in rebellion against God by causing fighting within humanity due to the differences produced by rival languages and cultures.

Even today, nothing has changed. Man's dream is still ultimately to solve humankind's problems through global unity and apart from God. This desire is clearly expressed today in the world peace movements that seek to unify mankind under a one-world government. The push toward globalism is on the rise. Yet, this very idea that somehow man can solve his own problems apart from God is at the root of *cosmic* thinking. In the Old Testament, this idea always manifested itself in human pride and defiance of God, human wisdom and knowledge, human power to control and manipulate, and vast human wealth.[4]

Pride and Defiance

First, worldliness manifests itself through *pride and defiance of God*. This is the very sin that brought Satan down, and it is the root of all sin (Isa. 14:13–14). Babylon typified this sin in the ancient world. Isaiah 47 gives a clear picture of how the Babylonians exalted themselves as the queen of the kingdoms (vv. 5, 7). In their arrogance, they believed that they could provide financial and military security for their people (vv. 8–9). This pride also produced an alternate religious system, (vv. 9, 12–15), somewhat like the contemporary New Age movement.

We see this same type of arrogance and defiance of God in our world today. Those who promote globalism think that human government is the solution to all of man's problems and that only a one-world government will be able to provide financial security and bring world peace. More often than not, these same people are promoting New Age ideas, which are a mixture of astrology, divination, sorcery, and various self-help techniques that either leave God out of the picture entirely or merely give Him lip service. Little difference exists between this and the mind set of the ancient Babylonians.

The major motivating principle used by the *cosmic* system and found increasingly within the church today is that of *self*. We are taught that self is the center of the universe: self-image, self-love, self-esteem, self-motivation. Self-absorption is one of the most prominent characteristics of the baby-boom generation in America. The result has been a breakdown in relationships and morality. (The high divorce rate is a result of this self-oriented thinking.) This kind of orientation to self is nothing more than an expression of pride, the trademark of Satan and his kingdom. This self-orientation breeds an attitude of rejection of any external authority, especially that exerted by God. Defiance of God is increasingly becoming the norm rather than the exception.

Wisdom and Knowledge

The second characteristic of worldly thinking places a high premium on *man's wisdom and knowledge* (Isa. 47:10). This characteristic not only involves man's attempts to answer the basic questions about life through the use of autonomous philosophy but also includes astrology and other occultic arts (Isa. 47:12–13): "All the nations were deceived by your sorcery" (Rev. 18:23).

Because modern men do not submit to God's wisdom and knowledge, man takes greater pride and satisfaction in his own thoughts. He has concluded that no one is going to save man except himself, whether by his own rational thought or by New Age mysticism. This explains why mankind has been so interested in human-viewpoint philosophy, whether of the rational variety or the mystical kind. This surely stems from pride, because historians of philosophy will be the first to admit that no one has been able to come up with a workable philosophy in all of human history and because the lure of occult secrets has always led to bondage or been a great disappointment. However, human viewpoint says that it is the *search* for truth which is important. And so this is all with which they are left—a search having no genuine hope of ever finding that for which they are looking: "always learning and never able to come to the knowledge of the truth" (2 Tim. 3:7).

This pride of human knowledge is often shown in the way we try to solve personal problems. In some cases, we look to humanistic psychology to find answers and help for our problems, not realizing that many of the ideas and concepts in modern psychology have their origin in demonic encounters.[5] At other times, people seek to resolve difficult situations on the basis of intuitive insights rather than biblical precepts. Often, as pastors we have counseled people in marital difficulty who have engaged in extramarital affairs because having this fantastic love seemed so right to them. They assume that God certainly wouldn't give them such a love and then expect them to walk away from it. Worldliness says, "Go with your feelings," which gives the flesh a real basis for operation. When intuition and emotion supplant the principles of Scripture, misery and self-destruction become inevitable.

The Power to Control

A third characteristic of worldly thinking involves *the power to control and manipulate*. On the national level, this characteristic is expressed through the accumulation of military and political strength, which our modern world uses not merely to restrain evil but to keep people under captivity to the state and its goals. Ancient Egypt and Babylon were perfect examples of nations that were trusting in great military and political strength, but God humbled them both.

In answer to Pharaoh's arrogant question, "Who is the Lord that I should obey His voice to let Israel go? I do not know the Lord" (Exod.

5:2), the Lord taught Pharaoh who He was and why even rebels must obey the Lord. The Lord redeemed the Israelites out of Pharaoh's hand through the ten plagues, and in the process Egypt's great military and political strength was smashed.

In Babylon, Nebuchadnezzar asked a similar question: "What god is there who can deliver you out of my hands?" (Dan. 3:15). Nebuchadnezzar in his pride was trusting in military and political strength to coerce his subjects to bow the knee and worship him as a god. Yet Nebuchadnezzar ended up realizing that "the Most High is ruler over the realm of mankind, and bestows it on whomever He wishes" (4:25). More recently, Adolf Hitler attempted to use military and political strength to forge his Third Reich, which was to last for a thousand years. It actually lasted only about ten years!

On a personal level, the pursuit of power has reached new proportions. Just think about the new terminology that we commonly use: *power dress*, *power suit*, *power lunch*, etc. This is one of the enticing appeals of New Age or metaphysical thought: it promises a new *power* to its adherents. Thus seminars such as the FORUM (formerly est), Silva Mind Control, and ONE offer customers new power over themselves and the ability to manipulate and control other people so that they may be more successful in their businesses. Unfortunately, the power to which some of their customers are introduced is demonic.

Money as Security

Fourth, worldliness sees *the accumulation of financial wealth as the means to security and happiness in this life.* An example in the Bible seems almost contemporary. The metropolis of Tyre (Ezek. 27) shows the classic pattern of how vast wealth operates in Satan's world system. The central drive behind ancient Tyre's success in the commercial world was her drive to please self—in other words, selfish ambition.

So captivated was Tyre by her own ability that she undertook daring expeditions, bold and unprecedented voyages. With her excellent charts of the ocean, her study of the stars, and carefully guarded records as to depths and distances, winds and currents, she was able to outstrip all other competitors by sailing during the night.[6]

Pride, conceit, self-absorption, a sense of grasping, and destructive covetousness all characterized Tyre and Satan's *cosmic* system. Tyre was famous for having the most aggressive merchants of the world; they could get along with anyone as long as there was a dollar to be made!

Someone has said that Americans are the salesmen of the world, which explains why the pragmatist, the person who gets the job done or closes the sale, is the most admired person in our culture. We live in a time in which more and more people pursue as the standard for happiness things that only money will buy. We have an unquenchable thirst for status, fame, luxury, ease, comfort, and entertainment.

Even within the church a whole new theology of health and wealth is proclaimed and practiced. This is a characteristic of Babylon and should be seen as the product of the spirit of this world. Wealth is not evil in itself, but the drive to accumulate wealth by any means and for the purpose of selfish desires is clearly contrary to Scripture. It is *the love of money* which is a root of all sorts of evil (1 Tim. 6:10). As with many modern Americans, wealth is pursued for its own sake. A contemporary bumper sticker reads, "Whoever dies with the most toys wins."

By now you have some insight as to how you can spot worldliness. At its very core, it is the assertion of man's independence against God. It is the idea that security and fulfillment in life can be attained apart from submission to God and orientation to His plan. Nimrod and his contemporary imitators seek to solve man's problems through global unity even at the expense of personal liberty. In their assertion of their independence, they turn to alternative religions, which are nothing more than thinly disguised forms of Satanism.

But lest we miss the brilliance of Satan's clever designs, we should note that the goals and ideals of worldliness are always very attractive. After all, who could be against world peace, nuclear disarmament, personal prosperity, saving the whales, or ending world hunger? These goals are not wrong in themselves; what is wrong is the fact that modern man has chosen to solve these problems on his own while denying his need for God. At the very core of man's efforts is his rebellion against God, his desire to make a success out of planet Earth apart from God. The idea that man can solve his problems on his own appeals to "the lust of the flesh, the lust of the eyes, and the boastful pride of life."

How can we escape the influence of worldliness? First, we must understand how the system really works.

How the System Works

None of us who have been through military boot camp will ever forget the experience. First, the drill instructor gives us a talk about how he is in charge and how we are under his absolute authority. Then he spends the rest of the day (from a very early start!) showing us that he has authority over us by constantly yelling at us, calling us all kinds of unrepeatable names, and making us do push-ups every time we do not do exactly what he commands us to do. He exerts this kind of control over us for the duration of boot camp, until finally, an hour before graduation, he manages a smile and makes a speech of appreciation for our accomplishments. One thing that we all knew about our drill sergeant was that he was in total control. The same is true of Satan's rule over his domain during this present age: he *is in control.*

The apostle Paul labels the age in which the world currently operates as "this present evil age" (Gal. 1:4).[7] It is evil because Satan is in charge of setting the agenda. Satan is said to be "the god of this world [age]" (2 Cor. 4:4), as well as "the ruler of this world" (John 12:31; 14:30; 16:11). Jesus Christ did not question Satan's right to give Him the "kingdoms of the world" if He would worship him (Luke 4:5-7). In fact, during the future Tribulation, Satan will confer authority over this world to the man of sin (Rev. 13:1-8), thus fulfilling the offer which he made to the Lord.

God has given Satan a certain freedom of operation, within divinely appointed limits, to act as God's opponent during the present age until the time when God will restrict him to the bottomless pit (Rev. 20:2-3), thereby removing his influence from the world. Indeed, it will be a new world when that day comes. Meanwhile, we should not forget that even though Satan currently occupies a high position and a certain degree of freedom, his days are numbered. God is sovereign, and His plan includes His rule over evil as well as good.

Satan rules over all the subjects under his domain, which includes both fallen angels and sinful mankind. John tells us that the scope of Satan's domain is the world: "The whole world lies in the power of the evil one" (1 John 5:19). The fallen angels are Satan's foot soldiers, who do his bidding in the spiritual realm. They are an organized group described in Scripture as "rulers," "powers," "world forces of this darkness," and "spiritual forces of wickedness in the heavenly places" (Eph. 6:12).

Those who do not know Christ as Savior are said to have been caught in "the snare of the devil, having been held captive by him to do his will" (2 Tim. 2:26). Every human being is at the beck and call of Satan, unless he or she has escaped his clutches by becoming a believer. Scripture describes unbelievers as those who walk "according to the course of this world, according to the prince of the power of the air, of the spirit that is now working in the sons of disobedience" (Eph. 2:2). All unbelievers are in bondage to Satan, making them his unwitting allies against God. He makes them dance in harmony to the tune of the world system.

This system operates similar to the way a radio station functions. Satan is the program director who selects the agenda for the station. The demons and fallen humanity produce the programming, which propagates and reinforces the agenda (false doctrine). The station then transmits the message over the air. However, you cannot pick up the station unless you have a receiver tuned to the right frequency. All of fallen humanity is tuned to radio station "WORLD" with the volume turned all the way up. The receiver is the flesh, which is attracted to Satan's frequency. All three aspects work in harmony: the world, the flesh, and the Devil.

The sin nature is sympathetic to the evil nature of the world system, so the two are attracted. The main difference between the two is that the world system characterizes the *corporate* expression of Satan whereas the flesh embodies these same characteristics on a *personal* level. When someone becomes a believer in Jesus Christ, this alignment is broken but only by expelling *cosmic* thinking from the soul by saturating our minds with the teaching of Scripture.

Winning the Battle

Jesus told the Pharisees in the temple that "you are of this world; I am not of this world" (John 8:23). Later, He said that His followers "are not of this world, even as I am not of the world" (17:14; see also v. 16). Christ then prayed to the Father on behalf of all believers that He not "take them out of the world, but . . . keep them from the evil one" (v. 15). We see from the New Testament that Christ is our model for how a believer should relate to the world. The well-known slogan often heard in Christian circles is true: Believers are to be *in* the world but not *of* the world.

The reason the believer is not of the world is that he has been chosen out of the world (John 15:19) and born of God (1 John 5:18). The believer has a new position in Christ because God has "delivered us from the domain of darkness and transferred us to the kingdom of His beloved Son" (Col. 1:13). His new nature no longer matches the tune being transmitted by the world system. The believer is now able to tune the dial to a new frequency and match his regenerated nature with the things of the Lord. He is now "the light of the world" (Matt. 5:14). He goes from being a resident of this world to being a cosmic tourist (Phil. 3:20). But how is he to conduct himself and relate to the world now that he is an outsider?

The believer's new relationship to the world system revolves around two simple aspects: *separation from the world* and *evangelism of the world*. We are left in the world to evangelize it, because in the world is the only place where we can call sinners to faith in Christ. On the other hand, believers are to be separate from the world because we are citizens of a heavenly country, have a different system of thinking, and follow a higher code of conduct.

Living in a Monastery?

Many New Testament passages command separation from the world. Some of them include the following injunctions: "Do not be conformed to this world" (Rom. 12:2); "instructing us to deny ungodliness and worldly desires" (Titus 2:12); "keep oneself unstained by the world" (James 1:27); "friendship with the world is hostility toward God" (James 4:4); "escaped the corruption that is in the world"

(2 Peter 1:4); "escaped the defilements of the world" (2 Peter 2:20); "do not love the world" (1 John 2:15).

Most Christians would agree that the Bible teaches us to separate from the world, but we would not all agree on what this teaching means or how it should be done. One popular answer has been *monasticism*. Monastics isolate themselves from any physical contact with the outside world. Usually, they build a large, stone edifice (if they are located in a populated area) and shut themselves in so that they will not come into contact with the world. They specialize in refraining from practices that they consider to be worldly. Their theory is that if they do not personally encounter the threat from the world, they will not have to deal with it. The modern commune is one such monastic approach to dealing with worldliness.

One of the problems with this approach is that the spirit of the world is usually transferred from a secular expression to a religious rite. Too often, the occupants within the monastery are surprised to find that the world actually resides within each of them. Monasticism is, in fact, just a worldly approach to spirituality.

The New Testament teaches that we accomplish true separation from the world by conforming to our new relationship to God and to the world. This conforming can be done only by changing the thinking in our soul to conform to God's way of thinking. Only by changing our thinking first will we see an internal transformation that produces a substantive change on the outside. The standard is the Word of God, which provides the basis for interaction with unbelievers and allows us to live before them such that they will see a difference in our attitudes and actions. Christ said in the Sermon on the Mount, "Let your light shine before men in such a way that they may see your good works and glorify your Father who is in heaven" (Matt. 5:16).

How do we do this? Because the world is out to benefit "number one" (i.e., self), we should display the opposite attitudes and actions by seeking what is best for others (i.e., love). Because the world takes God's truth and distorts it, believers should make it first a priority to learn God's Word. We cannot apply what we do not know, and we cannot know God's Word without making that the number one goal of our lives.

Only then from a transformed, Christlike character can we speak the truth in love. Living a life that contrasts sharply with the lifestyle of the world provides a sound basis for the other aspect of our relationship to the world: effective evangelism. First Peter 3:15 incorporates these two aspects in one passage: "Sanctify Christ as Lord in your hearts [separation from the world], always being ready to make a defense to everyone who asks you to give an account for the hope that is in you [evangelism], yet with gentleness and reverence [the Christian attitude as contrasted with the *cosmic* attitude of pride and arrogance]."

The believer separates himself from the world in two major areas: in *word* and in *deeds*. The epistles of the New Testament emphasize how a believer is to think and believe and then how to live in accordance with that doctrine. This is what is meant by not being conformed to the world but being transformed by the renewing of our mind (Rom. 12:2). The New Testament is full of teachings that describe how the believer is to think and live based on the dynamics of the Christian life provided by the Holy Spirit. If a believer loses his interest in doctrine and godly living, he is in serious trouble because he has no other effective basis to combat the world.

Shining in the Darkness

Evangelism is the other major way by which the believer relates to the world. Christ commanded His followers to "go into all the world and preach the gospel to all creation" (Mark 16:15). To accomplish this task from within the four walls of a monastery is impossible; to reach people, we must be in the world where people actually are!

In evangelism, one temptation is to make the gospel appealing to the world. The gospel is then watered down and reshaped to make it attractive to worldly people. All too often, Christians are drawn in by the trends and fads of the world as their platform for evangelism. Evangelism becomes based on salesmanship techniques. If the world has success through a certain kind of music, then we incorporate the world's music to attract them for evangelism. If the world has social and moral problems, then we become "Christian" sociologists and psychologists to show them how helpful Christianity is so that they will listen to the gospel. If the world uses certain tactics to effect political and social change, then the Christians will have their own similar version—except five to ten years behind the world's version! Sadly, many evangelicals have failed to realize the need to renovate their thinking radically and they have simply exchanged one vocabulary for another, one set of lyrics for another, and one social environment for another. Yet, they have failed to transform the way they think.

God has already given us a platform from which to attract the world so that we can preach the gospel to them. The New Testament calls this the "light shining out of a dark place"; it is the godly behavior of the believer and the message of the gospel of Jesus Christ.

Christ bore witness to the sinfulness of the world's conduct by demonstrating the moral perfection of God in His life. Likewise, the believer, by allowing the holy character of God to radiate in his life, exposes the sinfulness of the world's practices, showing that they are contrary to God's holy character. Christ also bore witness to the truth by showing men who God is and what He requires of them. Likewise, the believer bears witness to the truth, relating the life, death, and resurrection of the Lord Jesus. In these two ways the believer fulfills his responsibility of being a witness to the world.[8]

Truly Unique

We are to relate to the world by being *different*, not similar, in our lifestyles and our beliefs. Those of the world believe in themselves; we believe in Jesus Christ. Their goals are earthly; our goals are heavenly. Their trust is in their physical strength and beauty; our trust is in God and the Holy Spirit. They seek selfish fame and fortune; we seek selfless proclamation of Christ.

Unfortunately, many brands of Christianity today are simply worldly counterfeits. The world is materialistic, so Christians have their health-and-wealth gospel. The world holds to a situation ethic, so Christians have their licentious preachers who claim that we can freely sin because we are forgiven anyway. The world is entranced by spirits and psychic power, so Christians give undue attention to demons, spirits, deliverance, and exorcism. The world puts its faith in psychology to solve life's problems, so Christians blend the world's answers with the Bible's teachings and thus destroy both.

Because of our new position in Christ, John tells us that we have victory over the world: "Whatever is born of God overcomes the world; and this is the victory that has overcome the world—our faith" (1 John 5:4). We achieved victory over the false doctrine about who Christ is when we believed the gospel, but the battle is still raging. The world is in a pitched battle with us because we have become soldiers against Satan and his world system. Therefore, the world will do everything it can to remove us from the battle, either by luring us back into the fold through the attractions of the world (which still appeal to our sin nature) or by tempting us to renounce our allegiance to Christ through persecution or martyrdom. But whether tempted by bribery or torture, we have victory in Christ because He has overcome the world (John 16:33).

5

THE ENEMY WITHIN

*The deeds of the flesh are evident, which are: immorality,
impurity, sensuality, idolatry, sorcery, enmities, strife, jealousy, outbursts of anger, disputes, dissensions, factions,
envyings, drunkenness, carousings, and things like these.*

—Galatians 5:19–21

Russian by birth, Jewish by race, and British by choice, Sidney Reilly was perhaps the greatest spy of all time. (Ian Fleming, the creator of James Bond, at one time served with the British Secret Intelligence Service. When he first created the Bond character, he reportedly said that Bond was just a piece of nonsense that he had dreamed up—certainly no Sidney Reilly!) Perhaps the most harrowing of Reilly's feats was his infiltration of the German High Command in the First World War. But his greatest task of all was his final assignment.

With the threat of the Bolshevik revolution in Russia and Russia's consequent withdrawal from the war, British intelligence sent Reilly to Russia to overthrow the Bolshevik government, a task that Reilly nearly accomplished. It took the Soviets another seven years to stop him. His abilities to organize and mobilize people against the Bolsheviks was unsurpassed. People said that Lenin feared no enemy more than Sidney Reilly.[1]

Reilly was feared because his allegiance was to another government.

His secret activities were all aimed at subverting and overthrowing the rule of the Bolsheviks. Governments fear nothing as much as the traitor, the rebel within the camp, who covertly seeks to destroy their work. Just as governments have their traitors and spies within the camp, so Christians have theirs—the sin nature, called "the flesh" in Scripture.

The Internal Rebel

The flesh, the rebel within, seeks to hinder and suppress the work that God is doing in our lives. In previous chapters, we described the origin and nature of the first two enemies the Christian faces: Satan and the world. Yet, these two are *external* enemies; neither has the power to force any person to disobey God. What gives these first two enemies an opportunity to operate in the believer's life is that this internal enemy provides a foothold of influence within each of us. Satan (and demons) can tempt the Christian, and the world system supplies philosophies and ideas that offer a rationale for sin, but the individual makes the choices, yields to the temptation, or uses the philosophy to justify his sinful actions.

From the moment Adam first sinned in the Garden, he acquired something new. Some people might call it a principle, or a nature, or an influence, but whatever term is used, it is a predisposition, a desire, a hankering to assert one's own authority over God's authority. This nature has been passed on from Adam to every one of his descendants—except Jesus Christ, who "knew no sin."

The first mention of the power and control of sin is found in Genesis 4 in the familiar story of Cain and Abel. The account says that when the two men brought their sacrifices to God, God had favor on Abel's sacrifice but rejected Cain's sacrifice. Hebrews 11:4 explains that Abel's motivation was faith in the promise of God whereas Cain apparently relied on his own sufficiency. The result was that Cain became angry (a mental-attitude sin) and his countenance fell (he was depressed because of rejection). Modern man faces similar problems of anger and depression and looks for the solution in many places. Yet, he refuses to place the blame on his own volition and sin nature. God analyzed the problem for Cain and gave him the solution:

If you do well, will not your countenance be lifted up? And if you do not do well, sin is crouching at the door; and its desire is for you, but you must master it. (Genesis 4:7)

The Hebrew word for "crouching at the door" carries the image of a ravenous beast ready to pounce and devour its victim. This is what the enemy within seeks. The solution, simply put here, is to master this enemy. The result is that depression, resentment, and anger are conquered. The problem was not demons nor a parental disappointment in early childhood; the problem was *personal sin.* The solution was *mastery of the sin nature* through reliance upon the grace provision of God.

"And He has said to me, 'My grace is sufficient for you, for power is perfected in weakness.'" (2 Cor. 12:9).

The Flesh Within

In the New Testament, the word used most often to describe this sin nature is *the flesh.* The clear testimony of the New Testament is that the flesh, the rebel within, is the major and most influential enemy facing the Christian (cf. Rom. 7:14, 18; 8:1–17; Gal. 3:3; 5:13–21; Eph. 2:3). The twenty-one epistles in the New Testament were written to address the important issues confronting Christians in this age, the church age. One can reasonably expect that if anything is an important issue for the believer in this age, it will be given a comprehensive treatment in these letters; if something is not an issue, it will probably be ignored.

Seeing that His divine power has granted to us everything pertaining to life and godliness, through the true knowledge of Him who called us by His own glory and excellence. (2 Peter 1:3)

The silence of these letters in some areas speaks volumes. For example, demons (or evil spirits) are mentioned only ten times, and most of these instances simply relate to certain factual truths about demons. On the other hand, these same letters contain more than fifty references to the flesh as the primary enemy of the Christian (and *flesh* is only *one* term used to describe this sin nature). Obviously, the New Testament perspective emphasizes that the major source of our problem stems from our own sin nature.

Flesh in the Scriptures has three basic meanings. The first meaning is a reference to either a body or the basic material of a body (i.e., flesh and bone). The second sense focuses more on the limitations of man in contrast to the power and ability of God. The third sense is the one on which we are focusing in this chapter: the sinful nature of man. Although *flesh* sometimes refers to the physical body, and in some passages to sensual sin, it is not restricted to that meaning but covers the entire realm of sin (Gal. 5:19–21).

When you and I were born, we were in bondage to sin, "the flesh" (Rom. 6:6, 17). We were enslaved by it so that everything we did was marked by the flesh. Although some things that we did were relatively good, the Bible teaches that we could do nothing that was good in God's eyes. Isaiah 64:6 informs us that "all our righteous deeds are like a filthy garment." Paul echoes this thought in Romans 7:18, where he says, "I know that nothing good dwells in me, that is, in my flesh." The "good" to which he refers is that which is good in God's eyes. What we learn from this fact is that, in the light of God's righteous standard, everything that is produced by man is evil and sinful.

What Is Sin?

We must ensure that we understand how the Bible defines sin. Too often, people think of sin and the works of the flesh as only the baser activities, but the biblical concept of sin is much broader. Romans 14:23 says that "whatever is not from faith is sin," meaning that any thought, word, or deed, no matter how noble, helpful, or religious, if it is not done in dependence upon God (the meaning of faith) by walking by means of the Spirit (Gal. 5:16), it is done in dependence upon our own powers, and God calls that sin. That is exactly what Adam did in the Garden: rather than depend upon God and what He said, he depended on his own ability to handle the situation himself. That is the essence of idolatry and self-worship.

The flesh produces not only the baser activities that we associate with sin but also relative good. In Philippians 3:3–4 Paul warns us from his own experience not to put any confidence in the flesh, for the flesh produces a false religion, a religion based on human ability. Paul certainly understood this phenomenon because for years he was caught up in pursuing the religious standards of the Pharisees and hoping that these good works would have value in God's eyes. No one was more religious or moral than the apostle Paul before his salvation, but in Philippians 3:8 he states that all of his good works were no better than rubbish (literally "manure") in contrast to the true religion, which is based not on human works but on the finished work of Christ alone.

Besides producing evil works, the sin nature also produces works that often are thought of as good. The sin nature causes self-deception: "The heart is more deceitful than all else and is desperately sick; who can understand it?" (Jer. 17:9).

Paul emphasizes in Romans 8 the dangers of the mind controlled by the sin nature. Here we see a contrast between the person who is living "in" or "according to" the flesh and the person who is living "in" or "according to" the Spirit. Romans 8:9 clearly states that the person who is in the Spirit is a Christian: "You are not in the flesh but in the Spirit, if indeed the Spirit of God dwells in you. But if anyone does not have the Spirit of Christ, he does not belong to Him." At the moment a person trusts Jesus Christ as his Savior, God does a number of things for him, one of which is to give him the Holy Spirit, who indwells every believer. If a person does not have the Holy Spirit, then he is not a Christian; therefore, he is not "in the Spirit" but is still living according to the flesh.

The person who is in the flesh is in rebellion against God. He is not in a position of neutrality but—as harsh as it might sound—a position of hostility. Romans 8:7 tells us that "the mind set on the flesh is hostile toward God." The result of this hostility is that the mind that is operating on the sin nature rebels against anything that God commands. People often overlook this point. It is easy for us to think that some very nice people who seem to talk a lot about God and engage in "spiritual" activities do indeed have a desire to know God or perhaps even love God. But this is not what the Scripture says. No matter how moral, ethical, or religious a person might be, if they are walking according to the sin nature, believer or unbeliever, they are at enmity with God.

Operating on the sin nature is tantamount to operating on principles of the world system. Such affinity with and attraction to the world system is antagonistic to God and condemned as such. So the believer who is saved but is not operating on the principles of God's Word is at that point not only an enemy of God (James 4:4) but also living according to principles that are demonic (3:15).

There Is Hope

We have taken some time to detail what the Bible teaches about the flesh because too often we take our own sinfulness somewhat lightly. Today, many people think that self is basically good—perhaps a little misguided at times, but still basically good. The passages that we have examined, however, reveal the true degradation of the human race and how we are all defiled by sin. Yet, as horrible as this picture is, God's message of hope remains. When a person is saved, he is freed from this unholy dominion and the wicked hold that the sin nature has over each of us. Romans 6:18 tells us that when we are saved we are freed from sin and bondage to sin, and instead become slaves to righteousness. This doesn't mean that the flesh or our sin nature is eradicated but simply that its tyranny is broken. Remember: any sin you could commit as an unbeliever you can still commit as a believer; however, the flesh controls a believer only when he allows it to. That is the emphasis of Romans 6. Because the Christian has been identified with the crucifixion of Christ, "the old man" (the person he was in Adam before he was saved) is crucified, dead, and gone. The Christian is now no longer the person he once was. Instead, he is a new creature in Christ (2 Cor. 5:17). Yet, he still retains his sin nature.

The flesh is not removed until we die and receive our resurrected body. Romans 6:6 says, "Our old self was crucified with Him, that our body of sin might be done away with." The "old self" here is not the sin nature but our old, unregenerate self. Ephesians 4:22, 24 shows the contrast: "In reference to your former manner of life, you lay aside the old self, which is being corrupted in accordance with the lusts of

deceit . . . and put on the new self, which in the likeness of God has
been created in righteousness and holiness of the truth." Although
the English translation makes it appear that the believer is *to put off*
the old man, the Greek uses a construction here that is best translated "*you have put off* the old man with his works."

This fact is seen clearly by the parallel passage in Colossians 3:9–
10: "Do not lie to one another, since you laid aside the old self with its
evil practices, and have put on the new self who is being renewed to a
true knowledge according to the image of the One who created him."
We must recognize that the person we were before we were saved is
dead and gone, crucified with Christ. But although the *old man* is
dead, the *sin nature* continues. We still have a problem with the flesh.
This is why so many commands in the New Testament tell us to put to
death the deeds of the flesh, meaning to remove them from our lives.
We should live as the new creatures that we truly are in Christ.

Salvation in Three Phases

God's package called *salvation* is implemented in three phases.
Phase one occurs when a person trusts Christ as his Savior: he is
instantly freed from the penalty of sin, is credited with the perfect
righteousness of Jesus Christ, and receives eternal life (2 Cor. 5:21).
Because God's justice sees the righteousness of Christ, not our own
lack of righteousness, He judicially declares us to be righteous. This
act is known as *justification;* the believer is declared before the supreme court of heaven to be just because of who Jesus Christ is, not
because of who the believer is.

Phase two begins at the moment of salvation: we receive the Holy
Spirit, who enables us to have victory over the sin in our life. This
work takes place throughout the rest of our life and is a process known
as *sanctification*. During this phase, we learn to walk by the Spirit,
have victory over the present power of sin in our life, and renovate
our thinking based on the principles and precepts of the Word of God
(John 17:17).

Finally, when we go to be with the Lord and receive new bodies,
we will be saved from the very presence of sin. This third phase is
called *glorification*.

Although Christians are liberated from their *enslavement* to sin, this does not mean that they never sin or that resisting sin is easy. The sin nature is still very much present and is still set on asserting itself. Man's propensity to evil and rebellion against God is just as much there after salvation as it is before salvation. It's just that after salvation *he has a choice,* whereas before salvation he had no choice. He was a slave to sin (Rom. 6:17), he was "being corrupted in accordance with the lusts of deceit" (Eph. 4:22), he was spiritually dead (Eph. 2:1), and he was unable to perceive spiritual truth (1 Cor. 2:14). Before salvation, there was no choice; after salvation, however, we do have a choice. This is the power of the cross. The sin nature has power only if the believer chooses not to trust in God's Word and obey Him and, instead, places himself in a position of obedience to his past master.

This is where the central battle in the believer's spiritual life is taking place. The flesh is set against the Spirit and the Spirit against the flesh (Gal. 5:17). Peter tells us that these fleshly lusts wage war against the soul (1 Peter 2:11). It is not a battle that calls for demonic deliverance, exorcism, or any other sort of exotic practice that holds forth the empty promise that there will be no more struggle with a particular temptation or habitual sin. This battle takes place in your own heart. Are you going to "consider yourselves to be dead to sin" (Rom. 6:11)? This means that you must believe that sin no longer has power over you, and then you must live in light of that fact. It means that you must master sin (Gen. 4:7), and—through the power of God supplied through the Holy Spirit in conjunction with His Word—you can do so. To accept any notion of the Christian life that teaches that you can have a one-time experience and never struggle with sin and the flesh again is to accept unbiblical fantasy.

Several years ago, a news report described a number of immigrants from the Soviet Union who could not adjust to the freedom of the United States and so returned to Russia after a few years. They failed to adjust because many had not learned what was necessary to have a capacity to appreciate freedom and live on the basis of personal responsibility. Similarly, an unbeliever is born into a position of enslavement to a totalitarian regime with no freedom. If he emigrates, he is suddenly faced with freedoms that he never dreamed existed. At this point, he is faced with a choice: he can either continue to live as though he had no freedom, or he can believe that he is truly free and begin applying those freedoms to every area of his life. The people described in the article failed.

Most of us find it incredible that someone who has tasted freedom could then put himself back into a bondage relationship. Rejection of the grace of God is the reason. Israel did it at Kadesh Barnea in the Old Testament. Having been delivered from the slavery of Egypt, they faced the adversities of independence, rejected God's grace, and yearned to return to Egypt. Christians often follow that same pattern. Rather than living in light of their freedom from enslavement to sin, and then enjoying their freedom in Christ, in one or many areas they choose to continue living as though sin were still their master.

Morality Is Not Spirituality

Because the flesh can produce works that are disguised as morality and spirituality, it might be difficult for a person to tell whether his good deeds are simply the result of a sin nature that excels in producing good works (counterfeit good). As usual, the Bible does not leave us in the dark regarding the answer to this important question. One passage of Scripture is particularly helpful. As you read it, you might want to use it as a checklist for your own life.

In the epistle to the Galatians, the apostle Paul has to admonish the Galatians for following after the false teaching of the Judaizers, Jews who taught that salvation was not merely by faith alone in Christ alone, but that to truly have salvation and grow in the spiritual life, the Gentile Christian had to put himself under the Mosaic Law. They not only taught the necessity of circumcision but also enforced all of the mandates of the Mosaic Law. They were teaching spirituality by morality instead of spirituality based on the Holy Spirit (Gal. 3:3). This is not to say that spirituality is not moral, but that the life of the Christian demands a much higher basis for life, the Holy Spirit, and proclaims a system of ethics far beyond simple morality. Indeed, the Christian life is a supernatural life demanding a supernatural basis: walking by means of the Holy Spirit.

The Galatian believers were not an immoral or licentious congregation like the Corinthians. They were obsessed with morality and legal obedience. Yet, Paul castigates them for following a works- or morality-based approach to their relationship with God. Paul recognized that the flesh, the sin nature, can also produce morality, a good that perhaps imitates the behavior of the spiritually mature believer but that has the flesh as its source. In Galatians, he excoriated the congregation for attempting spirituality on the basis of the morality of the law, which was sin-nature generated, in contrast to walking by means of the Holy Spirit: "Are you so foolish? Having begun by the Spirit, are you now being perfected by the flesh?" (Gal. 3:3)

In Galatians 5:17–21, the apostle Paul describes the warfare existing between the Spirit and the flesh. To help us evaluate which is in control, Paul lists fifteen characteristics of the works of the flesh. No matter how good, moral, religious, or spiritual an activity might appear, if it is produced by the flesh, then these are some of the results that it will always produce.

These fifteen deeds of the flesh can be divided into four groups. The first group focuses on *sensual sin*. Immorality is based on the Greek word *porneia*, from which we get the English word *pornography*. It refers to any and all sexual activity outside the bounds of marriage, including homosexuality, premarital sex, and marital unfaithfulness. Any sexual activity between two people who are not of opposite sex and married to each other falls into this category. Impurity can refer to sexual sin, but it generally includes more than immorality. Sensuality, too, is broader than immorality and would include any sexual activity not necessarily involving fornication.

Physical and Mental Idolatry

The second category focuses on two activities typical of non-Christian religions—idolatry and sorcery. Idolatry is the worship of anything in the place of God. In ancient times (and in primitive cultures even today) people made idols as physical representatives of their gods. In America, our gods are usually more sophisticated idols of the mind, but even in ancient times idolatry started as a thought in the mind before it was formed into a physical image. Because we modern Americans do not usually fashion physical images, we often think that we are not idolatrous. Nothing is further from the truth! Modern man still thinks the same kinds of idolatrous thoughts as did the ancients, we just express them differently. We worship the abstract idols of success, money, career, sex, family, children, comforts, and the "good life." Any one of these can take the place of God in our lives and become a god unto itself. In one sense, we may be more deceived than the ancients because at least they were usually aware of what they worshiped. The average person today would never admit that his career or his children are his god.

The second activity in this group is sometimes translated "sorcery" but actually translates the Greek word *pharmakia* (from which we get *pharmacy*). Ernest De Witt Burton, in his classic commentary on Galatians, says of this word:

> . . . from Homer down [it] denotes a drug, whether harmful or wholesome. *Pharmakia* signifies in general the use of drugs, whether helpfully by a physician, or harmfully, hence poisoning. . . . In the LXX the word is uniformly employed in a bad sense, of witchcrafts or enchantments.[2]

This word encompasses all of the drug use and abuse so common today. Ultimately, it speaks of the reliance upon a drug (whether alcohol, cocaine, sleeping pills, or antidepressants) to provide the joy, peace, and freedom from anxiety in the midst of adversity that can come only through a right relationship with Jesus Christ (John 15:11; 17:13). (Of course, we are not talking about the legitimate use of medications for their healing benefits.)

Relational Fragmentation

The third group of works of the flesh contains eight deeds that show up in personal relationships: enmities, strife, jealousy, outbursts of anger, disputes, dissensions, factions, and envyings. Whenever people operate in the flesh, disruption and fragmentation results, first in the soul and then in relationships. As we examine this list of deeds, we cannot help but think about the large number of marriage problems and the high divorce rate among Christians today. Neither can we ignore the increase in child and spouse abuse that has become so widely recognized in the last decade. These are manifestations of sinful attitudes and living rather than living together to serve God and glorify Him.

The first of these words is one used rarely today: *enmity*. It carries the idea of antagonism and hostility. Fallen men are at enmity with both God and other men. The only other place in the New Testament that this word is found is in Ephesians 2:14–16, where the topic is the hostility between Jew and Gentile. Strictly speaking, in the context of the Bible, it has the definite connotation of anti-Semitism, but in broader application it would expand to the whole idea of personal animosity and hatred.

Strife, the second word of this group, is the practical outworking of the attitude of hostility. It focuses on the action of disruption and conflict. Like so many of these works of the flesh, it is the result of following self-serving desires rather than the desires of God.

Outbursts of anger, the third term, embodies the idea of temper tantrums or explosive bursts of anger rather than a deep, burning, long-term anger.

More Works of the Flesh

The next four words portray interrelated concepts: *disputes*, *dissensions*, *factions*, and *jealousy*. Each word describes similar works from a slightly different perspective. Each is based on self-seeking, self-serving, self-assertive attitudes that bring disruption of personal relationships from the family to the church. These actions characterized the Corinthian church. Because they were not serving Christ, but their own ends, the result was division. However, we must remember that not all division is evil (see 1 Cor. 11:19). Although the New Testament clearly exhorts Christians to be unified (see John 17:21; Eph. 4:1–6, 13), it is to be a unity based upon the clear doctrines of Scripture—a unity based *upon* doctrine and not *at the expense of* doctrine.

The final group of products of the flesh focuses on two acts that must be taken together: *drunkenness and carousings*. *Drunkenness* is clearly described here as a work of the flesh. Too often today, drunkenness and alcoholism are treated as a sickness. Yet, the works of the sin nature are clearly the results of our own choices. Although the Scriptures do not categorically prohibit the use of wine or alcohol, they are always to be used in moderation and never to the extent of producing inebriation or dependence. Although alcohol abuse might lead to a chemical dependency in some cases, the root problem is not physical but spiritual. Initially, the act was a sinful choice of the will. Although the chemical dependency, or physical problem, must be treated, the problem is only partially resolved if the sin issue is not dealt with.

The second word, *carousings*, is one not often used today. A more fitting word in today's vocabulary would be *partying*—having a celebration where liquor and drugs are freely used and abused, immoral activity is freely enjoyed, and fun and pleasure are indulged in at the expense of God's glory and holiness.

This litany of sins is as contemporary as the morning paper or the folks at last Sunday's church service. It is clear from this passage that these actions are not produced by demons, Satan, or the world but are the specific outworkings of a mindset and lifestyle that are controlled by the flesh and produced by the volition of the individual.

The Devil Made Me Do It?

The alarming fact is that a growing shift in belief exists among many Christians that places more and more responsibility for personal sin on demons or Satan. After reading articles and books written recently, we have seen references to demons named lust, murder, envy, gossip, and gluttony. Nowhere in Scripture is there any support for this concept, but Scripture explicitly says that these actions are a product of each person's sin nature and volition. In fact, as Galatians 5 clearly shows, these are not demons but works of the flesh. Believers who seek to blame demons for their failures are not being biblical in their handling of various issues.

Although those who teach such things may honestly desire to help Christians overcome the sin in their life, we believe that such teaching is nevertheless harmful because it supplies Christians with an unscriptural rationale for denying personal responsibility for sin: "The devil made me do it." Rather than accepting responsibility for our own bad decisions, we prefer to shift the responsibility to someone or something else. Rather than choosing the biblical solution of confessing known sin to God (1 John 1:9) and then ceasing the sinful thoughts or actions, many people attempt to solve the problem by "binding demons" or practicing "exorcisms."

Interestingly, passing the buck has been a convenient way of avoiding personal responsibility for sin ever since Adam and Eve. When God confronted Adam with his disobedience, Adam blamed Eve, and then Eve blamed the serpent. But God refused to accept this evasion and leveled a judgment on them because they were the ones who chose to yield. If you are a Christian, the issue is not who presents the temptation (Satan, demons, your sin nature, or your best friend) but whether you are going to trust God and obey Him or yield to the temptation. Christians who misplace their orientation on this matter are led astray from fighting the real enemy that Scripture says attacks in this area of warfare—their very own sin nature.

The Deep Cave of Sin

One reason many Christians fall into the trap of incorrect thinking on these issues is that too many people underestimate how incredibly evil their sin nature is and how its effects have permeated every aspect of their thinking. Because we are born in sin and in Satan's domain of darkness, it might be likened to being born deep inside Carlsbad Caverns with the lights off. When we move out in the direction of sin, it is like going even deeper into the caverns. Because we cannot see reality as it is, we attempt to construct a mental map of the cave and its appearance. Some aspects of this mental construct correspond more to reality than do others. Yet, the overall interpretation of reality is distorted by the lack of sight, the absence of an objective view of reality. This is how every member of the human race functions mentally until they are saved.

At salvation, the light of the truth of the gospel penetrates the darkness. We begin to see reality as it is, not merely as we have imagined it on our own to be. But that initial illumination is only the beginning. It provides us, we might say, with a flashlight so that we can see what is around us and begin to climb out of that darkness. The "flashlight" is analogous to the Spirit of God illuminating our thinking with the principles of God's Word. The more we use the light of God's Word, the more we see how things are in contrast to how we thought they were when we were in the darkness. But the process of reversing years of misconceptions and false ideas also takes time and discipline to study God's Word and the humility to accept its truth when it contradicts the "reality" that we constructed based on our experience. In our fast-food, drive-through, instant-gratification culture, we deceptively think we can achieve success over life-long habits of sin through some sort of quick-fix solution. We mistakenly believe that if we confess our sin, repent, or feel sorrow or regret for our sin, God will somehow lift us out of the cave by some spiritual elevator to the surface. But this just does not happen.

What *does* happen is that, by the power of the Holy Spirit and the light of God's Word, we are enabled to walk back out of the cave. It is a step-by-step process. It is not easy, but it is possible. This is God's perfect grace solution that is available to every believer (2 Cor. 12:9). As our thinking is transformed by the principles of God's Word, the Holy Spirit begins to produce a character transformation from the inside out. Unfortunately, many Christians have either tried some counterfeit gimmick to spirituality or have never really tried biblical Christianity, and they have subsequently given up in failure. They claim that the Bible just does not work. They then panic and turn to some quick-fix solution such as a emotionalism, mysticism, or secular psychology. One such solution that is currently popular is to blame deep-seated sin on the demons.

Defeating the Traitor

The flesh, like a spy or traitor, seeks its advantage through deception and secrecy. It seeks to avoid detection until its job of soul destruction is complete. It never surrenders, abdicates, or diminishes its power in this life. The confident promise of the Scriptures is that the sin nature's activity can be brought to light and at least partially neutralized by the ministry of God the Holy Spirit and the Word of God.

Galatians 5 gives us not only a description of how to recognize the symptoms of the flesh but also instructions for how to overcome the flesh. Christians (and only Christians) can do this because the tyranny of sin has been broken by our new position in Christ. Romans 6:6–7, 15–18 tells us that we are no longer under bondage to the sin nature; therefore, we are able to live in obedience to God. We achieve this goal as we walk by the Spirit.

In Galatians 5:16, Paul begins his instructions about the conflict between the flesh and the Spirit by simply commanding, "Walk by the Spirit, and you will not carry out the desire of the flesh." No mandate could be expressed more emphatically in the Greek language. In essence, Paul says, "Walk by means of the Spirit, and it will be impossible for you to fulfill the lusts of the sin nature." When the believer is living in moment-by-moment dependence upon God the Holy Spirit, in fellowship with God, and learning and applying doctrine, the sin nature is impotent. But the instant he chooses to yield to the enticing temptation offered by his sin nature, he comes under its control and begins to walk "according to the flesh."

The apostle then continues by describing the conflict between the two warring parties. He paints a vivid picture of what a person's life will be like depending on which of the two parties is in control.

The idea of *walking* involves a moment-by-moment faith in something. In the cavern analogy that we used earlier, it is that moment-by-moment walk up and out of the cave in dependence upon the light (the Holy Spirit and the Word of God). When we choose to operate in the flesh, the light goes out and we reverse the direction of our walk. Our step-by-step, moment-by-moment living is to be conducted in total reliance on the Word of God and the Holy Spirit. We are either moving forward or in reverse.

Walking pictures the believer's lifestyle as being dependent on the Holy Spirit moment by moment. We choose to follow the impulses of the sin nature, or we choose to depend on the Spirit. Too often, we rely on the flesh to do what only God can do, and that is why Paul penned this letter to the Galatian church. They had adopted the Mosaic Law from the Old Testament as their standard for living and were thereby attempting to live in reliance on the flesh. Although they were moral and religious, Paul warned the Galatians that they were attempting to do through their own power what only God can do through the Holy Spirit (Gal. 3:3).

Anyone, even unbelievers, can live a life that superficially appears to be in conformity to God's standard. But we know from Scripture that such living is done through dependence on the flesh. The Christian must know that he is not to try to live out his life in the power of the flesh. If he does, the effort will eventually manifest itself through the works of the flesh.

The walk by the Spirit is further clarified by the statement in Galatians 5:18, "If you are led by the Spirit, you are not under the Law." Because of the phrase "if you are led," some people might think that a Christian has an option in deciding whether to be led by the Spirit, but this is not the case because every person who has received Christ as Savior has been permanently indwelt by the Holy Spirit. From the point of salvation, the Holy Spirit continually leads the believer. Romans 8:14 tells us that "all who are being led by the Spirit of God [all Christians] . . . are sons of God." The context indicates that this is a leading in truth and holiness. Because we become children of God only when we receive Christ as Savior (John 1:12), we can be confident that the Spirit constantly leads us. *The issue is not whether we are being led but whether we are following.*

A New Understanding

When Jesus was preparing His disciples for the time when He would no longer be with them, He promised to send the Holy Spirit, who would guide them into all truth (John 16:13). This promise was fulfilled on the Day of Pentecost, as described in Acts 2. Once the Holy Spirit came, the new organism known as the church began and with it a whole new era in God's program.

Whenever a person in this age trusts Jesus Christ as his Savior, the Holy Spirit immediately comes to live in him. At this same time, the Holy Spirit also provides the ability to understand God's Word. This is not some kind of mystical, intuitive knowledge, and it is not simply picking up the Bible and immediately understanding it. What this basically means is that *we who were blind to spiritual truth and unable to understand the Word of God are now given the capacity to understand it.* As we study the Word, learn it, and meditate on it, the Holy Spirit enables us to understand it, and He applies it to our lives. Often, our understanding of some of the more difficult issues in Scripture might require years of study before we understand them accurately. Theologians call this "the illuminating ministry of the Holy Spirit." It is not a guarantee of infallibility when we interpret Scripture but a new, Spirit-directed capacity to understand what we could not understand before we were saved.

This new capacity enables us to understand the truth of God's Word and put it into practice. Throughout the New Testament is evident an important relationship between the Holy Spirit and the Word of God, both of which are said to be the means by which Christians grow. The Holy Spirit is the One who works in us and leads us whereas the Word of God is the means that He uses to bring this about. They are best friends and never travel alone. In addition, they never have an argument; they always agree. After all, the Holy Spirit is the agent that the Father used to write the Scriptures, so He knows them quite well! Therefore, the Holy Spirit would never lead anyone to do anything that conflicts with the written Word of God, no matter how convincing the circumstances or intense the experience.

The Mechanic's Tools

Suppose that we took a dented-up, poorly running 1957 Chevy to an auto mechanic for renovation. Our lives when we come to Christ may be compared to that Chevy. For years, we have been living in the flesh, and our lives reflect that fact. When we are saved, we do not automatically get a new set of ideas and a new set of circumstances. We have been regenerated, but now we must be transformed. Regeneration is the work of God in us that gives us a new nature and makes us willing to be transformed. Just as the auto mechanic renovates the car, the Holy Spirit transforms the wreck of our lives into something glorious for God.

If we took that old Chevy to a mechanic, no matter how talented and no matter how experienced he was, and expected him to renovate the car with only a screwdriver and a hammer, he would laugh us out of the garage. The mechanic personally has the ability to perform the task, but he is limited by the tools we allow him to use. The same is true of the Holy Spirit. The tools that He uses to transform our lives are found in the Word of God. The more tools we let Him use, the more equipped He is to perform the task. This is why we are commanded to renew our minds (Rom. 12:2) and to let the Word of Christ dwell *richly* within us (Col. 3:16). The failure of many Christians to allow the Holy Spirit to use all of the necessary tools is one of the major reasons why these same people often think that Christianity and the solutions of the Bible do not work. They then turn to a new experience that is supposed to enable them to deal with their problems, or they start to think that the Bible needs help from another source, such as psychology, to really help them with their problems.

The Spirit of God leads us through the Word of God. By learning God's Word, we give the Spirit the tools to renovate and transform our life. This process takes place in two ways. First, when we encounter temptation, the Holy Spirit recalls to our mind what the Bible teaches regarding that sin. When we choose to yield to the temptation and sin, we grieve the Spirit and shift from walking by the Spirit to walking according to the flesh. Second, the Spirit leads us through conviction, which takes place through our conscience to the degree that our conscience has been transformed by the new standards of God's Word. When we refuse to yield to temptation by applying what we have learned from the Word of God, spiritual growth takes place. We are now on the road to maturity, increasingly able to "discern good and evil" (Heb. 5:14). If we sin, when we are convicted by the Spirit we should turn away from our sin and back to God. Part of this turning involves confessing our sin, which, according to 1 John 1:9, is to be a standard characteristic of the Christian life.

The secret to controlling the flesh is *learning the Word of God—* letting it transform our lives and then living in accordance with this new standard. This explains Paul's second use of "walk by the Spirit" in Galatians 5:25, where the Greek word for "walk" is *stoicheo*, not *peripateo*. *Stoicheo* means to "follow a path, walk in the footsteps." The path that is laid out is the objective directions of the Word of God. Thus, we walk in moment-by-moment dependence, led by the Spirit down the path of God's Word.

Nine Kinds of Fruit

Over a period of time, walking by the Spirit (just like walking by the flesh) will produce certain results called fruit. The ninefold fruit of the Spirit is described in Galatians 5:22–23. These nine character traits are evident in the life of the Christian who is walking by the Spirit. God has given us these checklists so that we can evaluate our lives to see if we are walking by the Spirit or the flesh.

Love, the first fruit of the Spirit, is often misunderstood today. This is not an emotional or sentimental word. Several different words are used in Greek for love, each focusing on a different shade of meaning. The word used here is *agape,* which connotes a mental attitude of selfless concern for others rather than an emotional attachment. The best description of this love is found in 1 Corinthians 13 and in Christ Himself (John 3:16; Rom. 5:8).

The second fruit of the Spirit is *joy.* This is neither happiness nor exuberance, but a kind of stable, uplifted mental attitude that is neither disturbed nor upset by shifting circumstances. It is the attitude that Christians are to have when they face difficulties and suffering.

Peace is next. Most often in Scripture this word is used to indicate the opposite of anxiety. It is not a reference to world peace, military peace, or political peace but to a mental attitude that is relaxed and untroubled by worry and anxiety because it rests in the care and provision of God (Phil. 4:6–7).

Patience has the idea of longsuffering or not responding to immediate threats, but giving people time to change and come around. The perfect example of this is the patience that God has with us. This patience is manifested toward both people and events. This is not some grim, bleak hanging-in-there attitude but is linked with joy and peace.

Kindness and *goodness* are closely related ideas. Kindness is the attitude, and goodness is the action. Kindness is in some sense related to patience. It is an attitude of courtesy, respect, and consideration for people. Goodness describes the gracious actions toward others that are motivated by kindness.

Faithfulness expresses the idea of loyalty and consistency—values sorely needed in contemporary society. This characteristic includes loyalty to God, loyalty to one's spouse, loyalty to one's children, and loyalty to the church. Too often, commitments in these areas are honored only when they are convenient. Faithfulness is demonstrated when the commitment to these areas is neither convenient nor pleasant.

Gentleness is sometimes translated "meekness." Someone who is gentle or meek is too often pictured as being a wimp or a doormat, but nothing could be further from the biblical concept. The biblical idea of meekness is often contrasted with pride or arrogance, a central characteristic of the world system. In this sense, meekness is synonymous with humility. We must be reminded that "God is opposed to the proud, but gives grace to the humble" (James 4:6). Gentleness flows from recognizing who we are and submitting to God. This quality is in direct opposition to the self-assertive works of the flesh.

The last fruit of the Spirit mentioned is *self-control*, or self-mastery. This particular type of self-discipline is often associated with the control of sexual desire, but it also applies to every other area of life. As we continue to grow and to develop godly habit patterns in our life, the Holy Spirit strengthens our ability to master our sinful self and to control those fleshly desires so that we do not give in to sinful temptations.

The sin problem with which we so often struggle is the direct result of yielding to our own sinful nature. It is the flesh that wars against the soul. It is the flesh that is drawn and attracted to the temptations of the world and Satan. It is the flesh that is weak. Because neither Satan nor the world system can cause us to sin, the secret of deliverance lies in learning to walk in moment-by-moment, step-by-step dependence on the Holy Spirit.

6

INVASION OF THE KING

If I cast out demons by the Spirit of God, then the kingdom of God has come upon you.

—Matthew 12:28

Nolan Ryan is unique. Never in the history of major league baseball did a power pitcher maintain a ninety-five-miles-per-hour fastball at the age of forty-three. A few pitchers have survived that long, but none before Nolan Ryan had been able to maintain that degree of effective velocity on his fastball.

Jesus Christ is also unique, except He is infinitely greater. Never before or since in the history of mankind has there ever been a man who was also God. If Nolan Ryan is special in the field of baseball, then to an infinite degree Jesus Christ is unique to the human race. Never before was anyone like Him, and never again will there be anyone like Him. Jesus Christ is the eternal, infinite, unique Person of the universe.

God the Father sent Jesus Christ on a unique mission to the earth to accomplish a number of unique objectives. Chief among them was to live a perfect life to qualify Him to die on the cross as a perfect substitutionary sacrifice for the sins of the world. No other human in history could have accomplished this task because all others inherited Adam's sin and were disqualified. But Jesus Christ was uniquely born through the virgin conception and birth; therefore, He was untainted by Adam's original sin. Jesus Christ, the eternal second person of the Trinity willingly came to earth and fulfilled His mission, to free the human race from the penalty and slavery of sin that man might be restored to His original relationship with God to fulfill God's plan for mankind.[1]

The Unique Ministry of Christ

When it comes to establishing a biblical basis for many of the current deliverance ministries, many of them attempt to model their ministries after Christ's unique ministry, in which He came into direct conflict with Satan and his demons. But these events in the life of Christ were unique to His special, unique ministry. Although we are to be Christlike in emulating His *character*, many specific things that He said and did were related to His special, unique ministry as the God-man who came into the world to save sinners. How, then, do we distinguish those aspects of the life of Christ that we are to emulate from those that were part of His unique messianic ministry and that He alone was called upon to do? We believe that the New Testament Epistles were revealed to provide instructions on how Christians are to live during the current church age. Therefore, the Epistles instruct believers in only those things that they have been specifically called upon and equipped by God to do. Therefore, nowhere in the Epistles does one find commands or examples relating to the exorcising, binding, or rebuking of demons (more about this later).[2]

Although believers are mandated to imitate the *character* of Christ, His miracles and His conflicts with the powers of darkness were the calling cards to His unique messiahship. These miracles are not a pattern for the types of direct encounters with demons that many people within the deliverance movement claim. Although it is true that believers today are tempted as was Jesus the Messiah and that we are involved in spiritual warfare, we are to engage in warfare in a somewhat different way, as we will seek to demonstrate in the next chapter.

One reason many people get into trouble in spiritual warfare is that they fail to understand why Jesus encountered demons during His walk on earth and why these events are recorded for us. We will have a proper perspective of spiritual warfare only if we understand the purpose behind the unique ministry of Jesus.

Messiah Comes to Israel

The Gospel of Matthew was written to answer the primary question that the Jews had about the messiahship of Jesus: "If Jesus the Nazarene is truly the foretold Messiah, then where is the messianic kingdom?" Many Jews had erroneously concluded that Jesus was not the Messiah because the messianic kingdom had not yet arrived as anticipated. However, Matthew explains why the messianic kingdom did not come. It was not because Jesus is not Messiah, but rather because Israel in unbelief rejected their King, and there cannot be a kingdom without a King. This explains why the events of Matthew's Gospel build toward chapter twelve and the famous confrontation between Jesus and the Pharisees, who accused Christ of performing His miracles by the power of Beelzebul ("the ruler of the demons") or Satan (12:22–37).

At this point, Christ notes that Israel was committing the sin of "blasphemy against the Spirit" (Matt. 12:31) by rejecting the Holy Spirit's testimony that Jesus was Israel's Messiah. His claim to be Messiah had been certified through His many signs, wonders, and miracles, which included His power over Satan and demons, as the immediate context reveals (12:22–37). Not even the Pharisees could deny this fact. Therefore, instead of questioning the authenticity of the miracles of Jesus, they credited the source of His miracles to Satan rather than to God. Anything but admit the truth—Jesus was the promised Messiah.

Matthew contrasts this unbelief with the belief of John the Baptist in chapter 11. What gave rise to the expression of John's faith were the incidents related in Matthew 10, which tells us that Jesus gathered His disciples and gave them "authority over unclean spirits, to cast them out" (10:1) so that they could go throughout Israel announcing that the King was there ("the kingdom of heaven is at hand," 10:7). What was the confirming evidence that would demonstrate to the lost sheep of the house of Israel that Jesus was the Messiah? The ability to heal and cast out demons (Isa. 29:18–19; 35:5–6).

After this event, John the Baptist, who had been incarcerated by Herod, sent word to Jesus, asking if He was indeed the Messiah. Jesus responded by pointing to the confirmatory signs: "The blind receive sight and the lame walk, the lepers are cleansed and the deaf hear, and the dead are raised up, and the poor have the gospel preached to them" (Matt. 11:5). The parallel passage also includes the casting out of demons (Luke 7:21). John's response clearly reveals the divine purpose for these signs and wonders, including demonic deliverances. The result, John's faith in Jesus was reconfirmed. But his belief was in stark contrast to the unbelief of the Pharisees. When they witnessed the miracles of Jesus, they could not dispute them, so they attributed them to Satan. The point that we dare not overlook is that *Jesus' encounters with the demons were directly related to His claim to be the Messiah and His offer of the kingdom.*

Preview of the Kingdom

Most readers have undoubtedly seen a film preview, either on television or while attending another movie. The film trailer is designed to indicate something , but not too much, of what the movie is like. It sparks your curiosity to see that particular film. The trailer is designed to make a strong appeal so that you will decide to see the movie itself. In a certain sense, this was one of the purposes for Christ's first coming, and it explains some aspects of His ministry: to whet our appetite for the Second Coming and the messianic kingdom.

One of the major reasons Christ demonstrated He had power over sickness, nature, and the spiritual realm (including Satan and demons) was to provide a glimpse of what the messianic kingdom would be like if Israel would accept Jesus as their Messiah. But the kingdom would not arrive until the nation Israel acknowledged Jesus as their King. Instead, they rejected Him by choosing the rebel Barabbas in place of Jesus and said concerning Christ, "We do not want this man to reign over us" (Luke 19:14). Jesus proclaimed just before He gave the Olivet Discourse (Matt. 24–25), "Your house [Israel's temple] is being left to you desolate! For I say to you, from now on you shall not see Me until you say, 'Blessed is He who comes in the name of the Lord!' " (Matt. 23:38–39).

Israel's kingdom was related to their response to the messiahship of Jesus. Because they rejected Him, the messianic kingdom was postponed until the yet-future time toward the end of the Great Tribulation, when they will say, "Blessed is He who comes in the name of the Lord!"

The apostle Peter made a similar point to his Jewish countrymen in Acts 3:19–21: "Repent therefore and return, that your sins may be wiped away, in order that times of refreshing [the messianic kingdom] may come from the presence of the Lord; and that He may send Jesus, the Christ [Messiah] appointed for you [Israel], whom heaven must receive until the period of restoration of all things about which God spoke by the mouth of His holy prophets from ancient time."

Christ's first coming upon the earth did not result in the inauguration of His messianic kingdom *in any form*. Even though Christ offered it and provided a foretaste of what that time would be like, Israel rejected the King; thus, the kingdom was postponed until Christ returns to the earth in glory at the Second Coming.

By taking power and authority over Satan, demons, sickness, and disease, Christ gave a preview of the glorious conditions that will exist during the messianic kingdom, when the effects of the Curse (satanic oppression and sickness) will be lifted for a thousand years. How does this influence our study of Satan and demons? We shall see as we examine Christ's interaction with demonic forces during His first coming.

Stirring Up the Insects

In parts of Texas during the summer, you can look out at a field of Johnson grass and everything appears to be calm and inactive. However, when you walk through that field you stir things up. Often a wave of grasshoppers and other insects spring into action as you plod through the field. Some of them might cling to your clothing as you pass through, and occasionally you might come upon a jackrabbit or two or even a rattlesnake. What causes this kind of activity? Just the presence of a human being walking nearby upsets the normal, hidden activities that had been going on in this field of grass.

The same was true of Christ's ministry. Often it was just His presence passing through the land of Israel that caused the activity of the demonic realm to become noticeable. The activity had existed all along, but our Lord's messianic presence stirred up the spiritual realm and brought that activity out into the open. On one occasion, a demon asked Christ, "Have You come here to torment us before the time?" (Matt. 8:29), indicating his tremendous fear of the authority of the Lord of the Universe. Yes, Christ had come to stir things up at His first coming, but His final victory arrives only in the future, when Jesus establishes the messianic kingdom. Much of the demonic activity in Israel during that time can be attributed to the mere presence of Christ, the God-man.

That this heightened confrontation with the demonic realm during Jesus' life was related to His unique ministry is further seen by studying the way and frequency with which the New Testament talks about demons. The Greek word for "demon" *(daimonion)* and its related words are used seventy-seven times in the New Testament. Sixty-seven times the word is found in the four Gospels, seven times in the Epistles, and three times in Revelation.

A similar proportion is found in the forty-two times that the synonym for demons, "evil/unclean spirits," is used: twenty-three times in the Gospels, thirteen times in Acts, three times in the Epistles, and three times in Revelation.

The Three-Part Plan

The frequency and way in which the New Testament handles issues relating to the demonic is not consistent with the thinking and practice being advocated by many people in contemporary deliverance ministries. We are not setting one portion of the New Testament against another; instead, because these two sections are harmonious, we must recognize that the Epistles do not warn believers to look out for demon possession, nor do they describe how to become engaged in a deliverance ministry. Yet, these activities were central to the ministry of Christ and to a lesser degree of the apostles. Why was this the case?

We think that one of the primary reasons that 87 percent of the 119 references to demons occur in the historical section (Gospels and Acts) of the New Testament is because they are tied to the unique events associated with the messianic mission of Jesus and the beginning and establishment of the church. Complete victory over Satan and the demonic realm is scheduled to occur only when the messianic kingdom arrives. Jesus came to offer Israel this kingdom, but Israel rejected their King and His kingdom. Therefore, the messianic kingdom is delayed during the current church age, until Christ's second coming brings the removal of Satan and his demonic hordes from His thousand-year rule upon this earth. However, because Christ was on the earth during His first coming, He was engaged in direct battle with Satan and the demonic, whereas during His current absence the battle is carried out indirectly, or defensively, as we shall show in later chapters.

Make no mistake: Christ secured complete victory at the cross over Satan and the demonic. The realization of Christ's victory in our experience is implemented in progressive stages. *Phase one* of salvation is when we become believers, at which time we are justified (declared righteous, Gal. 2:20), we are given new spiritual life (regeneration, Titus 3:5), and we become new creatures in Christ (2 Cor. 5:17). All of which—plus much, much more—God does for us at the moment when we trust Christ alone for our salvation. During *phase two*, we live the Christian life; we still possess a sin nature and are still able to commit any sin that any unbeliever can commit, but we are also able not to sin. It will not be until *phase three*, however, when we receive our new, resurrection body which is free from a sin nature, that we will be totally and absolutely free from all aspects of sin.

God's plan is certain and sure because the price of our full redemption has already been paid by Christ on the cross. It is not an issue of whether He can do it; rather, His plan is being accomplished in different phases. So it is with Christ's victory over Satan and the demonic realm: it is being carried out in phases. This fact is crucial to understanding what is going on when Christ encounters Satan and the demonic powers in the Gospels.

Now let us take a closer look at how Jesus dealt with the powers of darkness.

Satan Attacks Jesus

At the beginning of His ministry, Jesus Christ went into the wilderness to pray and fast for forty days (Matt. 4:1-11). At the end of this fasting period, Satan appeared and tempted Him three times. When He was tempted, Christ countered Satan with Scripture but did not enter into extended dialogue with him or argue with him over the interpretation of a passage. On the third temptation, Christ rebuked Satan and told him to be gone. Satan left immediately, and no extended dialogue or argument ensued.

Satan did not try to cast a mystical spell over Jesus to bind Him to his will as though He were a mere robot. Instead, the force of Satan's temptations was based on the intended compulsion of his arguments. The first argument was an attempt to flatter Christ because He is God's Son (Matt. 4:3). Here Satan used a fallacious theology based on Jesus' deity. If Jesus had succumbed, He would have been operating independently of the Father's plan and thus would have compromised His mission. Jesus countered by correctly quoting and applying Deuteronomy 8:3, which emphasizes the priority of obedience to God over all else.

In the second argument, Satan became more sophisticated and quoted Scripture (Ps. 91:11-12). Indeed, it was both a misinterpretation and misapplication of the passage. Satan tempted Christ to put on a show of His miraculous power by leaping off the pinnacle of the temple (Matt. 4:5-6) and having the angels rescue Him, thereby gaining fame and notoriety. In other words, Satan attempted to get Christ to act by Satan's methods. Christ parried this argument by accurately interpreting and applying Scripture: "You shall not put the Lord your God to the test" (Matt. 4:7, quoting from Deut. 6:16).

In the third argument, Satan offered Christ the whole world if He would worship him (Matt. 4:8-9). Jesus did not dispute Satan's ability to make the offer; the Tempter was truly the "god of this world." But Christ's terse and pointed response in verse 10 was an accurate use of Deuteronomy 6:13: "You shall worship the Lord your God, and serve Him only."

Jesus' response to the attack of Satan serves as a prototype for how the believer is to handle such attacks. First, unlike Eve, at no time did

Christ give in to the logic of Satan's temptations. Instead, Christ penetrated the deceptive approach of Satan because He knew the Scriptures and was able to counter with God's way of thinking. He accurately used the "living and active" Word of God (Heb. 4:12). Second, the nature of this encounter was not mystical, two sorcerers attacking each other with their magical powers, as has been depicted in contemporary cartoons. Third, the power that enabled Jesus to defeat the temptations was the truth inherent in the Scripture, not a metaphysical power or use of the Holy Spirit. Remember that Jesus is handling these temptations in His humanity, and thus setting the pattern and example for us. This encounter with Satan is not designed to provide credentials, as was the case with casting out demons.

Christ's handling of Satan's temptations is the exact pattern of dealing with such temptation that is prescribed in the Epistles for believers. Since Satan and his demons are still tempting God's people during the church age by spewing out false ways of looking at life's issues in terms of *cosmic* thinking and doctrines of demons (1 Tim. 4:1; James 3:15), Christ's handling of the temptation serves as the model of how believers can stand firm and counter the attacks of Satan and the demonic powers. This is the pattern laid out in the Epistles as well.

Binding and Loosing

Some years ago, we witnessed a "deliverance" service conducted by a well-known pioneer in the field. Many bizarre things happened at the service. Many of the demons had names, such as the demon of lust, gluttony, worry, gossip, and criticism. One demon was even named after a particular food.

The "deliverance" evangelist had a routine that he followed in casting demons from people. First, he found out a little about the individual. He then asked him what his problem was. (He always assumed that it was caused by a demon rather than some other source.) Then he spoke authoritatively to the demon and commanded the demon to manifest itself. Having done this, he usually carried on a conversation with the demon, often quite humorous, as he would insult, question, and finally command the demon to leave "in the

name of Jesus" and "by the power of the blood of Christ." Some demons required several conversations before eventually departing. One
of the things he always did when he was commanding them to depart
was to bind them and send them to the "pit of hell."

The practice of binding Satan and/or the demons and evil spirits
is not only something that some Christians do during public and pri-
vate deliverance sessions but also is often a personal activity exercised regularly by an increasing number of Christians. Sometimes a
person will pray that Satan will be bound from blinding a person to
whom he or she is presenting the gospel in the belief that this will
improve the likelihood of the listener's trusting Christ as his Savior.
Or someone might pray that an upcoming event would be protected
from the influence of the demonic powers by binding the demons
from having influence in relation to that event. On other occasions,
people attempt to bind Satan and his demons from certain geographi-
cal locations, such as a new house into which the person will be moving, a new church building, or a particular location in a city or
neighborhood. Doing this, they believe, could improve the power and
moving of God in the lives of believers as well as unbelievers.

Many people view this practice as necessary for successful spiritual warfare. Let us look at the primary Bible passages from which
those who hold this belief say they have a scriptural mandate for such
a practice.

Mandate for Binding?

The misinterpretation of three passages in Matthew form the
primary basis for the popular "binding" teaching and practice. First,
we will consider Matthew 12:29, in which Jesus said, "How can anyone
enter the strong man's house and carry off his property unless he
first binds the strong man?" Christ made this statement as an
illustration in His refutation of the Pharisees' assertion that Jesus
"casts out demons only by Beelzebul the ruler of the demons" (12:24).
The Pharisees refused to admit, as many of the people were beginning
to suggest, that Jesus was truly the Son of David (12:23), the promised
Messiah of God. Therefore, they attributed His power to an alliance
with Beelzebul, their only other supernatural alternative in the

universe. Christ's response affirmed His sovereignty over Satan. The illustration pointed out that one would have to control the strong man before his house could be robbed. The logic of Christ's argument is that Christ was not in league with Satan but was casting out demons by the virtue of His inherent divine power. It would be wrong to conclude from this passage that Christ was laying down a universal pattern for believers to follow. Instead, this was a historic illustration of Christ's personal power over Satan.

A day will arrive when Satan, "the strong man," will be bound, along with his demonic host, and we do not have to speculate as to when that will be. Revelation 20:1–3 reveals that Satan will be bound for a one-thousand-year period during the Millennial kingdom immediately after Christ's second coming. He is not released again until the final days of the Millennial kingdom, when he instigates the last insurrection against the Lord in the Gog and Magog revolution. Following the Millennium, Satan will be deposited into the lake of fire for all eternity (Rev. 20:10). Meanwhile, during the current age, Satan is "a roaring lion, seeking someone to devour" (1 Peter 5:8). The antidote for the believer is not to bind him but to "resist him, firm in your faith" (1 Peter 5:9 with James 4:7). *Jesus Himself* will bind the strong man, Satan, on behalf of His followers at a future time. He never uses believers to act on His behalf in this area.

The Keys of the Kingdom

I will give you the keys of the kingdom of heaven; and whatever you shall bind on earth shall have been bound in heaven, and whatever you shall loose on earth shall have been loosed in heaven. (Matt. 16:19)

Truly I say to you, whatever you shall bind on earth shall have been bound in heaven; and whatever you loose on earth shall have been loosed in heaven. (Matt. 18:18)

The focus of these passages is on the word *bind (deo)*. How is this word used in context, and what does it mean? The word has the basic meaning of "to tie up by binding." The result is inactivity on the part of the one bound. Here, the word *bind* is used with its opposite, "loose." In these contexts, the idea of binding and loosing has the force of the judicial notion of "forbidding" and "permitting." Israel's religious leaders used this phrase in Christ's day to refer to what was forbidden (bound) and what was permitted (loosed). This is why our Lord told Peter that He would give him "the keys of the kingdom of heaven; and whatever you shall bind on earth shall be bound in heaven, and whatever you shall loose on earth shall be loosed in heaven" (Matt. 16:19).

Peter was to become one of the apostles upon whom the Christian church would be founded (Eph. 2:20). Therefore, Peter and the apostles would be the human agents through whom entrance into the kingdom of heaven would be denied or allowed, depending upon whether one's key matched the lock. The words *shall be bound* and *shall be loosed* as used in the Greek perfect tense mean that the binding and loosing in heaven will precede the binding and loosing on earth.

A translation that brings out this aspect of the original Greek would read as follows: "I will give to you the keys of the kingdom of the heavens, but whatever you bind on earth is that which shall already have been bound in the heavens, and whatever you loose on earth is that which shall already have been loosed in the heavens." Peter was to bind things upon the earth, but only what had already been bound in heaven. Peter was to set the standard on earth for entrance into the kingdom of heaven based upon the standard that God had already set in heaven—those who respond to the gospel of faith alone in Christ alone will be eternally secure in their salvation. Peter was to be a mediator of the Word of God between God and man, and that standard is what Peter stated in Matthew 16:16, namely, that Jesus was "the Christ, the Son of the living God." The instant that a person trusts Christ as Savior, he is "bound," destined for eternity in heaven. When a person rejects Christ as Savior, he is "loosed," that is, "judged already, because he has not believed in the name of the only begotten Son of God" (John 3:18).

Affirming God's Will

"Binding and loosing" are used in exactly the same way in Matthew 18:18, which is literally translated as follows: "Truly I am telling you, whatever you may bind upon the earth shall be that which has already been bound in heaven; and whatever you may loose upon the earth shall be that which has already been loosed in heaven." Jesus is saying that believers can have confidence that when they justly excommunicate someone on earth, they are fulfilling the will of God that has already been determined in heaven. This truth should give them confidence in what they are doing. So in this context binding and loosing carry the idea that corresponds to our modern judicial language of declaring someone guilty (binding) or innocent (loosing). The court decision does not make someone guilty or innocent but simply determines whether his past acts violate or conform to God's heavenly standard.

In both passages, neither word suggests anything similar to the contemporary notion of binding Satan or the demonic powers. Instead, these references refer to carrying out God's heavenly will upon earth as it has already been determined in heaven. In fact, the contemporary idea of binding and loosing has more in common with the methods related to the casting and removal of spells found in the occult than with anything related to biblical Christianity. Therefore, we as believers must be extremely careful when we adopt practices that are not mandated by the Scriptures. One scholar in commenting on these two passages has said:

> A purely magical binding and loosing such as may be found elsewhere in Greek and Rabbinic usage [passages outside of the Bible] is ruled out by the context. Jesus does not give to Peter and the other disciples any power to enchant or to free by magic. The customary meaning of the Rabbinic expressions is equally incontestable, namely, to declare forbidden or permitted, and thus to impose or remove an obligation, by a doctrinal decision.[3]

Neutral Practice?

Someone might claim that this is a neutral practice used either for good or for evil. This is the same logic that is often used in magic. Those who believe that they use magic to do good call it white magic whereas an evil use of magic is called black magic. The problem is that the Bible does not teach the use of this technique *at all*. It is an unproven assumption that extrabiblical practices can be used for good. The Bible teaches us to do God's will in God's way. We are not saying that everyone who uses this approach is necessarily flirting with the occult, but we are saying that it is possible for sincere use of this technique to result in the occult practice of casting and countering spells because the Bible does not advocate this type of technique.

From Revelation 20:2, 10, this kind of direct conflict with Satan and the demonic powers seems to be carried on in the heavenly realm, not the earthly realm. God either directly moves to limit Satan and the demonic powers or He uses His elect angels to accomplish His will in this regard. As we shall show in the rest of the book, God's strategy for humanity is to deal with the specific issue or sin through which Satan and the demonic powers might be attacking us, and to deal with that sin or issue directly. Believers are never authorized to engage Satan or demons directly. When we obey God's will relating to the issue, God and His angels will deal with Satan and the demonic powers behind the scene.

Christ's Conflict with the Demonic Powers

Demon-related material occurs on eleven occasions in the first three Gospels. It is helpful to notice the following breakdown of this material (parallel passages in parentheses). Three *general* statements about casting out demons: (1) Matthew 4:24: ". . . they brought to Him all who were ill, taken with various diseases and pains, demoniacs, epileptics, paralytics; and He healed them" (cf. Mark 3:11; Luke 6:18); (2) Matthew 8:16: "When evening had come, they brought to Him many who were demon-possessed; and He cast out the spirits with a word, and healed all who were ill" (cf. Mark 1:29–34; Luke 4:38–41); (3) Luke 7:21: "At that very time He cured many people of diseases and afflictions and evil spirits; and He granted sight to many who were blind."

Eight *specific* incidents are also described: (1) Mark 1:23–28 (cf. Luke 4:33–37); (2) Matthew 8:28–34 (cf. Mark 5:1–20; Luke 8:26–40); (3) Matthew 15:21–28 (cf. Mark 7:24–30); (4) Matthew 17:14–21 (cf. Luke 8:2); (5) Mark 9:14–29 (cf. Luke 9:37–43); (6) Matthew 12:22 (cf. Luke 11:14); (7) Luke 13:10–17; (8) Matthew 9:32–34. Two passages cover the disciples and the demonic: (1) Matthew 10:1–16 (cf. Mark 3:13–19; Luke 9:1); and (2) Mark 6:7, 13. One incident of teaching was related to the Pharisees' accusation that Christ's power came from Beelzebub (Matt. 12:43–45; cf. Mark 3:22–30; Luke 11:14–26).

In the first section, we see three general statements relating to Jesus' casting out of demons. In the first incident, many people were bringing the sick and demon possessed to Jesus, and He was healing them and casting out "many demons" (Mark 1:34). The purpose for these events was to demonstrate that Jesus was the Son of God, as some of the demons were testifying (Luke 4:41). This point is consistent with the purpose of the first three Gospels: to demonstrate that Jesus was the Messiah because He had power and authority over the demonic realm.

One reason why this fact is significant goes back to the first prophecy about the Messiah in the Bible, found in Genesis 3:15: "I will put enmity between you and the woman, and between your seed and her seed; he shall bruise you on the head, and you shall bruise him on the heel." The Messiah would gain victory over Satan, and Jesus demonstrated this to Israel. Because He had power and authority over Satan and the demonic powers, He was the promised Messiah.

When Jesus cast out the demons, many of them were "crying out and saying, 'You are the Son of God!' And rebuking them, He would not allow them to speak, because they knew Him to be the Christ [the Messiah]" (Luke 4:41). This incident is in stark contrast to many people within the contemporary deliverance ministries who carry on conversations with demons. Generally, Christ did not permit them to speak, or even to convey the truth that He was God's Son, apparently because He did not want otherwise lying spirits to testify to the truth.

Only once did Jesus ask them to identify themselves (Mark 5:9). Jesus wanted Israel to believe the truth because it came from the mouth of *God* and not from the mouth of *demons*. Also, He did not want to give the people who were weighing the evidence of His deliverance an opportunity to reject Him because the testimony came from an unreliable source, thus affirming the principle that a right thing done in a wrong way is still wrong. The ends never justify the means. Man cannot compromise with evil—even to achieve an alleged noble end.

Jesus' unique ministry is again seen in the third general statement of casting out demons. This incident involved John the Baptist, who had been imprisoned by King Herod because he offended Herod's wife with his preaching. While in prison, John began to wonder if Jesus was really the Messiah after all. He sent a messenger to Jesus to inquire about the matter, and Jesus' response is described in Luke 7:21: "At that very time He cured many people of diseases and afflictions and evil spirits." This description of what Jesus was doing was enough to remove all doubt from John because it was a description of indisputable messianic activity.

Category	Scripture		
	Matthew	**Mark**	**Luke**
Three general statements of casting out demons	8:16 4:24	1:29–34 3:11	4:38–41 6:18 7:21
Eight specific incidents described with details	15:21–28 8:28–34 17:14–21 12:22 9:32–34	1:23–28 5:1–20 7:24–30 9:14–29	4:33–37 8:26–40 9:37–43 8:2 11:14 13:10–17
One incident of teaching related to the Pharisees' accusation that Jesus' power came from Beelzebub (Satan)	12:43–45	3:22–30	11:14–26
Two occasions regarding the disciples	10:1–16	3:13–19 6:7, 13	9:1

The Specific Cases

The seven specific incidents described in the first three Gospels follow the general pattern that we observed earlier. In the first incident, Jesus entered a synagogue, a place of worship, and an unclean spirit cried out of someone, "What do we have to do with You, Jesus of Nazareth? Have You come to destroy us? I know who You are—the Holy One of God!" (Mark 1:24). Once again, Jesus commanded the demon to be quiet, and then He cast the evil spirit out of the man. This incident brought Jesus notoriety regarding His authority over the demonic powers.

Undoubtedly, the most extensive narrative relating to the demonic powers occurs in the incident often titled "The Gadarene Demoniac" (5:1–20). This is the story about Jesus' casting demons out of a man and into a herd of swine. As usual, the encounter began when the demons in the man recognized Christ as "Jesus, Son of the Most High God" (v. 7). Jesus then cast out the demons, but here He commanded the unclean spirit to first give Him his name. The demon replied, "My name is Legion; for we are many" (v. 9). Notice that the demon was not named lust, gossip, adultery, hate, or any of the other names often given to demons by those involved in contemporary deliverance attempts. "Legion" is more of a generic description that shows that many unclean spirits were within the man. It could not have been a proper name unless the entire multitude all had the same name—a highly unlikely possibility. Instead of the current popular belief that names of demons are related to the sin or habit that they inflict upon their subject, the Bible reveals something quite different.

This is the only place where Jesus carried on any extended dialogue with demons, but it was not to acquire information from them, as some contemporary deliverance practitioners advocate but rather to accommodate a request from the demons as to where they would be going. When the man was delivered, Jesus forbade him to travel with Him, but instead instructed him to return "home to your people and report to them what great things the Lord has done for you, and how He had mercy on you" (v. 19). Christ did not allow the demons to testify to who He was, but He did want this delivered man to testify to God's mercy and grace, which was the basis for his deliverance.

Incidents three through seven follow the same general pattern as is noted in the previous examples.

One of the most significant observations we can make is that *not a single one of these cases reveals someone who came to Jesus in order to be delivered of a demon!* Each person was brought by someone else, except for the Gadarene. And in that instance he did not come to Jesus to be delivered, but "he ran up and bowed down," indicating worship, and asked, "What do I have to do with You, Jesus, Son of the Most High God?" Then he begged Jesus not to torment him. This man clearly was not coming for deliverance. If anything can be inferred from these examples, it is that demon-possessed people do not seek deliverance.

A second observation regards terminology. Never is it said that Jesus or the disciples exorcised a demon. The English *exorcism* is a transliteration from the Greek *exorkizo,* which is always used of the magical, ritualistic attempts of unbelievers to remove demons. In the biblical accounts, Jesus and the disciples only "cast out" *(ekballo)* demons—a vital distinction in methodology. The practices of modern deliverance practitioners, whether extremist or more moderate, have more in common with the exorcists of Jesus' day than with the disciples.

The Disciples and the Demons

The twelve disciples of Jesus became involved in casting out demons when Jesus sent them out to declare to their fellow Israelites that the kingdom of God was at hand. Mark seems to indicate that this commissioning occurred twice, in 3:13–19 and 6:7–13. Clearly, the reason Jesus delegated this power and authority over the demonic realm to His disciples was as an authenticating sign to their fellow countrymen that their Rabbi was indeed the Messiah. Only Messiah could truly deliver those under the domain of the demonic powers. This was a power and authority given only to the twelve disciples, and lest there be any misunderstanding who they were, they were specifically named in Matthew 10:2–4. Jesus instructed them, "As you go, preach, saying, 'The kingdom of heaven is at hand.' Heal the sick, raise the dead, cleanse the lepers, cast out demons" (Matt. 10:7–8).

Just like the ministry of Christ, so the ministry of the twelve disciples in relation to casting out demons was a sign pointing to the coming of the messianic kingdom.

All of this evidence that Jesus was the Messiah led to a head-on collision with the Jewish leaders of Christ's day. They feared that they would lose their positions of leadership if Jesus really was the Messiah. So when they were backed into a corner, having to admit the genuine messianic quality of the miracles and demonic deliverance that Jesus demonstrated, they tried to say that the source of His power and authority came not from God, but from a deal that Jesus worked out with Satan himself so that He could put on a good show.

Lucid Claims

The central role of Jesus' demonstration of His power and authority over Satan and the demonic powers comes center stage in the drama of the Gospels. One particular incident was triggered by Jesus' deliverance of a demon-possessed man (Matt. 12:22). The response of the people was that of amazement as they wondered, "This man cannot be the Son of David, can he?" (v. 23). When the scribes and Pharisees heard this, they accused Jesus of being in league with Satan himself. Christ refuted them personally first, then went on to refute the logic of their charge, showing it to be false. The point is clear: Jesus' rule over Satan and the demonic powers was a sign that He was Messiah because only Messiah would be stronger than Satan.

7

STRATEGIES OF THE ENEMY

*When the unclean spirit goes out of a man, it passes through
waterless places seeking rest, and not finding any, it says,
"I will return to my house from which I came." And when
it comes, it finds it swept and put in order. Then it goes
and takes along seven other spirits more evil than itself,
and they go in and live there; and the last state of that
man becomes worse than the first.*

—Luke 11:24–26

Tonight was the night for which several of us had been waiting
all week. The evangelist was going to hold a deliverance service
on the final night of a week of meetings. This "deliverance minister"
had been teaching us all week about Satan and the demonic powers,
and now the time had finally arrived to see him practice what he had
preached.

Our carload of Christians focused our discussion on Jane as we
expectantly drove to the other side of town. After hearing the teaching that week, Jane had come to believe that the demon of gossip
resided in her. We were all attempting to discern, on the basis of what
we had been learning, if the reason Jane spent six to eight hours a
day on the phone gossiping was because she had a demon or, as her
husband thought, simply because this was the area of sin to which
she easily succumbed. Jane decided that she would go forward that

121

night to be delivered from a demon that she was convinced was the root of her problem.

As we pulled into the packed parking lot, we knew that this night would witness the largest crowd of the week. We wormed our way through the crowd to the pew we had occupied all week and sat down, charged with anticipation. We were not disappointed. During the course of that evening we saw some truly amazing things. Among the incidents were the following: Multiple voices shrieked out of one woman. A second woman keeled over with convulsions when the minister commanded the demon to depart in the name of Jesus, and then a young boy passed out and lay on the floor unconscious for a long time. Another lady literally vomited up what the minister called the demon of gluttony in response to the evangelist's command to that evil spirit to leave. Virtually every case handled by the deliverance minister seemed bizarre and required his vast experience and discernment finally to see through the nefarious bag of tricks implemented by the demons in their always-futile efforts to continue to control their victim.

Jane made it to the front as nine o'clock approached that evening. The evangelist motioned to her that she would be next. He rapidly began his interrogation of Jane in the style that had preceded the deliverance of the others.

"Are you a Christian?"

"Yes."

"Have you renounced all of the works of Satan from your past?"

"Yes," she proclaimed.

"Then what is the nature of your oppression?" he asked in an effort to find the basis of her plight.

Jane then confessed her excessive participation in gossip. She renounced it 'in the name of Jesus' as the minister ordered the demon to manifest himself. When the evil spirit finally spoke, the minister demanded to know the demon's name.

"Chatter!" the voice screamed back. "I love to talk about other people!"

"Well, your use of this child of God's vocal cords is about to cease, because I am sending you to the pit," proclaimed the minister. He then commanded the demon to leave Jane in the name of Jesus as he "pled the blood" over his subject. The demon let out a sudden, high-pitched screech that startled most of us in the room and then departed. Jane returned to her seat having apparently gained victory over Satan.

Time ran out shortly after Jane's deliverance, so the evangelist had all of who believed that they had some kind of demonic oppression raise their hands. Almost every hand in the place shot into the air. He then led them through a group deliverance and gave a few parting words on how to keep delivered and not return to the bondage of demonic oppression.

Deliverance Expert?

I (Thomas) recall the next few months. Every time I had any kind of problem in my life, I instantly believed that it was some kind of demonic oppression. I would go through the steps that we had learned at the meeting for casting out demons, just in case they were still there.

My friend Jane quickly developed into our local deliverance expert, and she spent much time on the telephone repeatedly casting out demons from our friends anytime they encountered the slightest problem. Jane's life went from one crisis experience to another. Her husband was transferred out of town a few months later, and about a year after that I heard that they were experiencing severe marital problems, which eventually led to divorce. After that, I never heard from either of them again.

I was a young Christian when I went through this exposure to contemporary deliverance teaching and practice. After years of studying the Scriptures, however, I have become convinced that this kind of teaching and practice is not authorized by the Bible at all. As I look back on what I went through then and see this same kind of approach to Satan and the demonic powers growing by leaps and bounds in our own day, a number of questions repeatedly come to mind. How much control does God allow Satan to have over people? More specifically, what can Satan do and not do to believers? However, the most provocative question of all—which neither the deliverance minister, myself, nor my friends brought up for discussion at that time—was whether a true, born-again believer could even be demon possessed. If Christians cannot be demon possessed, then the whole notion of a believers' deliverance ministry is not scripturally valid. If a Christian *can* be indwelt by a demon, then a whole different scenario would follow for spiritual warfare. To understand the answers to these questions, we must first understand how much control Satan has over people.

The Power of God

The book of Job is considered by many Bible scholars to have been the first book of the Bible given to man from God. At the beginning of the story, when all of the angels (both the holy and the unholy) came to present themselves before the Lord, He said to Satan, "From where do you come?" Satan answered, "From roaming about on the earth and walking around on it" (Job 1:7). Why was Satan "cruising" the earth? A similar expression is found in 1 Peter 5:8, where Peter says that "your adversary, the devil, prowls about like a roaring lion, seeking someone to devour." The answer is clear: Satan roams and walks around the earth to find someone whom he can devour. However, as we continue to follow the development of Satan's dialogue with the Lord, we find that even though the evil one is *capable* of attacking human beings, this does not mean that he is *permitted* to.

A major emphasis in the book of Job is the sovereignty of God. We need to recognize that nothing happens in God's creation without God's permission, including evil. God is not the author of sin, but His plan for His creation allowed for man's choice and the presence of evil. Satan and mankind are responsible for introducing and maintaining sin in God's world. Despite this, God is still sovereign over the evil that happened to Job.

First, God appears to have had a regular time in which all of the angels, both the elect and the evil, had to report to Him (Job 1:6; 2:1). This indicates His authority over both domains. Second, the Lord initiated the conversation with Satan by asking him if he had "considered My servant Job." Third, Satan then sought permission from the Lord to harm Job. Surely Satan would not be seeking permission on such a matter if it were not necessary! Fourth, Satan recognized that the Lord had put a hedge (fence) around Job and his house that pre-

vented Satan from stalking Job without divine permission. Fifth, after granting Satan permission, God limited the extent of suffering
that Satan would be permitted to inflict (Job 1:12; 2:6).

God's sovereignty over His creation means that Satan does not have
a free hand to run roughshod over God's creatures, especially His
children, without the Lord's permission. The psalmist says, "Surely
the wrath of man shall praise thee: the remainder of wrath shalt thou
restrain" (Ps. 76:10 KJV). The interaction between God and Satan in
Job illustrates this point. However, some people advocate the view
that we have to "pray a hedge of thorns" around fellow believers to
protect them. The Scriptures indicate that God automatically erects
a hedge of thorns around His children. Like any loving Father, God
moves to protect His family members from the moment of salvation.
Praying for a hedge of thorns is unnecessary.

We must keep in mind God's sovereignty over *all* of His creation if
we are to avoid two common errors. First, when some people learn
about the things that Satan can do, they might respond as if God does
not restrain Satan's activity. Another people might claim to know that
God is sovereign but then fail to apply that aspect of His character to
their thinking by acting as if protection from Satanic or demonic attack depended on their own actions. Once again, they admit in *theory*
that God is sovereign, but they *behave* in a way that actually denies
His sovereignty. Those who are especially vulnerable to this incorrect
perception worry constantly about whether they might have some
unknown sin, curse, or family heritage with which they have not specifically dealt and that could be the basis for a "satanic stronghold."
This error fails to realize that God sovereignly applied all aspects of
His salvation to our lives when we became His children.

Second, if we do not take into account God's sovereignty as we study
what Satan can do to people, then we might react to this information
fatalistically. Knowledge of the many ways in which Satan might attack
people could cause us merely to throw up our hands in surrender and
say, "What's the use of trying to battle against impossible odds?" This is
the flip side of the first error. The biblically oriented believer should
respond with an active trust in God characterized by a quiet confidence
in God's protection.

God's sovereignty is like a filter that protects us from anything that He has not planned to bring into our lives to mold us into the image of our model—Jesus Christ. Now that we have our filters snugly in place, we will examine what Satan does to people.

Satan's Subordinate Power

Satan and demons can affect people in many ways. Yet, just because they have this capacity does not mean that all of the things we will list happen with the same frequency or to all people, or even that they are necessarily demonic in origin in a particular case. We are pointing out the things of which Satan *is capable* and that he has done *at one time or another* as revealed in Scripture.

We have already seen that Satan is the opponent of God, which explains why all of his activity seeks to distort what God has made. Jesus makes this point in John 10:10: "The thief comes only to steal, and kill, and destroy; I came that they might have life, and might have it abundantly." Jesus creates something, but Satan destroys it.

If God has given us a gift, Satan wants to steal it. God has given us life, but Satan wants to bring death. If God has built or created something, Satan wants to smash and destroy it. God gave Adam and Eve the gift of a beautiful life in Eden, but Satan said that God was still holding back something good. When the first couple fell for that lie, they lost the gift of Eden and were cast into a wilderness as a result.

God has given to each person life, both physically and spiritually. Satan often attempts to persuade people that death is to be preferred over life. This may take many forms. He may encourage one person to take the life of a fellow human being, as Cain did to Abel. Or he may try to convince a person that the only way out of his problems is to take his own life—to commit suicide, as King Saul did. Or Satan might use a worldly rationale, such as "I need to reach my full potential" to convince a man that he could be happy only if he left his wife and four children. But Christ came to give life back to fallen man through salvation, as well as to instruct us how to live a lifestyle that is called often in Proverbs "the way of life." Proverbs 15:4 informs us that what we say now affects the quality of life we live now: "A soothing tongue is a tree of life, but perversion in it crushes the spirit."

God is the One who created the marvelous world in which we live. Satan, on the other hand, is continuously attempting to destroy the work of God. Satan loves to destroy relationships such as marriage and the family. Satan is like the malicious little child who breaks everything on which he can get his hands. Satan wants to destroy and pervert our relationship with and worship of God by promoting idolatry and false religion. He does this by distorting who Jesus really is, by making people feel good about their false worship and idolatry, and by teaching that we can achieve salvation by doing good works. Satan and his demons are the source of false doctrine. Paul called this kind of deception "doctrines of demons" produced by "deceitful spirits" (1 Tim. 4:1). James went further, identifying all nonbiblical thinking as "earthly, natural, demonic" (James 3:15).

Satan's Other Powers

Satan also has an impact upon nations and human history. Daniel 10:13 records the incident of a heavenly struggle, lasting three weeks, between an elect angel and the "prince of the kingdom of Persia," representing the demonic realm. It became necessary for the elect angel to gain the assistance of a higher-ranking angel, Michael, because he could not handle the prince of Persia alone. This event took place in relation to God's revelation of His plan for Israel and the Gentile nations. Therefore, this angelic conflict affects the affairs of nations upon earth. Revelation 16:13–16 is an example of a similar effect that demons will have in influencing the plans and actions of leaders during the Tribulation. Possibly the rapid changes that have taken place in Eastern Europe have been the result of angelic interference. But whether this is so is not the concern of the believer. The principles for living the Christian life and the response to external circumstances do not change, whether the attack is from fallen humanity, fallen angels, or our own fallen nature.

Unfortunately, some people have used these passages to develop the doctrine referred to as "territorial spirits." At the root of this teaching is a small element of truth—that demons do, according to Scripture, indeed exercise a certain geopolitical influence. However, this is all that Scripture says about the subject. The vast majority of what is said today about territorial spirits is developed from experience, not from the Bible. Remember that it is not the glass of water but the small amount of cyanide in the water that harms you.

The Scriptures contain no indication, mandate, or authorization for believers to pray away the influence of these demons or that it is even necessary to free a city, neighborhood, or nation from the influence of these demons as a precursor to evangelism. Once again, this view reflects a "devil-made-me-do-it" approach and subtly shifts responsibility for personal decisions away from the individual and onto some other entity or event. Advocates of this doctrine assume that people in a given area fail to respond to the gospel because they are being kept from it by demons. Could it not be that they simply reject the gospel and suppress the knowledge of God by their own volition (Rom. 1:18–20)? The Scripture never presents the problem as anything other than an issue of personal volition. Although it is true that all unsaved people are being blinded by Satan (2 Cor. 4:4), Scripture contains no example or command urging us to pray away these demons before there can be a gospel impact. In fact, every believer in human history, including the Pharisee Saul of Tarsus, was initially blinded by Satan until they responded to the truth of the gospel.

Paul and his associates certainly never practiced a deliverance prayer ministry in the book of Acts. This idea is really based on too low a view of God's power and too high a view of Satan's power.

Besides blinding people to the gospel, Satan and his demons may also inflict physical disease and even death upon people. This fact is illustrated in the first two chapters of Job, where the Lord gives Satan permission to harm Job with physical sickness and then to kill his children. Some of the physical diseases listed in the Bible that might have a demonic source include epilepsy (Matt. 17:15–18), dumbness (Matt. 9:33), blindness (Matt. 12:22), deafness (Mark 9:25), and physical deformity (Luke 13:11, 16). Although disease might have some demonic source, however, Satan still must work in and through the biological laws that God created. These maladies are not mystical diseases that befuddle physicians and are cast away by magical incantations as in paganism. A disease caused by Satan would still have all of the pathology of a disease that is brought on naturally; the same cure that worked on the latter would work on the former.

Some mental disorders may also be induced by demons (Mark 5:4–5). Such bizarre behavior may include violence (Matt. 8:28), outbursts of abnormal strength (Mark 5:4), raving/crying/screaming (Mark 5:5), self-mutilation (Mark 5:5), foaming at the mouth (Mark 9:20), nakedness (Luke 8:27), and grinding of teeth (Mark 9:18).

It is absolutely imperative to state that *these conditions are not always caused by demons.* Often, believers mired in the self-destructive emotional and mental consequences of their own bad decisions may become delusional, psychotic, and divorced from reality and may imitate many characteristics that are associated with demon possession. King Saul is one example from the Scripture. In addition, not every bona fide demon possession has identical effects. Today, many people may make the incorrect mental leap that a violent person must be demon possessed simply because one symptom may sometimes be a characteristic of demon possession.

Moreover, even when the ultimate cause of the disease or problem is supernatural, the biblical solution does not necessarily lie in a direct engagement with the demon. Scripture always presents the solution in terms of steadfast progress in spiritual growth through learning biblical principles and applying them consistently to the thinking and lifestyle of the believer. Never does the Scripture authorize or even hint that believers should engage in identifying, rebuking, or attacking the demons. (We will say more about this issue in the next chapter.)

What happens when a person accepts Jesus Christ as his Savior and becomes a Christian? In what way does this influence how Satan and his demons can affect that person?

What Is Demon Possession?

How does the Bible describe and define demon possession? To understand properly the biblical teaching about spiritual warfare, we must begin with a clear understanding of what Scripture means when it refers to demon possession. A wrong perspective on this matter will result in our misunderstanding God's Word as He has spoken it, causing us to rely instead on human opinion.

Because the Old Testament contains no clear example of demon possession, our examination will concentrate on the New Testament. The New Testament uses more than one term to refer to demon possession. First, the Greek word *daimonizomai* is a participial form of the more commonly used noun for demon *(daimonion)*. *Daimonizomai* is usually translated "to be possessed by a demon," or, when it is used to describe a person in that condition, it is rendered "demoniac." The word is used thirteen times,[1] all in the Gospels. It is increasingly popular to dilute the meaning of this word by translating it as "demonized."[2]

The second term in the Greek is *daimonion echein,* "to have a demon." This phrase is used eight times in Matthew, Luke, and John.[3] The Greek grammar conveys the idea that the subject is characterized by having a demon indwell him.

A classic definition of demon possession is that by the late Merrill Unger:

> Demon possession is a condition in which one or more evil spirits or demons inhabit the body of a human being and can take complete control of their victim at will. By temporarily blotting out his consciousness, they can speak and act through him as their complete slave and tool. The inhabiting demon (or demons) comes and goes much like the proprietor of a house who may or may not be "at home." When the demon is "at home," he may precipitate an attack. In these attacks the victim passes from his normal state, in which he acts like other people, to the abnormal state of possession.[4]

So far, this is a fairly accurate definition; however, as Unger subsequently develops his definition, it becomes apparent that he is relying, at least to some degree, on experiences with what he believed to be demonically possessed people.

Extrabiblical Confusion

We believe that a sound definition of demonization must be based solely on the information in the Bible. Unfortunately, some people today let experience determine even more of the definition:

> The difficulty with Dr. Unger's definition is that although it
> may be correct in some cases, it may not be broad enough to
> function in all cases of demon possession.[5]

This writer critiques Unger's biblically derived definition from the vantage point of his own experience. Like many others, he offers his own autonomous definition of demon possession. He elevates his interpretation of his experiences to the same level as scriptural accounts. Then, on the basis of this assumption, he uses the combination of biblical events and contemporary clinical events to derive conclusions about possession. This is the type of invalid methodology that usually leads people to the conclusion that Christians can be demon possessed.

Once a person moves beyond Scripture as the sole authority, anything becomes possible if it is carried to further extremes. (And there always seem to be some people who are willing to push an idea further than the contemporary consensus.) The following list reveals what people in the seventeenth century believed to be symptoms of a demon-possessed person:

1. to think oneself possessed;
2. to lead a wicked life;
3. to be persistently ill, falling into heavy sleep and vomiting unusual objects (either natural objects—toads, serpents, worms, iron, stones, etc.—or artificial objects—nails, pins, etc.);
4. to blaspheme;
5. to make a pact with the Devil;
6. to be troubled with spirits;
7. to show a frightening and horrible countenance;
8. to be tired of living;
9. to be uncontrollable and violent; and
10. to make sounds and movements like an animal.[6]

Even in the seventeenth century definitions of demon possession were based on human experience, or human experience plus the Bible, not on the Bible alone.

If we allow any basis at all for extrabiblical thought on this matter, it opens a floodgate of errant thought. For example, who could say that the preceding seventeenth-century list is wrong if the Bible alone is not the standard? Everyone's opinion becomes just as possible as anyone else's opinion. Let's see how the Bible *alone* describes demon possession.

The Clarity of the Context

Because the Bible contains no systematic definition of demon possession, the best way to understand this issue is to examine the characteristics in the biblical examples that define these words for us. We see from the two basic terms noted earlier that someone who is said to be "demonized *(daimonizomai)*" or "to have a demon *(echo daimonion)*" is a person who has one or more demons dwelling *within* him, they have taken up residence inside the body, not inside the soul or spirit. For example, while the Gadarene demoniac is labeled as "demonized" in Mark 5:15–16, 18, the same person is said to "have a demon" in Luke 8:27. A variation of this synonymous usage occurs when demon-possessed people are said to "have an unclean spirit" (Mark 5:2, 8). If our information about demon possession was limited to these three words, then it might be legitimate to conclude that these are merely generic terms describing some sort of demonic activity in relation to human beings. In fact, this view is exemplified in an approach that is becoming increasingly popular today. The claim is made that the idea of demon possession per se is not in the Greek of the New Testament:

> To be demonized means to be under the control of one or more demons. Demonization is not a matter of extremes, such as the either/or idea of being completely free or totally bound; it's a matter of degrees.[7]

This writer claims that the English terms *demon possession* and *demon influence* are merely theological inventions that do not accurately reflect the original language of the Bible. All that the Bible says, so the reasoning goes, is that people are demonized. But is this true? Absolutely not! A correct understanding of the Greek reveals

that the standard way of translating this Greek term as demon possession has been correct all of the time.

This approach commits the fallacy of defining a word based on its
root meanings, or etymology, rather than on how the word is actually
used and defined in context. *Demonized* and *to have a demon* are
used in Scripture of only one extreme type of demonic activity: to
have one or more demons take up residence inside the body of a person and exercise control by overriding the individual's volition in relation to their bodily functions. The person's soul, his identity, is still
there, although perhaps unconscious. His volition to believe or reject
the gospel is still there, but his ability to control his body is not. These
words never describe a case involving anything less, such as mere
influence or putting ideas into someone's mind. For example, these
terms never describe Satan's activities of accusation, temptation,
deception, or persecution; they describe only the extreme case of being inwardly controlled by a demon.

Jesus gives us a picture of demon possession in one of His dia-
logues with the Pharisees. In Matthew 12:28–29, 43–45, Jesus pictures the possessed victim as a house in which demons dwell. Casting
out the demons is analogous to throwing the inhabitants out of the
house. Therefore, demon possession clearly includes evil/unclean
spirits (another term for demons) indwelling an individual. This point
is further reinforced by the terms used to describe the moving in and
eviction of demons from their captive. Both transitions are recorded
in Mark 5:13, with the "coming out" *(exerchomai)* of the demons
from their human hostage as they then "entered into" *(eiserchomai)*
the herd of swine. Mary Magdalene is described in Luke 8:2 as the
woman "from whom seven demons had gone out *(exerchomai)*."
These precise terms provide clarity for the meaning of *daimonizomai*,
making it indisputable that the word means nothing less than the
indwelling of a demon in the body of a human host.

Dr. Unger's earlier definition describes well how, once inside a person, demons can then "speak and act through him as their complete
slave and tool. . . . When the demon is 'at home,' he may precipitate an
attack. In these attacks the victim passes from his normal state, in
which he acts like other people, to the abnormal state of possession."[8]

In the Bible, demon possession is the direct, inward control by demons (also called evil spirits) of their victim by their residing in him. We will now examine the crucial issue of whether Christians can be demon possessed. Can this happen to Christians?

Can a Christian Be Demon Possessed?

We do not believe that the Bible teaches that a Christian can be possessed, which means to have his body, or the physical home of the immaterial soul, indwelt by a demon. We *do* believe, however, that Christians can be severely influenced or oppressed by Satan and the demonic powers. The key issues on this matter revolve around the differences between *internal* control/inhabitation and *external* influence.

The Holy Spirit. Scripture clearly teaches that the Holy Spirit indwells each believer. First Corinthians 6:19 says, "Do you not know that your body is a temple of the Holy Spirit who is in you, whom you have from God?" The Holy Spirit lives inside every believer in the church age. He has converted their physical body into the dwelling place of the Trinity. In addition, 1 John 4:4 tells us, "Greater is He who is in you [the Holy Spirit] than he who is in the world [Satan and the demonic powers]." Therefore, a demon is not able to enter into and take control of a believer's physical body because the Holy Spirit lives there. Think of it thus: because the Holy Spirit lives in the material house of a believer, then every time a demon knocks at the door the Holy Spirit answers. Since God the Holy Spirit is stronger than any demonic being, including Satan himself, then no demon or evil spirit could enter. It's that simple: God is greater than Satan; thus, He protects His children.

Jesus used this same analogy when He refuted the Pharisees: "When the unclean spirit goes out of a man, it passes through waterless places, seeking rest, and does not find it" (Matt. 12:43). In this illustration, the demon is searching for a new home because he was cast out of the individual whom he once occupied. The word for "cast out," *exerchomai,* is the same word used of the departure of a demon in other possession episodes. Then the homeless demon says, "I will return to my house from which I came" (v. 44). The demon and his friends can only enter the house if it is empty, that is "unoccupied." Because the house is vacant, the demons entered, *eiserchomai*, another technical term for demon possession. In the case of all believers, the house is *occupied*, and God the Holy Spirit answers the door even if repossession is attempted. This passage is saying that only *empty* houses—unbelievers—can be reoccupied; therefore, Christians cannot be demon possessed.

Kept from the evil one. Several other New Testament passages indicate that Christ's victory over Satan and the demonic powers was so extensive and His power is so vast that it totally protects believers "from the evil one." First, Jesus prayed in His great high-priestly prayer that the Father "keep them [Christians] from the evil one" (John 17:15). But what exactly did He mean, "keep from?" As one writer notes, if this is a prayer to protect believers from simple influence or temptation, then it was a vacuous prayer that was never answered.[9] Such would not be in harmony with the intercessory power of the second person of the Trinity, so something else must have been intended.

The preposition *ek* here is used to indicate severance or separation. Whatever else our Lord intended, this would exclude the invasion of the body of a child of God by unholy demons. Because we know that the Father has heard and is fulfilling Christ's request, this must at least include protection of all believers, both the obedient and the disobedient, from demon possession.

The apostle John later wrote that each believer is kept by God and that "the evil one does not touch him" (1 John 5:18). The context of 1 John 5:18–19 reflects the Lord's intercessory prayer in John 17:19. He also refers to the believer living in the world, in the very power sphere of the Devil. This particular passage is one that involves several technical difficulties that must first be resolved before accurate interpretation is possible. First, the identity of he "who is born of God" (a perfect participle) is undisputed and refers to the regenerate believer. Second, the identity of he "who was born of God" (an aorist passive participle) is debated. Some people argue that the shift in tenses indicates a shift in reference, so that the second participle refers to the Lord Jesus Christ.[10] Thus, the verse would be translated, "We know that no regenerate believer sins; but Jesus Christ, the One who was born of God keeps him. . . ." This translation would again indicate that our Lord keeps and protects us from demon possession. However, those who want to say that Christians can be demon possessed reject this interpretation. Although we agree that the preceding view is the best interpretation, we will assume, for the sake of argument, the alternate position.

This raises the second difficulty with this passage. The object of the verb *keeps* is *him* in some but not many ancient manuscripts. An alternate reading found in the Majority Text might be understood to mean "himself." Those who believe that Christians can be demon possessed attempt to avoid the implication of this passage by rejecting the standard reading of the Greek text in favor of the Majority Text alternate reading.[11] But even if we grant for argument's sake that this is the correct reading and interpretation of the text, it nevertheless still supports the view that a believer cannot be demon possessed. Majority Text advocate Zane Hodges, who follows the same alternate reading that C. Fred Dickason suggests, concludes that the passage still means that believers cannot be demon possessed.

> John thus affirmed that "the one who has been born of God *keeps himself* (there is no word for safe in the original)." This restates the truth of [1 John] 3:9 in a slightly different form. A believer's new man (or "new self"; Eph. 4:24; Col. 3:10) is fundamentally impervious to sin and hence the evil one (cf. 1 John 2:13–14; 3:12), Satan, does not touch him.[12]

It is not the textually disputed phrase but the verb in the final clause that clinches the argument against demon possession of the believer. The Greek *hapto* in the middle voice means "to touch, take hold of, or hold."[13] This word indicates touch with intent to harm, which means that Satan cannot touch or do any serious damage to the believer.[14] Because this interpretation would include at the least indwelling by an unclean spirit, the Christian is clearly protected from demon possession. The final clause, "the evil one does not touch him," is not conditioned upon the previous clause but is an additional reality. It is hard to imagine how a believer could be demon possessed but also be said to have not been touched by the evil one! Certainly this passage would add weight to the teaching that believers cannot be demon possessed.

Paul declared in 2 Thessalonians 3:3 that "the Lord is faithful, and He will strengthen and protect you from the evil one." The Greek preposition *apo*, translated "from" here, is different from the previous passages. Here the preposition has the idea of being kept away from something, and when it is used in combination with the infinitive *to guard*, it means to protect something "so that it is not lost or damaged."[15] This protection is based upon the Lord's, not man's, faithfulness. Nothing in the context indicates it applies only to believers who are walking in obedience. To assume that view is to presume one's interpretation to predetermine the conclusion. No wonder some writers believe that the Scripture is unclear on the matter!

It is hard to believe that our faithful Lord's protection would allow one of His children to become demon possessed. It doesn't make sense in the light of Scripture. Why, then, do some people assert that believers can be open to some form of demonic possession?

Is Experience More Lucid than the Scriptures?

A popular approach today supports the claim that Christians can be demon possessed on the basis of case studies. Dickason is typical of some who conclude that Christians can be demon possessed. Following a lengthy analysis of biblical arguments used to support or deny demon possession, he concludes that the biblical data are inconclusive: "From the survey and analysis for arguments pro and con, we conclude that we cannot say with reasonable certainty that either position is correct."[16] How does he seek to resolve this alleged tie? He enters into the realm of "scientific investigation." After citing many case studies from reputable sources, he concludes, "We must allow the distinct probability that biblically guided investigation and counsel has shown in experience that some Christians have been demonized. The evidence is heavily weighted toward that conclusion."[17] Apparently unable to interpret the Bible decisively on this issue, he is able to analyze and interpret human experience outside the realm of Scripture such that the scales are tipped in favor of Christian demon possession. Dickason's interpretation of these case studies leads him to declare that the "burden of proof lies with those who deny that Christians can be demonized."[18] Why? In a tie, no burden is assessed on either side. But we think that Scripture is clear, and the burden of proof is with those who think that the Scripture is unclear.

Like many other people who have struggled to answer this question, Merrill Unger changed his view, although the change was not the result of further Bible exegesis or insights into word meaning. He shifted away from the statement "To demon possession only unbelievers are exposed"[19] to the statement "Demon influence [including demon possession] may occur in different degrees of severity and in a variety of forms, both in Christians and non-Christians." What changed Unger's mind? As with Dickason, it was the interpretation of *experiences* of Christians. Unger wrote, "Since the first publication of *Biblical Demonology* in 1952, the author has received many letters from missionaries all over the world who question the theory that true believers cannot be demon possessed. . . . The claims of these missionaries appear valid."[20] But how can anyone this side of eternity know with certainty that these were believers or were demon possessed?

To summarize this position, we see Dickason and Unger claiming that the Scriptures are fuzzy and that God has not sufficiently clarified the issue of demon possession. Man is left to his own resources to determine the answers to this important question. Under this cloud of uncertainty, man must enter a different arena to decide the issue— the arena of experience. This experiential evidence is so overwhelming, they assert, that we must break the tie in favor of the concept that Christians can be demon possessed.

However, this approach has some serious problems and fatal flaws.[21]

Back to the Bible

First, the whole idea that any area of thought is removed from the divine-viewpoint authority of Scripture is a fallacy. Scripture is to be the source from which we derive a biblical framework so that we can then enter the other fields of thought to extend our learning and develop wisdom. Without definite conclusions from the Bible to guide us in the unseen spiritual realm of the demonic powers, we are no different from someone trying to explore Carlsbad Caverns in the dark. When we do this, we have, in effect, abandoned God's Word in this area and substituted our own thoughts and experiences instead of interpreting our experiences within the light of the Bible. Jesus told Nicodemus in John 3 that He descended from heaven specifically for the purpose of revealing heavenly things (vv. 9–13), which we earth-bound creatures cannot discover at all if God does not tell us. So case studies and experience are not the way to break the alleged tie found in Scripture.

Second, Dickason interprets so loosely the biblical data for why a Christian cannot be demon possessed that he naturally concludes that the Bible is not clear. Because he believes that he has accurately interpreted his experience, he assumes that valid arguments must exist that indicate that a believer can be demon possessed. He is predisposed to declare the Bible totally inconclusive on this subject. The fact that the Trinity indwells and protects the believer should be reason enough for anyone to conclude that Christians cannot be demon possessed. Furthermore, when this fantastic truth is combined with the reality that demon possession is not even mentioned as something with which believers should be concerned after the resurrection of Christ and the coming of the Holy Spirit on the day of Pentecost, then it should remove any lingering doubt. The burden of proof lies with those who believe that Christians can be demon possessed because the Scriptures do not support that point of view. Valid proof must flow from the Scriptures, not from experience.

Dickason and others go to enormous lengths in their tapes and books to show from their case studies that the Christians whom they counseled were under such great demonic bondage that only a diagnosis of demon possession accounts for their symptoms. This is anecdotal theology, not exegetically sound, biblical theology. Often, the believer, in dealing with his or her problem, is pictured as having tried unsuccessfully all of the techniques of the Christian life as found in the New Testament. The point that is often emphasized is that if the person had not realized that he was demon possessed and been delivered, he would never acquire the means to overcome his problem by applying the God-given principles found in the Bible.

A Reverberating Silence

But if Christians can be possessed, then why do the New Testament Epistles, those letters written specifically to teach believers how to live a victorious Christian life until the return of Christ, not tell us that believers can be demon possessed, or command us to cast out demons from Christians, or otherwise tell us how to deal with this problem? It is unthinkable that the Epistles would not deal with a subject as important as this.

If Scripture is foggy as to whether Christians can be demon possessed, as is claimed, then it certainly cannot be clear as to how to deal with Christians who are demon possessed. Conversely, if the Epistles gave instructions on how to cast out demons, then it would be clear that Christians could be demon possessed. Therefore, because no instructions exist for dealing with demon-possessed Christians in the New Testament, and assuming that believers can be demon possessed, then once again it is back to experience and trial-and-error as our teacher for functioning in this area.

To those who suggest that some of our arguments are based on the silence of Scripture, we believe that such silence speaks volumes. In chapter two, we showed that the Bible clearly claims to give us *everything pertaining to life and godliness* (2 Peter 1:3) and is *adequate to equip us for every good work* (2 Tim. 3:17). Christian demon possession is certainly a vital matter pertaining to godliness for which we should be equipped. If the Bible claims to give *everything* pertaining to godliness but ignores this particular subject, we can be absolutely confident that Christians need not worry about demon possession. Therefore, those who teach Christian possession are by implication denying the sufficiency of Scripture and are going beyond its authority by promoting the authority of their own experience. They have forgotten the warning of Paul: ". . . that in us you might learn not to exceed what is written, in order that no one of you might become arrogant in behalf of one against the other" (1 Cor. 4:6).

Unger in his earlier book, *Biblical Demonology*, made the following helpful observation:

> To demon possession only unbelievers are exposed; to demon influence, both believers and unbelievers. In the one case, the personality is actually invaded, the body inhabited, and a dominating control is gained; while in the other instance, attack is made from without, through pressure, suggestion, and temptation.[22]

This statement accurately expresses our own view and properly distinguishes the demonic impact upon unbelievers and believers. The major characteristic of *possession* is an internal assault upon the unbeliever. Demonic *influence* upon believers is an assault from without and is related to ideas and thought, more aptly described as the thinking of the world, which is characterized as demonic (James 3:15). The difference is as great as having an enemy *within* your house who has a gun pointed at your head making you obey his wishes versus having someone *outside* who is trying to persuade you to do something. As Unger noted, demonic influence from without takes the form of persuasion "through pressure, suggestion, and temptation."[23] The believer, therefore, is not under the type of bondage that those who believe that a Christian can be demon possessed often imagine. Instead, the will has been freed by Christ to obey, although the believer may choose to submit to the sin nature and follow Satanic ideas rather than Christ in a given instance. On the other hand, if he were truly demon possessed, he would have to be delivered before he could be free to obey.

Some Christians make a similar distinction between possession and influence in theory but then define what they mean by "influence" such that for all practical purposes they are saying that a believer can be demon possessed. We have heard one version of that view expressed something like this: "Demon possession really means demonization in the New Testament. A Christian cannot be demon possessed, but he can be demonized." (As we saw earlier, to be demon possessed *is* to be demonized and vice versa.) This view, then, describes "influence" upon believers such that it is really the type of internal *possession* that affects unbelievers.

No Demon-Possessed Believers in the Bible

"Satan can and does demonize believers," declares John Wimber.[24] He attempts to support his belief that Christians can be demon possessed from several biblical passages. His first example is King Saul, whose story is told in the book of 1 Samuel. We agree with Wimber that Saul was a believer because Samuel indicated that they would be together in paradise (1 Sam. 28:19). However, Wimber wrongly equates the fact that Saul was tormented (16:14) with demon possession.

For several reasons, this situation could not have been a true case of demon possession.

1. The evil spirit is said to have been sent from God, not Satan (16:14).
2. The evil spirit would leave when David played his harp (16:23), and no demon is said in Scripture to depart at the playing of music. Instead, demons are cast out in the name of the Lord.
3. Saul later repented of his sin (26:21). The New Testament presents a demon-possessed person as a victim who needs freedom, not repentance.
4. The Hebrew prepositions clarify that the evil spirit would come *upon* Saul or depart from *upon* him; it is never said to have entered *into* Saul, as would be expected if demon possession was the intended idea. We saw earlier that the language of demon possession is that of *entering into* and *exiting out of* a person, not coming upon. The description in this passage is consistent with an external attack that does happen to believers. Finally, because the case of King Saul is considered the strongest candidate for demon possession in the Old Testament, it follows that there are no genuine cases of demon possession recorded in the Old Testament.

Wimber cites Luke 13:16 and the fact that Jesus called a woman who had been demon possessed for eighteen years "a daughter of

Abraham." He thinks that this statement means that she was a believer. First, he has not proved from this that a New Testament believer can be demon possessed, especially a post-Pentecost Christian. Second, "daughter of Abraham" is a nationalist term for a female citizen of Israel. Many Israelites were believers, but most of them were not. Nothing in the text indicates whether she was at that time a believer.

A third suggestion is that Judas was a believer because he was one of the twelve disciples. There is no question that Judas was demon possessed. John 13:27 uses clear "demon-possession" language (cf. Luke 8:30) in describing the fact that "Satan then entered [eiserchomai] into him [Judas]." It should be equally clear, however, that Judas was *not* a believer. First, Jesus commented in John 6:70, "Did I Myself not choose you, the twelve, and yet one of you is a devil?"[25] Judas is singled out as that devil in the next verse. This is hardly a term for a Christian. Certainly the burden of proof would be on someone to demonstrate that Judas was a believer after a comment like that on his résumé. Second, Jesus tells the Twelve in the Upper Room that all of the twelve disciples were "clean," *except Judas* (John 13:10–11).[26] "Clean" *(katharos)* in this context clearly indicates salvation. Third, Judas, the "son of perdition" perished *(apolummi)*, the same word used of those who fail to believe in Christ alone for salvation (John 3:16). It is wrong to equate a disciple as necessarily being a believer because not all of Christ's disciples were believers.

Peter is said by some to have been demon possessed when he was rebuked by Jesus in Matthew 16:23: "But He turned and said to Peter, "Get behind Me, Satan! You are a stumbling block to Me; for you are not setting your mind on God's interests, but man's." Once again, this is an inferential assumption that can be demonstrated to be wrong. Satan's influence was that of persuasion from *outside*, not an operation from *within*. Why? Because Peter had accepted a wrong view about the role of Messiah: Peter did not want Jesus to die. But this was contrary to God's plan for Jesus, so Jesus rebuked Peter to let him know the source of that type of false thinking. False thinking is equated to demonic thinking (James 3:15).

Earlier, when Peter had declared that Jesus was "the Christ, the

Son of the living God" (16:16), Jesus had said that the source and inspiration of *that* thought was a revelation from God. However, when Peter rebuked Jesus for following the revelation of God's will for His life, Jesus wanted to ensure that Peter knew that the source of this thinking was not *God* but *Satan*. Notice that Jesus explained after His rebuke that Peter was not setting his "mind on God's interests, but man's" (16:23). This statement is a picture of Satan's using persuasion from outside Peter to try to convince him to believe false teaching.

Ananias and Sapphira are other candidates for examples of believers who were "demonized" to lie because "Satan *filled* your heart to lie to the Holy Spirit" (Acts 5:3). The reasoning is that someone whose heart is "filled" with something is experiencing internal control and thus demon possession. We will not debate whether Ananias and Sapphira were believers, but we will assume that they were. The difficulty with this verse is that so little information is given. It is possible to understand the phrase "Satan filled your heart" in two ways. The first view is that Satan, the "father of lies" (John 8:44), influenced the heart of Ananias to lie. This situation would be similar to the type of external, mental persuasion that we saw in the previous event involving Peter. The second view, the way in which deliverance practitioners understand it, is that Satan himself entered the heart of Ananias. However, if this were the case, then it would be Satan who lied; yet, it was *Ananias* who lied and was punished. Had Ananias been Satan—or demon possessed—it would have been Satan inside him who was lying, and the solution would have been to cast out Satan because Ananias would be the innocent victim and not the perpetrator that the Bible declares him to have been. The next verse says, "Why is it that you [Ananias] have conceived this deed in your heart?" (Acts 5:4). Ananias, like every believer, is in control of his thoughts and responsible for his thinking, decisions, and actions, not Satan. Therefore, this situation is an example of Satan's using the rebellious thinking of a Christian as a base of operations, influencing him with "doctrines of demons" (1 Tim. 4:1).

A final example focuses on the incestuous man in 1 Corinthians 5. Some people contend that he was a believer whose behavior was a symptom of demon-possession. Thus, Paul placed this man out of the church and into the sphere of Satan for discipline, with the result that the man could lose his physical life, even though this would not affect his eternal destiny (v. 5). However, Satan does not have to possess a person internally to kill him. King Saul was not demon possessed, but he was driven to death by an evil spirit (1 Sam. 31). Job was certainly in no danger of being demon possessed, but the Lord told Satan that he could do anything to him except kill him. Paul was given a thorn in the flesh to buffet him, a demonic messenger (called an *aggelos* or "angel" from Satan, 2 Cor. 12:7), yet he was not demon possessed.

A Sliding Scale

When answering this important question of demon possession of Christians, especially in the light of various experiences that seem to indicate demonic possession of Christians, we find it helpful to use the following chart.

The line represents the entire spectrum of demonic activity toward people. The intensity of this activity increases from left to right on the line. The first section, between lines A and B, covers the general attacks of Satan toward all people, including believers. This assault includes temptation, opposition, and attempts to influence and control through false doctrine. The second section, between lines B and C, covers all areas of intensified demonic *oppression* from outside the body. This assault may include influence through false teaching and even occult activity. The third section, between lines C and D, covers demon *possession*, the internal dwelling by a demon or demons. The Bible itself does not give us a full description of everything of which demons are capable. Because of this lack of complete information, in light of the satanic ability to deceive, combined with our own shortcomings in the area of discernment, it is likely that certain activities—such as vocal chord control or even a demon's throwing someone on the ground—*may* be caused by a demon without requiring internal habitation, but it imitates possession. This point is indicated by the shaded area. To say anything more definite on this issue goes beyond the information that Scripture has given and is pure speculation on our part.

In the final analysis, it is unnecessary for us to define these differences because God has not called us to be spiritual diagnosticians. No matter what the degree of demonic influence, the solution is the same: Christians are to "submit therefore to God. Resist the Devil and he will flee from you" (James 4:7). At no point in Scripture is the solution for the believer phrased in such deliverance terminology as "binding" or "rebuking" the demon.

The Apostles and the Demonic Powers

On three occasions the apostles are said to have been involved in the casting out of demons (Acts 8:5–8; 16:16–18; 19:11–12). None of these passages involves a debate over whether those delivered were Christians; everyone would agree that they were not. The significance of these events is as signs that the apostles had the authority from their risen Head (Christ) to act and speak on His behalf, as was demonstrated by the fact that they had authority over Satan like their Master. Once the foundation of the church had been laid by the apostles (Eph. 2:20) and the boundary and nature of the gospel message was established, the norm for dealing with demon-possessed unbelievers had become *the preaching of the gospel.*

Upon belief in Christ as Savior, an unbeliever is delivered not only from his sin but also from any demon possession that might have afflicted him. So the proper biblical way to deliver an unbeliever from demons is to *preach the gospel to him.* It does not benefit the victim for someone to cast out demons (if possible) only to have him remain in his unsaved condition. Christ told the Pharisees in Matthew 12 that when the demon comes back to his old house and finds it swept and clean, he will go and get seven other demons, so that the state of the person will be worse than at the first. Any believer can deliver another person from demons by leading him to Christ. The Scriptures do not require a second step of deliverance for a believer that he may be freed from the demonic powers; Christ sweeps the house clean at the moment of salvation and the Holy Spirit fills it.

Our True Focus

Because Christians cannot be demon possessed, they need not be delivered from demon possession. Satan can influence us from *without*, but God the Holy Spirit protects His children from internal repossession after salvation. One of the tragedies of the contemporary deliverance ministries is that they are attempting something that is a complete waste of time—trying to deliver Christians from demons. As we have noted in previous chapters, true spiritual warfare is focused primarily on the world and the flesh, not on preoccupation with demons. The focus of the Christian should be on proper ethical conduct in accordance with God's Word, not on a metaphysical battle with Satan and his demons.

Increasingly, Christians today seem to be getting caught up in preoccupation with Satan and the demonic powers. This distraction has caused them to forget that there is a three-front war going on—not just with the Devil, which is very real, but also with the world and the flesh. Many Christians have become so obsessed with Satan that they are being overrun on the other two fronts—the world and the flesh. In fact, many of the false teachings today about Satan and the demonic powers are really products of this world system. Also, some of the very people at the forefront of the deliverance ministries are being overwhelmed by the sin nature in many areas of their lives because they think that they are possessed by the Devil instead of their own lusts.

The call for today is to let the Bible tell us who our real enemy is, what our battle plan involves, and how to carry it out. As Christians, we must be completely submissive to Jesus Christ and His Word. Satan wants you to get your eyes on him; God wants you to get your eyes on Him and His Word.

8

RESISTING THE ATTACKER

Submit therefore to God. Resist the devil and he will flee from you.

—James 4:7

The forces of darkness influence and, in extreme circumstances, oppress Christians. Satan goes about as a roaring lion seeking whom he can devour. He and his demonic forces are an ever-present enemy against Christians. In the previous chapter, we saw the many ways that Satan and the demons can influence and affect Christians. What, then, is our defense against these enemies?

One form of popular teaching today focuses on the solution of deliverance or exorcism. According to this view, deliverance is not only for Christians but also for non-Christians. Usually, deliverance is presented in terms of exorcism, rebuking, or binding Satan. However, it is exceptionally strange that we do not find any instructions or commands in Scripture for rebuking or binding Satan; instead, we find the important command to *resist* the Devil. This command is found in three crucial and similar passages in the New Testament: Ephesians 6:10–18; 1 Peter 5:6–9; and James 4:7. These passages not only strengthen our confidence in spiritual warfare but also supply certain assurance that we cannot be blindsided by Satan.

The Problem of Fear

Much popular teaching today fosters an attitude of fear among Christians. Recently, an example of this came across my desk. The writer of this story is a former missionary who now engages in a deliverance ministry.[1] At one time he did not believe that Christians could be demon possessed, but then he had an experience that he says completely changed his worldview. Such a reversal is common. But rather than coming to this change because of intensive Bible study, people change their views because they have some sort of experience that does not quite fit their previous understanding of Scripture. Although we do not believe that Christians can be demon possessed and so question this writer's interpretation of his experience, other factors in the story raise an even greater concern: He fosters fear and anxiety among Christians instead of promoting confidence in Christ and the sufficiency of His Word *plus nothing*.

The episode that this author relates occurred in the 1960s when his daughter was a young teenager. While he was away from home, he received a very upsetting phone call from his wife, who insisted that he return home immediately because their daughter was acting strangely, and the wife believed the young girl to be demon possessed. At that time he rejected this explanation, not believing that Christians could be demon possessed. Nevertheless, he quickly returned home and discovered a very frightened and confused daughter.

He began questioning her about her relationship with the Lord. Her response, as he relates it, indicates a young girl who *seemed* to be walking with the Lord. She said, "Dad, help me. I'm scared. I love Jesus, and I want to do what's right. What's wrong with me?" As he prayed with his daughter, he noticed a pentagram on a chain hanging around her neck. In response to his inquiries, she said that it was a gift from a friend. When he asked what it symbolized she replied, "I don't know; I guess it's kind of a good luck charm. It's found on the dustcovers of some musical albums. A lot of kids wear them."

After discovering the significance of the pentagram as a symbol of the occult, he told his daughter that she needed to remove it and renounce the spirit forces associated with it. As she obeyed, he says that they were immediately involved with a face-to-face confrontation with evil spirits. He prayed and renounced the demons associated with it, and, after a second episode later that night, he relates that she was finally delivered.

While it is beyond our intent and knowledge to explain exactly what was taking place in this young girl's life, the way the story is told leaves us with some very significant, unaddressed questions.[2] If this interpretation of the event is, in fact, correct, then we should have a legitimate fear that we, too, might unknowingly pick up a demon and become demon possessed. At first glance, the father seems to present his daughter as a fairly mature Christian for her age and one who is walking with the Lord. In complete innocence, she had been introduced to occult symbols and practices by a friend and thereby picked up a demon. Anyone who hears of such an experience would wonder if he might innocently pick up a demon by unknowingly having an occult object lying around the house. If he or she walked through or by a store that sells such objects, might he not "pick up" a demon? In the story the father does seem to give some indication that the girl knew more than he first realized. Not only did she have the one pentagram necklace but also she had an entire box of occultic trinkets and had been exposed to heavier rock music and transcendental meditation (TM).

Asking Questions

The thinking Christian should pose several questions at this point. Can a Christian unknowingly be exposed to occultic objects and thereby pick up a demon and become demon oppressed or possessed? Second, if the involvement is innocent and done out of ignorance, where is the protection of a loving and sovereign God? Third, if this sort of thing happens (demonic oppression but not possession), what is to be the believer's response? What is the Christian to do to ward off the attacks of Satan in this age?

First Peter 5:8 is a well-known passage describing the strategy of Satan during this age as a roaring lion: "Be of sober spirit, be on the alert. Your adversary, the devil, prowls about like a roaring lion, seeking someone to devour." God in His wisdom not only warns us about the attacks of Satan but also provides clear instruction on how to deal with these attacks: "But resist him, firm in your faith, knowing that the same experiences of suffering are being accomplished by your brethren who are in the world" (1 Peter 5:9). This further explanation clarifies the way in which the Devil prowls.

Peter wrote this epistle to believers who were scattered and undergoing persecution for their faith. It was not Satan personally attacking them but an indirect assault through the *cosmic* system: the culture, the ideas, and the unbelievers around them whose thinking was dominated by those false, human viewpoint ideas, which are also termed demonic in James 3:15. The context of 1 Peter strongly suggests indirect attacks of Satan through the cosmic system and not direct engagements with Satan and demons. Nevertheless, whether we are attacked directly or indirectly by demonic forces the solution is always the same: "Resist the devil and He will flee from you."

Some might think that resistance includes exorcism, so before we can understand the meaning of resisting the Devil, we must first examine exorcism.

Is Exorcism an Option?

With the popularity of the movie *The Exorcist* (as well as the emphasis by deliverance teachers), the answer that many people expect the Bible to give to the problem of demonic oppression or possession is *exorcism*. However, as we have seen, this is not what the Bible actually teaches. The only people the Bible ever says cast out demons by the power of God were the Lord Jesus Christ, the apostles, and Philip. However, the Bible also records that unbelieving Jewish exorcists attempted to cast out demons in Jesus' name (Acts 19:13) and that there would be many people at the final judgment who had cast out demons in Jesus' name and performed many miracles in His name, but Jesus would reject them, saying, "I never knew you; depart from Me, you who practice lawlessness" (Matt. 7:23). The fraudulent or even real casting out of demons neither validates the experience nor indicates that its practitioner is a child of God. In a recent interview, Paul Hiebert, professor in the World Mission department at Fuller Seminary, told of exorcism episodes that he had witnessed in India in which Hindu gurus performed exorcisms and people were apparently delivered from demons. Clearly, this was not done by the power of God.

A prevalent attitude that seems to be communicated by deliverance ministries is that anyone who is oppressed or possessed by a demon should be delivered. It might surprise some people to learn that this view apparently was not held by the apostle Paul. Acts 16 says that when Paul and Silas were in Philippi, a slave girl who had a spirit of divination (a demon who gave her fortune-telling ability) followed them around, giving an accurate testimony of their message. Many people would think that Paul would have dealt with this problem early on, but he did not. Acts 16:18 tells us that "she continued doing this for many days." Finally, Paul became "greatly annoyed" and commanded the spirit to depart from her. Notice that he did not command the spirit to depart so that he could witness to the girl, nor did he command the spirit to depart so that he could have a better reception to his message, nor did he command the spirit to depart out of compassion or care for the girl. Instead, he commanded the spirit to depart because he was annoyed, probably because he did not want the truth that he proclaimed to be validated by a testimony from an evil spirit.

Signs and Wonders

When we examine the New Testament, we find that the casting out of demons was one of the many miracles that came under the classification of signs and wonders. Acts 5:12 says, "At the hands of the apostles many signs and wonders were taking place among the people." The passage goes on to describe in detail of what these signs and wonders consisted, healing the sick as well as those afflicted with unclean spirits. Signs and wonders were specifically designed to authenticate and validate the ministry of the apostles; they were unique to the apostles and the people who were closely associated with them. If others in addition to the apostles could perform these signs and wonders, then the apostle Paul could not have said: "The signs of a true apostle were performed among you with all perseverance, by signs and wonders and miracles" (2 Cor. 12:12). These passages clearly show that the only legitimate practice of casting out demons as a sign or wonder was apostolic.

In some churches today are those who maintain that the apostolic office has continued. Although it is beyond the scope of this book to go into a lengthy discussion of this matter, let us say that the Bible does not support this view. Apostles were men who had witnessed the Lord's life and resurrection and had been directly commissioned by Him (Acts 1:21–22). This office was a foundational office and thus unique to the beginnings of the church (Eph. 2:20). Those who maintain the continuation of the office do so without scriptural basis. Because this gift/office has ceased, signs and wonders have also ceased, and with them the casting out of demons.

This fact does not mean that God no longer performs miracles or delivers the afflicted from demons. During the time of our Lord's ministry on the earth and the beginning years of the church, God delegated the ability to perform miracles to a chosen few. These men performed those miracles through the power of God at their own discretion. They determined when they would perform these miracles and whom they would heal. God mediated the miracles through these individuals. Today, God still performs miracles and frees people from demons, but He performs these actions *directly* rather than indirectly through His people. (Of course, He may do it in response to the prayer of one person for another or in response to the prayer of an unsaved person who turns to Christ and seeks salvation.) The writer of Hebrews, which was written late in the apostolic period, recognized that even by the late apostolic period, signs and wonders were a thing of the past (Heb. 2:3–4). Clearly, the biblical solution to demonic oppression or possession in this age is never expressed in terms of casting out demons but rather in terms of resisting the Devil.

How to Resist the Devil

The only command given to believers for dealing with Satan is to *resist* the Devil. It is significant that this command is given three times in the New Testament (1 Peter 5:9; James 4:7; Eph. 6:13). The word translated *resist* means "to stand against" or "to oppose." It is a compound of the Greek preposition *anti*, meaning "against," and *histemi*, which means "to stand." The word came to mean "to set oneself against, to oppose, to resist, to withstand."

Ephesians 6:10–18 instructs the believer to put on the full armor of God so that he will be able "to resist" or stand against the Devil. Notice that when Paul explains why we are to put on the armor, he says not only that it will enable us to stand against *(antihistemi)* (v. 13) but also that we may be able to stand firm. The word for "stand firm" is simply another form of the Greek word used for "resist." It is the word *histemi,* which means "to stand." We resist the Devil by putting on the armor of God.

This word group reflects a military usage. It is the word used in orders given to a sentry. His responsibility was primarily *defensive* rather than *offensive,* since a sentry's responsibility is to guard the encampment or fortress and to watch for the enemy. If the enemy is spotted or seeks to infiltrate the camp, then the guard is to alert the troops so they can defend their position. It is not the guard's responsibility to go on the offensive, to seek out and engage the enemy.

It is extremely important to pay attention to the *defensive* aspect of this command because it is just the opposite of what some people are teaching today about spiritual warfare. The ideas of binding, rebuking, performing exorcisms, or taking dominion over Satan and demonic strongholds are *offensive* ideas. When believers go on the offensive against Satan, they are stepping out of their legitimate bounds by becoming involved in situations that the Lord has never intended for them. This offensive type of response was described by Peter as characteristic of false teachers (2 Peter 2:10–11). Often, this response opens the door to demonic oppression in the believer's life.

Just as a guard who spotted the enemy and went out to engage him would be dangerously exposed to the attacks of the enemy, so a believer is vulnerable to increased satanic attack when he stops resisting and starts attacking. Perhaps the reason some churches have so many people who have problems with demons is that they are involved in an aggressive campaign against Satan that has put them in a position of biblical disobedience and opened them up to demonic oppression. We must recognize that the battle is the Lord's, not ours. No amount of spiritualizing with religious terminology can transform binding and rebuking into some form of defensive language.

Standing Firm

A beautiful example of what is meant by standing firm is found in the flight of Israel from Egypt. As the Israelites followed the Lord's command to leave Egypt, they were followed by Pharaoh and all of his chariots and calvary and infantry. Pharaoh represented the greatest military establishment at that time, and he threw everything he had against the Israelites. This threat surely overwhelmed them and struck fear in their hearts—a situation not very different from the Christian who is the target of Satan. When the Israelites in their fear accused Moses of bringing them out of Egypt to be killed, Moses demonstrated the kind of attitude and action that Christians are to have in spiritual warfare: "Do not fear! Stand by (*histemi* in the LXX) and see the salvation of the Lord. . . . The Lord will fight for you while you keep silent" (Exod. 14:13–14). As they obeyed and stood firm, the Lord delivered them first by opening up the Red Sea as a path of escape and then by drowning the army of Pharaoh in the waters as they closed back on them.

The Israelites were to stand firm; that was their responsibility. The Lord would deliver; that was His responsibility. In the same way believers today are to stand firm against Satan; that is our responsibility. We are to stand our ground in our position in Christ. God then deals with Satan. We are on the defensive, and God exercises the option of the offensive.

How to Put on the Armor of God

When we ask specifically how we are to resist or stand firm against the Devil, the Scriptures are clear: Christians are to resist or stand against the Devil by putting on the full armor of God. Twice Paul states this fact in Ephesians 6 to ensure that we get the point. Just as a guard would put on his armor and collect his weapons before going out to his watch post, so the believer is to put on his armor so that he will be able to stand firm.

This passage on spiritual warfare begins by instructing the Christian to "be strong in the Lord, and in the strength of His might" (Eph. 6:10). This reminds us not only of Moses' statement to the Israelites that they were to stand still and see the deliverance of the Lord but also of David's statement that "the battle is the Lord's" (1 Sam. 17:47).

One of the titles given to God in the Old Testament is that of Lord of Hosts, or Lord of the Armies. This title refers to His position as Commander-in-Chief over all of the angelic hosts. Once we become citizens of heaven, we are to submit ourselves to His authority as the Commanding General. It is in *His* strength that we fight and according to *His* orders.

This point means first that we must submit ourselves to Him and His lordship if we are to have victory in our spiritual combat. Submission involves the attitude of humility. This is why the two other passages related to standing against the Devil emphasize the attitude of humility and submission to God. Peter tells us, "Clothe yourselves with humility toward one another, for God is opposed to the proud, but gives grace to the humble. Humble yourselves, therefore, under the mighty hand of God, that He may exalt you at the proper time" (1 Peter 5:5–6). James's command is almost identical in 4:6 and 4:10. Sandwiched between these two sentences he says, "Submit therefore to God. Resist the devil and he will flee from you."

This is a fantastic promise from God. When we submit ourselves to God as our Lord and as the Commander-in-Chief of the warfare, then we are exhibiting humility. It is no longer *our* will but *His* that we follow. This attitude of humility was exemplified by Jesus Christ when He clothed Himself with humanity by taking the position and form of a bondservant and humbling Himself by becoming obedient to the point of death (Phil. 2:8–9).

The essence of humility is to put ourselves in the position of a servant of God and to give up all claim to personal rights. Jesus expressed this principle when He said, "If anyone wishes to come after Me, let him deny himself, and take up his cross, and follow Me" (Matt. 16:24). If we are going to take up the full armor of God and operate in His strength, we must first humble ourselves under the mighty hand of God.

Only with such an attitude of humility are we able to submit ourselves to God and put on the full armor. But before we look at the armor, we must understand some things. First, the armor passage is simply an analogy. We must be careful not to read too much into each piece. The armor is simply a visual aid to help us understand what it means to put on Jesus Christ (Rom. 13:14). "Putting on Christ" means to put on the *character* of Christ. In essence, putting on the armor is an illustration of the Christian life: By putting on His character, we will be able to stand firm against the schemes of the Devil, just as Jesus did when He was tested in the wilderness.

Six Pieces of Armor

Putting on the full armor of God involves two aspects. The first aspect looks at putting on the full armor whereas the second aspect looks at each individual piece. When we decide to follow the Lord Jesus in spiritual warfare and submit to Him, in one sense we put on the full armor. This does not necessarily mean that every piece is fully in place, needing no more adjustment, but that the armor as a whole is in place. When we first trust Christ as our Savior, we become identified with Him and receive His righteousness. This condition is called *positional sanctification* or *positional holiness*. Because our position is "in Christ," in the eyes of God we are credited and clothed with His perfect righteousness.

Yet, although we are positionally righteous and holy, we still sin and we still need to grow as Christians. This growth process is known as *progressive sanctification*. It is the progressive, sequential, daily walk of the believer in which he gradually learns the principles of God's Word, applies them consistently, and advances toward spiritual maturity. To summarize, *positional sanctification* is putting on the full armor of God whereas *progressive sanctification* focuses on each piece of the armor.

In the book of Joshua, the Israelites invaded the land of Canaan to take it for themselves, as God commanded. When they first entered the land, they had a few pitched battles and conquered some key towns, such as Jericho and Ai. After these victories, they were basically in control of the land, but the battle was not over. They were in control *positionally* but not *totally* because they still had to carry on a mopping-up operation, which involved years of taking out different pockets of resistance.

The armor that Paul described in Ephesians 6 contains six pieces. Many interpreters believe that the idea of this illustration came to

Paul as he was in Rome under house arrest, probably chained to one or two members of the Praetorian Guard. As he observed their armor and readiness for battle, he used this equipment to illustrate how the believer is to defend himself against the schemes of the Devil. Paul clearly used this illustration to make a particular point because he did not mention every piece of armor that a Roman soldier might wear. It is especially important to note the order in which he presented these pieces.

The belt of truth. The first thing we need to do to be successful in spiritual warfare is to *put on the belt of truth.* For a Roman soldier, the belt was a very important piece of equipment. A Roman soldier normally wore a long, free-flowing tunic. Obviously, such a garment would get in his way if he were in a battle, hindering his movements. So he would strap a belt around his waist, then pull the loose ends of the tunic up through it to keep it out of his way. This prepared him for action and kept him from stumbling or being hindered by the tunic.

Jesus used this same phrase in Luke 12:35: "Be dressed in readiness." The idea of putting on the belt emphasizes *readiness, preparation, watchfulness,* and *alertness.* This same idea of removing hindrances is found in Hebrews 12:1, where the analogy is a race. We are to "lay aside every encumbrance, and the sin which so easily entangles us." Using the soldier illustration in his second letter to Timothy, Paul reminded him that a good soldier wouldn't get tangled up with the affairs of this life because it would hinder his success as a good fighter (2 Tim. 2:4).

The belt that removes the hindrances to our fight and prepares us for the battle is the belt of *truth. Truth* in this verse refers to *the Word of God as objective truth.* Some people have suggested that this refers to truthfulness or integrity because the sword that is mentioned later is also the Word of God. But there the idea is the Word of God put to use in *specific situations.* The belt of truth cannot refer to general truthfulness and personal integrity because these are inadequate as a preparation for warfare against satanic forces. It is only *the Word of God* that prepares us and instructs us about sin in our lives, so that we may remove the sin that hinders us in our spiritual warfare. The truth of God's Word also is the anchor of our soul, just as the belt helped tie down the breastplate and held the sword.

Jesus stressed the necessity of the Scriptures for sanctification when He said, "You shall know the truth, and the truth shall make you free" (John 8:32). Only when we personally put on the belt of truth, committing ourselves to the absolute truth and sufficiency of God's Word, are we freed from hindrances in spiritual warfare. Many Christians today are ineffective in their Christian life and in spiritual warfare because they have not committed themselves fully to the Word of God, which alone is sufficient to prepare them for every situation in life. Often, the Christian today falls into the trap that we explained in chapter two: merging the Bible with other forms of truth. Rather than taking the Bible alone, many people today are merging the divine viewpoint of the Bible with the human viewpoint of psychology, sociology, or self-help techniques. They are trying to solve the problems in their lives not by Christ alone but by Christ plus something else. This tendency has left them dangerously handicapped in carrying out their resistance against Satan. In fact, by taking the Bible plus something else, they are doing exactly what Satan wants them to do.

The breastplate of righteousness. No Roman soldier would ever go into a battle without wearing his breastplate. At times, Roman soldiers used breastplates made of leather or animal hooves, although the most common breastplate was a solid piece of metal that covered the front of the soldier's torso from the base of the neck to the upper thighs. This plate protected all of his vital organs, including the heart and the bowels.

In the Bible, the heart and the bowels are very significant because they represented the immaterial part of man. The word *heart* was often referred to the mind, and the word *bowels* represented the emotions. Proverbs 3:5 instructs us, "Trust in the Lord with all your heart, and do not lean on your own understanding." Proverbs 4:23 warns us, "Watch over your heart with all diligence, for from it flow the springs of life."

In the original languages of the Scriptures, the bowels or kidneys are used to represent emotions. Many times when we are in a very emotional condition, such as worry or anger, we feel it in our stomach. The King James Version translates Philippians 2:1 literally, ". . . if any bowels and mercies." Often the word translated "compassion" in English has the sense of "bowels" in the original Greek.

The point of all of this information is that our thoughts and emotions are to be protected from Satan's attacks by the *breastplate of righteousness*. Some of Satan's primary tactics are to influence people through false doctrine and reliance upon their emotions rather than on the truth of God's Word. To protect the mind and emotions, the Christian is to put on the breastplate of righteousness.

This righteousness has two aspects. The first aspect is the *righteousness of Christ*, which has been imputed or credited to us: "To the one who does not work, but believes in Him who justifies the ungodly, his faith is reckoned as righteousness" (Rom. 4:5). Righteousness refers to our right standing before God. Satan and his demons often attack the Christian by raising doubts about his salvation or his relationship with God, or by accusing the believer because of sin in his life. The only basis we have for response to such attacks is that our standing before God has nothing to do with our own righteousness but is based solely and completely on the righteousness of Jesus Christ. However, there is more to putting on the breastplate of righteousness than just enjoying our positional righteousness in Christ.

The second aspect involves our *personal righteousness*. This does not refer to our own goodness, for we have none. Instead, it refers to the righteousness and holiness that the Holy Spirit produces in our lives as a result of our growth in Christ, obedience to divine precepts, and living in dependence upon the Holy Spirit (Gal. 5:15–26). This aspect is the progressive part of our sanctification.

Although every believer is positionally righteous in Christ, he is also responsible to pursue holiness in his life by being obedient to Christ and having his character transformed and conformed to the character of Christ. This process takes place in a believer's life as he recognizes the sin in his life and then turns away from it to Christ. Peter also relates this process to dealing with the lusts of the flesh: "As obedient children, do not be conformed to the former lusts which were yours in your ignorance, but like the Holy One who called you, be holy yourselves also in all your behavior; because it is written, 'You shall be holy, for I am holy'" (1 Peter 1:14–16).

This is part of what is meant by standing firm against the Devil. In James 4:7–10, we see that this concept is related not only to the idea of submission and humility but also to cleansing from sin. James 4:8 says, "Draw near to God and He will draw near to you. Cleanse your hands, you sinners; and purify your hearts, you double-minded." Although the basis for the believer's cleansing from sin is the redemption of Christ, believers still sin (1 John 1:8). The solution to sins committed after salvation is confession, admission of known sins to God (Ps. 32:5): "If we confess our sins, He is faithful and righteous to forgive us our sins and to cleanse us from all unrighteousness" (1 John 1:9).

Whenever a Christian sins, he is, in essence, giving his loyalty to Satan and rebelling like a child against his Father. At this point, the Christian is being influenced by either his flesh or the world to follow Satan in obedience. At the point of sin, the Christian opens himself up to satanic attack. Once this breach in his defense occurs, if he does not turn from his sin but continues in it, the toehold that Satan has in his life may be expanded. Eventually, the believer can be living in full-blown rebellion against God. At some point, the believer possibly can become involved with some aspect of the occult and become oppressed by a demon. This is exactly what happened in the life of King Saul in the Old Testament, and it eventually resulted in demonic oppression, severe depression, and involvement in the occult.

However, as with Saul, the solution to the problem of demonic oppression is to confess your sin and begin living in obedience to God. Many times God gave Saul the opportunity to turn from his sin, but because he never did, God continued to discipline him through the demonic oppression.

This same thing occurred in the New Testament. In two different instances, the New Testament tells about Christians who had fallen into serious and prolonged sin, and, because they failed to turn from it, they were given over to Satan for discipline (1 Cor. 5:5; 1 Tim. 1:20). The solution to this problem is never presented in the Scriptures in any other way than submission to the plan, precepts, and principles of God. If the believer does this, Satan will flee.

Feet shod with the preparation of the gospel of peace. Today shoes are often purchased on the basis of fashion rather than function. But anyone who works on his or her feet (or jogs or hikes) knows the value of a well-made pair of shoes or boots. Roman soldiers also valued their shoes because they realized that their effectiveness in combat could well depend on the sureness of their footing. They wore sandals, heavy soles bound to their feet with leather straps. The bottoms of the soles were reinforced with hobnails or studs to give added protection against spikes or stakes stuck in the ground for defense.

Likewise, the spiritual shoes worn by Christians give them both a sure-footed stance against the Devil and protection. The shoes are described as "the preparation" of the gospel of peace. Literally, that means *readiness*. What prepares or makes us ready, what gives us stability and protection against the attacks of Satan, is the "gospel of peace."

Scripture tells us that before we were saved we were enemies of God, but the death of Christ is the basis for our reconciliation: "If while we were enemies we were reconciled to God through the death of His Son, much more, having been reconciled, we shall be saved by His life" (Rom. 5:10). When we trust Christ as our Savior, we are justified by faith. The result is that we now have peace with God: "Therefore having been justified by faith, we have peace with God through our Lord Jesus Christ" (v. 1). This is the gospel of peace—the fact that we are at peace with God, that we have been transferred permanently to the kingdom of His Son, and that we are now on His side against the rebellion of Satan. This is our new position in Christ, and it is on the basis of this new position that we are able to resist the Devil.

Therefore, whenever we find ourselves tempted to doubt or to sin, because of our position in Christ as a child of God (and because we are at peace with God), we can stand firm. Satan can attack and tempt all he wants, but it need never phase us. We can remain steadfast and immovable because our feet are firmly grounded on our immovable relationship with God.

The shield of faith. Although Roman soldiers carried one of two types of shields, the larger one is mentioned here. This shield was a very large oblong shield, some four feet tall and two and one-half feet wide that the soldier used to hide behind for protection from the arrows and flaming missiles that the enemy would hurl at him.

The shield that protects the Christian is the shield of *faith.* To exhibit faith means to trust God. No matter what the situation and no matter how difficult God's instructions might seem, we are to trust in God. "Without faith it is impossible to please Him, for he who comes to God must believe that He is, and that He is a rewarder of those who seek Him" (Heb. 11:6). Only by *believing* God can we avoid the traps and snares that Satan sets for us. Adam and Eve fell into Satan's trap in the Garden of Eden because they trusted in their own ability rather than in God's Word. Satan's major weapon is to get us to distrust God's Word. Whenever we sin, we are believing Satan and giving our allegiance to him. Remember, faith means that God's Word is more real to us than our experiences, feelings, and circumstances.

With the shield of faith, we are not only able to extinguish in a general sense the missiles that Satan throws at the world but also to extinguish *all* of the missiles that Satan throws at us. God's Word is sufficient to handle every temptation, every assault, and every problem that Satan throws at us, not by launching an assault of rebuke, not by binding, and not by exorcism but by standing firm and putting on the armor of God. By trusting God and obeying Him, we need not worry about any attack that Satan might use; every trick that he tries can be handled by simply trusting God.

The helmet of salvation. The Roman soldier's helmet was made of leather and metal and was designed to protect his head against arrows and swords. What protects the Christian is his *salvation.* However, Paul is not saying that the person needs *to get* saved because he already is saved; otherwise, he wouldn't be wearing the other pieces of the armor.

In earlier chapters, we mentioned the three phases of our salvation that the New Testament describes. The first phase is called *justification,* which takes place when a person puts his trust in Christ for his salvation. This is salvation from the penalty of sin. The second phase is *sanctification,* which is the phase known as the Christian life, when we learn God's Word and apply it to be delivered from the power of sin. The third phase is *glorification,* which occurs when a Christian goes to heaven and is freed from the very presence of sin.

The helmet of salvation speaks of the application of God's Word to our present life on earth. This is phase two of our salvation. Paul speaks of it in Philippians 2:12, where he instructs us to work out our salvation with fear and trembling. We put on the helmet of salvation by letting the principles of God's Word renew and transform our minds.

The sword of the Spirit, which is the Word of God. The sword mentioned here is the short sword that the Roman soldier carried. It was used in close combat and was a weapon that had to be used very precisely. Its function was primarily defensive because it was used to ward off the close-range attacks of the enemy. It was not the large broadsword, which would be the weapon of choice in an offensive campaign.

The sword that the Christian carries is described here as the Word of God. But this is not the Word of God generally. The term translated "word" here is not the Greek *logos*, but *rhema*, which refers to a *specific* word or utterance, such as a promise or a principle from Scripture. In spiritual warfare, it is not enough to have merely a *general* knowledge of the Scriptures; we must also have a *specific* knowledge of the Scriptures and use this knowledge correctly.

Our Lord graphically demonstrated this point when He faced His temptation in the wilderness. When Satan tested the Lord, Jesus did not attack or rebuke Satan but countered his thrusts with specific parries from Scripture. When Satan tempted the Lord, he displayed a knowledge of Scripture, but he twisted it and used it inappropriately. Because Jesus had an excellent and accurate knowledge of the Scripture, He was able to defend Himself against Satan. In the same way, the Christian is able to defend himself against the attacks of Satan by using Scripture accurately. This fact means that we must know Scripture well enough to use it in any situation and to use it correctly. Many Christians are ineffective in the battle against Satan because they have only a partial (and in many cases inaccurate) knowledge of Scripture.

God's Promise to You

We are to take up a defensive posture against Satan and submit ourselves to God. As we resist the Devil with an attitude of humility and submission to God, we are promised that God will take care of the battle for us, and Satan will flee. The picture here is of two different forces. On the one hand is the believer, whose responsibility is the defensive whereas, on the other hand, is the Lord and the holy angels, whose responsibility is the offensive. When we rest in our proper position, the Lord and His angels attack from the flank and defeat Satan.

Perhaps you have been plagued by demonic manifestations. Perhaps you were involved in the occult before you were saved, or have become involved since then. But whatever the reason, perhaps you are facing serious spiritual oppression. If so, the significance of Ephesians 6 must not be lost on you because it is a passage of great comfort. When you are under attack by Satan, you must rest in your position in Christ, trust in His Word, and submit to God. The result will be that Satan and his hosts must flee. This is God's promise to you.

9

THE GREATEST WEAPON

Confess your sins to one another, and pray for one another, so that you may be healed. The effective prayer of a righteous man can accomplish much.

—James 5:16

In the previous chapter, we learned that the Bible gives us clear instructions on how to have victory in our struggle with the forces of Satan: we are simply to put on the whole armor of God and thereby resist the Devil. Although this instruction is simple in concept, it is not so easy to do in actual daily living. As Paul concludes his description of the armor, he makes a very pointed statement that we all too often overlook in our practical daily experience:

> With all prayer and petition pray at all times in the Spirit, and with this in view, be on the alert with all perseverance and petition for all the saints. (Eph. 6:18)

The action that undergirds and strengthens the armor is twofold: *prayer* and *perseverance.* These actions are so vital for today yet so lacking in the lives of many Christians that we want to take two chapters to focus on what these two things mean and how they apply in daily spiritual warfare.

Does Prayer Really Change Things?

Prayer is so often mentioned and commanded in Scripture that its necessity can hardly be questioned. But why should we pray? After all, if God is sovereign and works all things after the counsel of His will (Eph. 1:11), why bother asking God to do something if He has already determined what He will do? This question is sometimes phrased, "Does prayer really change things?"

Prayer is simply communication to God by a Christian. Prayer as seen in Scripture may contain one or more of the following elements: confession, adoration, praise, thanksgiving, intercession for others, and petition for oneself. Prayer is the means by which a believer's communion with God is strengthened. In prayer, we pour out our souls to God; in the process, our souls are nourished, our spirits are revitalized, our attitudes are conformed to God's character, and our focus is sharpened by the promises of God. In short, our ability to stand firm is strengthened.

Three aspects of prayer are important in spiritual warfare. The first aspect is *thanksgiving*. Often in the heat of the battle, when we are faced with discouragements or suffering, we are strongly tempted to become self-absorbed and to succumb to self-pity and the "poor me" syndrome. We begin to focus on the problem and the conflict and forget that the Lord is battling for us. As time goes on, spiritual fatigue sets in. This is why prayer and perseverance are so often linked together. In prayer, we are rested, refreshed, and refocused on the work of God in our lives.

The second aspect of prayer that is vital in spiritual warfare is *confession*. Confession means that we recognize sin in our lives and admit it to God. The attitude underlying confession is humility. We recognize that we have disobeyed God and acknowledge our culpability. Underlying confession is the realization of our own dependence upon God and the reality that Christ has already paid in full for that sin. First John 1:9 promises, "If we confess our sins, He is faithful and righteous to forgive us our sins and to cleanse us from all unrighteousness." The word translated "cleanse" here is the same word used in James 4:8: "Cleanse your hands, you sinners." As we saw in the previous chapter, the statement of James 4:6–10 must be taken in its entirety. That passage is framed in verses 6 and 10 by commands to be humble because true humility involves confession of sin. This is part of submitting to God and resisting the Devil. This is what it means to draw near to God. As we do so, we are promised that God will draw near to us. Jesus linked our level of obedience to a greater disclosure of God: "He who has My commandments and keeps them, he it is who loves Me; and he who loves Me shall be loved by My Father, and I will love him, and will disclose Myself to him" (John 14:21).

The third aspect of prayer that is vital in spiritual warfare is *petition*. As we encounter opposition and hostility in the world from the flesh, the world, or Satan, we call upon God to come to our aid. This again demonstrates the basic attitude that is foundational to spiritual warfare—*humility*. In prayer, we adopt an attitude of submission and humility toward God. We call on Him to intercede in our behalf.

Total Dependence

The primary image of prayer in the Bible is that of a subordinate coming to his superior to make requests. It emphasizes the attitude of total dependence, even when the request is known beforehand to be the will and the desire of the superior. Although an employee (let's say a sales manager) might know that his boss wants him to conduct regular training sessions with the sales force, he still must go to his boss to arrange times, coordinate the meetings with other events, and confirm permission for what he is doing. This consulting demonstrates the sales manager's submission to his boss and his recognition that he serves a higher authority.

In prayer, we go to God in dependence, asking for what we already know is generally the will of God, requesting God's aid in certain areas, and then waiting on the Lord to work out the details. Sometimes our request might be generally within the will of God but in this specific instance outside God's sovereign will. It might be a matter of timing (when God is simply saying "wait"), or it might be a matter of God's simply denying the request. Sometimes God's denials are hard for us to comprehend, especially when they involve prolonged suffering, poverty, unemployment, sickness, or living in a difficult relationship.

At those times, we are tempted to attempt impatiently to solve the problem on our own terms rather than to wait on the Lord. We need to *persevere in our dependence.*

Sometimes we wonder why God does not answer certain of our prayers, especially when they seem to us to be completely within God's will. After all, we have the promise in 1 John 5:14–15: "This is the confidence which we have before Him, that, if we ask anything according to His will, He hears us. And if we know that He hears us in whatever we ask, we know that we have the requests which we have asked from Him." This passage clearly states that when we ask according to God's will, He will answer.

Other prayer promises that Jesus made also indicate that when we come to the Father in Jesus' name, He will hear and answer us.

Whatever you ask in My name, that will I do, that the Father may be glorified in the Son. If you ask Me anything in My name, I will do it. (John 14:13–14)

If you abide in Me, and My words abide in you, ask whatever you wish, and it shall be done for you. (John 15:7)

Everything you ask in prayer, believing, you shall receive. (Matt. 21:22)

Must God Answer Prayer?

These great promises of Scripture that indicate God's certain answers to our prayers raise another question. If we follow all of the guidelines presented in the Bible for prayer, does that obligate God to answer our prayers? The answer to this question is both yes and no. It is *yes* in the sense that when we pray according to God's clear promises to us, God is obligated to answer (exactly what we mean by this will be clarified later in the chapter), although the timing is up to Him. But the answer is also *no*, for three reasons. First, we often link the "when" and the "how" to the general prayer request, thus putting man, the creature, in control of God, the Creator. In current spiritual-warfare practice, the prayers of many people, although expressed in words that indicate a request, are in fact nothing more than commands by the believer toward God to intercede in a particular way. This is pride, not humility. A proud approach in prayer makes this type of prayer satanic rather than holy. Whenever we do anything in pride, we are following Satan in his rebellion.

Petition is essentially the request of a child to a father to intercede and protect. How this is done and when it is done are left completely to the sovereign will of the Father.

A very important prayer promise is found in James 5:16b: "The effective prayer of a righteous man can accomplish much." James then draws upon the prayers of Elijah to illustrate this principle. But before we look at Elijah to find several principles that are characteristic of efficacious praying, we must first ask what "efficacious praying" is.

The King James Version translates this phrase "the effective fervent prayer," which is similar to the New American Standard translation, and implies that fervency somehow makes prayer more effective. Some people interpret this to mean that the harder we pray the more effective the prayer, thereby treating prayer as something mystical or magical. Some churches have been known to promote marathon prayer sessions based on this interpretation. However, the Bible always distinguishes between prayer and magic.

The difficulty with this verse is the unusual Greek construction. Without laboring the point, we suggest that the most consistent way to understand this verse is to realize that it is not the *prayer itself* that is strong or efficacious but rather *the One who answers*. In essence, "the prayer of a righteous man accomplishes much when it is effective."[1] Elijah furnishes the example of how much can be accomplished through prayer.

Elijah and the Promise

Effective prayer is based on the promises of God. The specific instance mentioned by James occurred at the beginning of Elijah's ministry. James 5:17–18 states, "He prayed earnestly that it might not rain; and it did not rain on the earth for three years and six months. And he prayed again, and the sky poured rain, and the earth produced

its fruit." (The incident to which this passage refers is recorded in
1 Kings 17:1–18:45.) Elijah's ministry was to the northern kingdom of Israel during the
time of the divided kingdom. Ahab, the king of Israel, had married
Jezebel, the daughter of the high priest of Baal worship in Tyre, who
used her position as queen to impose and advance the worship of
Baal in the northern kingdom. She instigated a policy of executing
any known prophet of God. (This time was one of the darkest periods
in the history of Israel.) The few prophets who remained alive were
hiding in caves, and the people gave themselves completely to the
idolatrous worship of Baal and the Asherah.

At this time, Elijah suddenly appeared on the scene, announcing God's
judgment on Israel for their rebellion. The judgment announced is
grounded in the promise of God in the Mosaic Law. As Israel prepared to
enter the land that God had promised to give them, Moses reminded the
people of their covenant obligations to obey God. Part of the covenant
contained promises of blessing for obedience and warnings of judgment
for disobedience. A specific judgment was mentioned for idolatry: "Be-
ware, lest your hearts be deceived and you turn away and serve other
gods and worship them. Or the anger of the Lord will be kindled against
you, and He will shut up the heavens so that there will be no rain and the
ground will not yield its fruit; and you will perish quickly from the good
land which the Lord is giving you" (Deut. 11:16–17).

Elijah was able to stand before the powerful king of Israel and announce this judgment on him because he knew the promise of God.
We are not told whether God specifically told Elijah to confront Ahab
or whether Elijah simply knew the promises of God and applied them
to his situation. (We believe that the latter case is more likely, especially because 1 Kings 18:1 specifically states that God told Elijah to
go to Ahab to announce the end of the drought.) In either case, however, Elijah's actions were grounded on the promise of God.

Between the time that God instructed Elijah to announce to Ahab
the termination of the drought and the coming of rain, two things
happened: Elijah confronted the prophets of Baal, demonstrating the
impotence of their god, and he prayed to the Lord. This prayer yields
principles of effective praying.

First, it was a prayer that was based on the promises of God. Peter tells us,

> His divine power has granted to us everything pertaining to life and godliness, through the true knowledge of Him who called us by His own glory and excellence. For by these He has granted to us His precious and magnificent promises, in order that by them you might become partakers of the divine nature, having escaped the corruption that is in the world by lust (2 Peter 1:3–4).

Is Every Promise Made to Me?

At this point, we must warn against wrongly applying God's promises. Someone has stated that the Bible contains more than seven thousand promises, but not all of those promises are for Christians. It is important to distinguish between promises to specific individuals, promises to the nation Israel, promises to the disciples, and promises to the church.

Some promises are individual in nature. For example, God made specific promises to David, Moses, Elijah, Mary, and the disciples. These promises were conditioned by certain historical events and are not to be applied to anyone else, as we will see. One example of an individual promise that is often used in contemporary spiritual-warfare contexts to justify the practice of casting out demons is Jesus' statement to His disciples in Matthew 10:7–8: "As you go, preach, saying, 'The kingdom of heaven is at hand.' Heal the sick, raise the dead, cleanse the lepers, cast out demons; freely you received, freely give."

Based on just these two verses, it would seem justifiable to suggest, as some people do, that these four activities should accompany the proclamation of the gospel. This view has come to be known as "power evangelism." Casting out demons, it is suggested, should be one thing that accompanys the true preaching of the gospel. But before we decide whether this is true, we must consider Jesus' entire statement. These two verses must not be removed or isolated from the entire commission that Jesus gave His disciples at that time. For example, not only did He command them to heal the sick and cast out demons but also He prohibited them from going to the Gentiles, limiting them to only the house of Israel (Matt. 10:5–6). Immediately after His instructions regarding the message that they were to proclaim, Jesus also prohibited His disciples from accepting any money or taking any supplies or luggage with them—even an extra change of clothes or shoes. We suggest that if this promise of Jesus to cast out demons is valid for today, then these other conditions must also be met. This is the kind of problem that results from misapplying Scripture and taking verses out of context.

Other Promises

Another type of promise is that given exclusively to the nation of Israel. The Old Testament is filled with promises that were meant only for Israel and are related explicitly to their obedience to the Mosaic Law. Yet, often these verses are taken out of context, and God is expected to fulfill promises to the church or the United States that were meant only for Israel.

One example of this error is the use of 2 Chronicles 7:14: "If . . . My people who are called by My name humble themselves and pray, and seek My face and turn from their wicked ways, then I will hear from heaven, will forgive their sin, and will heal their land." Even a superficial look at the surrounding verses shows that this was a statement made to Solomon concerning God's people Israel at the dedication of the temple. The phrase "heal their land" is a reference to the judgment of drought mentioned in the previous verse, which itself is a restatement to Solomon of the passage quoted earlier (Deut. 11:16–17). In 2 Chronicles 7, God is reaffirming His covenant promises to Israel with Solomon. Because the Mosaic covenant was made with Israel, the promise of verse 14 must be understood in that context and applied only to Israel.

Still another type of promise is general or universal. Although many promises in the Old Testament are specifically addressed to certain individuals or to Israel, many others are general. We are certainly not trying to imply that the Old Testament has no relevance for Christians today; we simply wish to caution you to ensure that when you hold God to a promise, that promise was not intended for someone else.

Here are some general New Testament promises to Christians:

I can do all things through Him who strengthens me. (Phil. 4:13)

God has not destined us for wrath, but for obtaining salvation through our Lord Jesus Christ. (1 Thess. 5:9)

We know that God causes all things to work together for good to those who love God, to those who are called according to His purpose. (Rom. 8:28–29)

I am convinced that neither death, nor life, nor angels, nor principalities, nor things present, nor things to come, nor powers, nor height, nor depth, nor any other created thing, shall be able to separate us from the love of God, which is in Christ Jesus our Lord. (Rom. 8:38–39)

Using God's Promises Correctly

All promises, even general ones, ought to be used correctly. One often-misused promise is found in Matthew 18:19, immediately following Jesus' statement that "whatever you shall bind on earth shall have been bound in heaven; and whatever you loose on earth shall have been loosed in heaven" (v. 18). In chapter 6, we discussed the meaning of this passage. The context is one of church discipline, and the language is that of a courtroom. This is also true for Matthew 18:19: "Again I say to you, that if two of you agree on earth about anything that they may ask, it shall be done for them by My Father who is in heaven."

Often, this passage is applied to any type of prayer: whenever any two Christians agree together in prayer, then God is obligated to answer that prayer. But the context shows that this is a promise related to the execution of *church discipline,* or excommunication. The "two" mentioned in verse 19 and the "two or three" mentioned in verse 20 are the same two or three witnesses that testify against the accused in verse 16. Christians must be careful not to be led astray into wrong prayer methods by incorrectly applying this verse.

Elijah could have the boldness to confront Ahab and announce the drought because he correctly understood and applied the promise of God in Deuteronomy 11. Because this was a national promise of divine discipline on Israel for idolatry, Elijah could confidently expect God to fulfill His promise. After three years of drought, God directed Elijah to go to Ahab and announce the return of rain. This was an individual promise to Elijah, so Elijah could confidently expect God to bring rain to the land.

Because God made this specific promise to Elijah, why did Elijah still pray for rain? In 1 Kings 18:41–42, Elijah announced the coming rain to Ahab and immediately went to the top of Mount Carmel and began to pray. Often, we make the mistake of generally trusting God without backing it up with prayer, but Elijah continued to humble himself in prayer even though God had specifically promised the rain. Often, our general reliance upon God without specific prayer reveals a subtle influence of pride. But Elijah shows us that although we have a specific promise from God, we must continue to pray to God. Perseverance in prayer is critical.

Get Alone with God

Too often in our busy lives, pressed as we are by the demands of people and the overcrowding of our calendars, one thing that gets lost is our personal time alone with God. Yet the prayer lives of the great saints of Scripture reveal how often they took time to get alone with God. After announcing the coming rain to Ahab, Elijah withdrew from the crowds to pray. He recognized that crushing crowds and crunching calendars might destroy communion and fellowship with God. We simply *must* withdraw and get alone with God.

When our Lord was on the earth, He recognized the same truth. Several times the Bible mentions that after busy times of ministry, when the press of the crowds and the demands of ministry closed in around Him, Jesus withdrew to be alone with God. One busy day began with the news that John the Baptist had been executed. In response, Jesus withdrew to be alone (Matt. 14:13). But His disciples found Him, the crowds followed Him, and He spent the rest of the day healing the sick. When evening came, He miraculously multiplied five loaves of bread and two fish to feed them all. After a busy day like that, many of us would crash on the couch in front of the TV or head off to bed early, but not our Lord. He realized that He was in need of spiritual revitalization, so "after He had sent the multitudes away, He went up to the mountain by Himself to pray; and when it was evening, He was there alone" (Matt. 14:23). Jesus recognized the importance of time in communion with the Father. If He who was one with the Father needed to spend time in prayer alone with the Father, how much more do we who are His children, yet still sinners, need to be alone pouring out our hearts to the Father?

As reports of Jesus' teaching and healing ministry traveled through-out the land, people poured out of the villages to hear Him and to be healed. We can only imagine the demands that this put on Jesus' time. Yet, in spite of this, He never failed to get alone with God and pray. "The news about Him was spreading even farther, and great multitudes were gathering to hear Him and to be healed of their sick-nesses. But He Himself would often slip away to the wilderness and pray" (Luke 5:15–16).

Another important time for prayer is during times of decision-making. Jesus exemplified this fact before He chose His disciples. We are not told for what He prayed but simply that He prayed. And He didn't pray for just fifteen or twenty minutes; "He spent the whole night in prayer to God" (Luke 6:12).

We must ask ourselves at this point how often we spend even a single morning in prayer. Would we even know what to do during an extended time of prayer? Would we fall asleep, or get bored and day-dream, or use the time to think about other things, or plan our com-ing week? Too often, we think of prayer as just one-way communication with God, and we just do not have that much to say, especially since God knows everything anyway.

Or we might realize that prayer is two-way communication with God but fall prey to the fallacy that God speaks directly to us during prayer, so we just sit and wait for God to speak to us. Then we either get bored in the silence and go to sleep or mistake our own thoughts for the words of God.

How God Speaks to Us Today

Prayer is clearly two-way communication with God, but today *God speaks to us through His Word*. Even in the days when God spoke directly to people, His direct communication was rare and to only a select few, so people were encouraged to meditate and memorize whatever Scripture had already been revealed. Repeatedly, the psalmist expressed the importance of meditating on God's Word while praying. Psalm 5:1–2 clearly shows the connection: "Give ear to my words, O Lord, consider my meditation. Hearken unto the voice of my cry, my King, and my God: for unto thee will I pray" (kjv). The word used here for meditation is a word that has the idea of murmuring or muttering. The object of meditation is the person and work of God and His Word.

The vivid picture painted by this word *meditate* reminds us of our days in seminary when students were learning the basic verb and noun forms in Greek. We wrote these words on index cards and carried them around in our pockets so that we could review them at any opportunity. We took them out of our pocket to look at them and then repeated them over and over to ourselves as we walked along. You can always spot the first-year language students at seminary because they are walking around muttering verb forms under their breath!

This is what we as believers are to do. As we pray without ceasing (1 Thess. 5:17), we are also meditating day and night (Ps. 1:2), praying God's Word back to Him and giving Him the tools that He uses to work in our lives. The result of this continued meditation produces wisdom that guides us through life (Ps. 119:99). As the Word enters our souls, the Holy Spirit uses it to convict us of sin and shows us how to apply the Scriptures to our lives. Meditation also provides us with a knowledge of God's promises, which, in turn, reinforces and strengthens our prayer life as we learn more about that for which we should be praying. If we, like Elijah, are going to be effective in our prayers, we must be often alone with God in prayer and meditation.

Persist in Prayer

We have already noticed that Elijah did not simply rest upon God's promise to provide rain, but when the time came, he prayed for the rain to come. But when we look at that prayer, we see that he prayed continually until the rain finally came. He began to pray then sent his servant to see if the rain was coming. When it wasn't, he prayed again. This went on seven times, until finally a cloud began to appear. Elijah was effective in his prayer because, knowing the will of God, he was persistent.

Jesus emphasized this same point to His disciples when they asked Him to teach them how to pray. In Luke 11:5–10, He related the following illustration:

> Suppose one of you shall have a friend, and shall go to him at midnight, and say to him, "Friend, lend me three loaves; for a friend of mine has come to me from a journey, and I have nothing to set before him"; and from inside he shall answer and say, "Do not bother me; the door has already been shut and my children and I are in bed; I cannot get up and give you anything." I tell you, even though he will not get up and give him anything because he is his friend, yet because of his persistence he will get up and give him as much as he needs. And I say to you, ask, and it shall be given to you; seek, and you shall find; knock, and it shall be opened to you. For everyone who asks, receives; and he who seeks, finds; and to him who knocks, it shall be opened.

Jesus again emphasized this point in Luke 18:1–8. At that time, He used the illustration of a widow coming for protection to a judge who neither feared nor respected God. At first, he was unwilling, but he finally gave in because of her persistence. Jesus then made the point: "Shall not God bring about justice for His elect, who cry to Him day and night, and will He delay long over them?" (Luke 18:7). The point in both passages is that if sinful men are moved by persistence, how much more God will be moved.

However, mere persistence is not necessarily the basis for God's answering our prayers. If something is not God's will for us, no matter how persistent we may be, He will be even more persistent in saying no. An episode of this type is found in the life of the apostle Paul. In 2 Corinthians 12, Paul tells his readers that he was given a "thorn in the flesh, a messenger of Satan to buffet me" (v. 7). Even Paul came under demonic attack! How did he respond? He neither bound nor rebuked Satan. Instead he prayed! "Concerning this I entreated the Lord three times that it might depart from me" (v. 8). Although Paul prayed, God's answer was no because He had a reason for allowing the attack: it was to keep Paul humble, to teach him that God's grace was sufficient, and to teach him to persevere. Again we see that prayer and perseverance are linked.

Strengthening God and Angels?

Some people claim that our persistence or lack of it strengthens or weakens God's ability to answer. Recent teaching among some groups of Christians has been that the angels that God uses to answer our prayers are strengthened to perform their task by the prayers of the saints, and if there are no prayers then the angels are weakened and are defeated in their combat with the demons. This approach views prayer as a great battery charger that energizes the angels for action. Although it is true that God uses the angels to carry out His answers to requests, nowhere in the Bible is there any indication that God's answers are determined by the prayers of the saints.

This false teaching is the same basic error that is prevalent among positive-confession advocates, which places God in a position of obligation to man and puts the creature in a position of control over the Creator. This error denies the clear biblical teaching of the sovereignty of God. God will certainly work out His purposes and plans for man and is not limited by the prayers of the saints.

The only passage that we can find that someone might use to suggest that angels gain strength from the prayers of the saints is Daniel 10:12–21. Daniel had been praying for three weeks for understanding from God, but no answer had come. During that time, he continued to pray and to fast, but still no answer came. Finally, at the end of the third week, an angel appeared in answer to his prayer. It took three weeks to get an answer because the angel had been in combat with the "prince of the kingdom of Persia," a clear reference to the chief demon working to influence the government of Persia. Some people might be tempted to think that it was Daniel's prayer and fasting that enabled the angel to persevere, but that is not what the Scripture says. The passage does not contain a cause/effect connection between Daniel's prayer and the angelic action. The angel who came to interpret Daniel's vision was clearly sent on the first day in response to the prayer, but the delay was because he was opposed by an evil angel. He was able to overcome the demon not because of Daniel's continued prayer and fasting but because Michael, "one of the chief princes of God," assisted him in winning the battle. Nowhere in this conflict are Daniel and his prayer in any way related to helping the angel get through to Daniel. All that we see is the conflict and opposition viewed from below. To infer that Daniel's prayer helped the angel get through is illegitimate speculation.

Expecting Answers

There was no doubt in Elijah's mind that God would bring rain. Because Elijah prayed on the promise of God, because he knew the God behind the promises (because he had spent much time alone with God benefiting from His grace), and because he was persistent, he was completely confident in God's answer. When Elijah saw the small cloud in the sky on the edge of the horizon, he turned to Ahab and warned him to hurry home so that he would not get caught in the downpour. What a tremendous example of confidence!

This is the same attitude that the believer is to have in his prayer life. Jesus told the disciples, "Everything you ask in prayer, believing, you shall receive" (Matt. 21:22). We know from Scripture that without faith it is impossible to please God (Heb. 11:6). This fact does not mean, however, that God is obligated by our faith but that in those areas where God desires to give us certain things, He withholds them because we do not trust Him. This is why James says, "You do not have because you do not ask" (4:2).

These four principles should govern our prayer lives: we should pray on the promises, we should cultivate a time for being alone with God, we should be persistent, and we should be confidently expectant.

Prayer is the communication lifeline of the believer. Just as a soldier behind enemy lines relies heavily on his radio to communicate with his support team, so the believer living in Satan's world must rely heavily upon prayer for his support team. If we are going to be effective soldiers in our defense against Satan, we dare not allow ourselves to be cut off.

10

TRIUMPHANT WARRIORS

Therefore, since we have so great a cloud of witnesses surrounding us, let us also lay aside every encumbrance, and the sin which so easily entangles us, and let us run with endurance the race that is set before us, fixing our eyes on Jesus, the author and perfecter of faith.

—Hebrews 12:1–2

I (Thomas) remember the Saturday afternoon as if it were yesterday. When the phone rang, it was one of my best friends, Gary. During the previous couple of years, we had done much together—studied the Bible, prayed, worked, evangelized, traveled, and fellowshipped. Gary was the kind of guy who would give you the shirt off of his back if you needed it, probably without having to ask.

I said hello to Gary and asked him what was up. Gary informed me that he just wanted to let me know that he was quitting the Christian life. *"What?"* I asked. "Quitting the Christian life? *Why?"*

"I'm tired of confessing my sin," Gary replied.

"But you don't just quit Christianity—it doesn't work that way!" I responded.

Unfortunately, Gary is just one example of many believers who start with a bang but then stray from the course. Some people, like Gary, completely quit the race whereas others just wander around in a state of spiritual confusion. Probably you also have friends who have followed a similar path. Why don't some Christians finish the race?

On the other hand, I also know believers who have endured even under great pressure. Some of them have had everything against them, humanly speaking, yet they continued to exhibit steady faith in the Lord Jesus Christ.

Anyone who is a fan of racing knows that mere speed is not enough to win races consistently. Effective contenders must also have *endurance*. Many auto races come down to a contest of who can stay in the race until the end. During a race, a car may be knocked out of competition for various reasons. Some drivers might blow an engine; others might crash into a wall or collide with other cars. A fire in the engine, an electrical failure, or a flat tire can lead to an early exit for a given contestant, even if he is leading the race at the moment. *Endurance* is a primary ingredient for any racer.

Endurance is also a primary ingredient in the Christian life. What, then, are some of the roadblocks that a growing believer will encounter in the marathon of the Christian life?

Suffering in a Feel-Good Society

We cannot think of a single instance of believers wanting to quit the Christian life that does not relate in some way to suffering. This point is especially true in our modern, feel-good society. A person grows weary or is disappointed by what is required of him. Endurance, perseverance, and patience all require that a person suffer at some point, but suffering certainly does not feel good. As the writer of Hebrews put it, "All discipline for the moment seems not to be joyful, but sorrowful" (Heb. 12:11). Therefore, many Christians want to quit the race when they begin experiencing some pain or discomfort. The second half of Hebrews 12:11 goes on to say, "Yet to those who have been trained by it [discipline], afterwards it yields the peaceful fruit of righteousness." Suffering is an inevitable part (though not all) of the Christian life. If suffering is not handled with endurance and faith, a believer will be tempted to drop out of the race.

Because suffering, if not properly understood and handled, often leads to an early exit from the race, we must look at suffering from the perspective of God's Word. The Bible teaches that God, being good, did not directly create evil. Instead, evil entered the universe through God's rebellious creatures. However, now that evil has entered God's creation, He sovereignly uses evil for His own good purposes (Gen. 50:20; Exod. 3:18–20; Prov. 16:4; Rom. 8:28).[1] God is in control of all evil, and the suffering that we experience in this life He will use to help us mature into Christlikeness.

The Ultimate Good

The greatest example of how God turns evil into good is seen in the death of Christ. First Corinthians 2:6–9 tells us that those people who were involved in crucifying Christ did it out of an evil motive. However, Scripture also informs us that this was something "which God predestined before the ages to our glory" (1 Cor. 2:7). The death of Christ resulted in the greatest of all blessings to mankind—our salvation from sin. Paul goes on to explain that God kept certain aspects of His plan a secret because had the rulers of this age understood it, "they would not have crucified the Lord of glory" (v. 8). This passage further explains that future blessings are included in the plan of God that He has not yet revealed but that are going to be worth waiting for. The implication is that just because we cannot understand everything that God is doing in our lives at the present time, including the suffering, does not mean that God has no glorious purpose in store for us. The Bible teaches that there is a divine purpose behind all of the suffering that evil brings upon God's children.

It is not as important to know in each case of suffering into which of the preceding categories we fall as it is to endure suffering with joy, hope, and endurance. Regardless of the purpose that God might have for specific events of suffering in our lives, we should handle each situation with the same Christian character. The future will reveal many of the specific reasons why we have suffered, as can be seen from the life of Job, but our calling in the present is to trust God to know what He is doing in our lives.

Scripture reveals at least four reasons why Christians suffer.

1. *Christians suffer because of the curse resulting from Adam's fall.* Christians, like all of the rest of humanity, suffer under God's curse

upon creation as a result of the fall of Adam into sin (Gen. 3:8–24; Rom. 5:12–21). This is the broadest purpose behind moral and physical evil and suffering. Those who have suffered the loss of a loved one (especially if it was sudden and unexpected) or have been associated with someone with birth defects have experienced firsthand the effects resulting from Adam's fall. This kind of suffering and pain is not part of God's original creation, but it is something resulting from man himself. Sometimes Christians realize this fact but still react bitterly toward God because He could have prevented the loss of a loved one but did not in their specific case. Although God is gracious, we should realize that God is also fair and just in His dealings with us. We just have to trust Him in these kinds of matters. Scripture recognizes the abnormality that Adam's sin has brought upon the human race and teaches that our only hope is in God's plan.

The pain related to the Curse is noted in Romans 8:18–25. Paul contrasts "the sufferings of this present time" to "the glory that is to be revealed to us" in the future (v. 18). Why does humanity experience present suffering? Paul explains that it is due to Adam's fall (vv. 20–21). The point of this passage is to let believers know that we have a hope for the future that will one day release us from the pain of present suffering. This is not a hope for unbelievers because their destiny is eternal suffering in the lake of fire. Because we have the hope of future glory and know that suffering and pain is only a temporary feature for the Christian, "with perseverance we wait eagerly for it" (v. 25). Paul is saying that the future hope of glory produces *perseverance* in the present life of a Christian.

2. *God disciplines His children and uses adversity to produce spiritual maturity.* This is probably one of the primary reasons for Christian suffering (Heb. 12:3–15). When we respond to these experiences with patience, we learn what it means to be conformed to Christ (Col. 1:24; James 1:2–4; 2 Peter 1:5–8). Anyone who has ever been involved in athletics knows that disciplined workouts are required, not because the coach is angry at his players but because players must have a competent endurance level to compete in a game. The same is true of a soldier who is preparing for combat. Similarly, training in righteousness requires the tough exercise and discipline of learning to

follow God's will instead of our own selfish and often lustful feelings, regardless of the pain that might be involved in crucifying the flesh. But this kind of discipline produces the godly characteristic of perseverance needed to finish the race.

3. *Some Christians suffer in a hostile world because we are identified with Christ.* Jesus made this truth clear to His disciples in His farewell address to them in the Upper Room: "If the world hates you, you know that it has hated Me before it hated you. If you were of the world, the world would love its own; but because you are not of the world, but I chose you out of the world, therefore the world hates you" (John 15:18–19). People who have not trusted Christ as their Savior from their sins have an innate animosity toward Christ and His people when they are challenged about their relationship to God. Often, they take out their hatred toward Christ on His messengers. Christ is telling every believer that we can expect this type of response. In a sense, this behavior is normal, so we should not be surprised when it occurs. Our goal should be to respond to this kind of suffering the way the early disciples did as recorded in Acts 5:41: "They went on their way from the presence of the Council, rejoicing that they had been considered worthy to suffer shame for His name."

4. *Christians sometimes suffer that they might be to all creation a testimony of God's grace.* They are a testimony to angels (Eph. 3:10), other Christians (2 Cor. 1:3–6; 4:8–12), and non-Christians (1 Peter 2:12–20; 3:13–17). When we respond to suffering and hardship properly, that response can be an encouragement to other believers of the grace of God. We can be an encouragement and not a detriment to others, as Paul explains: "If we are afflicted, it is for your comfort and salvation; or if we are comforted, it is for your comfort, which is effective in the patient enduring of the same sufferings which we also suffer" (2 Cor. 1:6).

In addition to encouraging other believers, we learn from Ephesians 3:10 that angels ("the rulers and the authorities in the heavenly places") are learning lessons "through the church." What lessons do they learn? Ephesians 3:4–7 indicates that as history unfolds they are learning about God's grace as expressed in Christ. The angelic realm cannot personally experience saving grace, so they must learn about it from believers in Christ.

Non-Christians are part of the "all creation" cited in this reason. When non-Christians observe the way that Christians handle suffering, they can see a testimony of Jesus Christ working in our lives. First Peter 3:17 says, "For it is better, if God should will it so, that you suffer for doing what is right rather than for doing what is wrong." Thus, "those who revile your good behavior in Christ may be put to shame" (3:16). Unbelievers often watch us believers who have spoken out for Christ to see how He has affected our lives. What better testimony to the world than the way we handle adversity and suffering? Perseverance, endurance, and patience are the biblical response of the Christian to suffering.

Suffering God's Way

Christians can learn much about the nature of perseverance by understanding the Greek word for perseverance in the New Testament. The verb *hupomeno* is made up of two smaller Greek words: *hupo*, meaning "under," and *meno*, meaning "to remain." Taken together, they mean "to remain under." Remain under what? It depends on to what the word is referring. If it is talking about the sufferings related to trials, as in 1 Peter 2:20 ("when you do what is right and suffer for it you patiently endure it, this finds favor with God"), then perseverance, endurance, or patience refers to the ability to remain under the pressure of a given situation rather than seeking to escape it for the temporary relief from the pain of suffering.

How does this apply to the issue of spiritual warfare? Some deliverance teachers say that many of our problems and trials can be dealt with simply by rebuking Satan, and then these trials will be removed instantly from a believer's life. This idea is very appealing to many modern Christians who have grown up in a society where we don't have to wait very long for anything. However, this is not the way God normally works. In the first place, many of our problems stem from the flesh. Therefore, God wants us to learn how to resist sin in our lives through the often-painful process of learning to trust Him to overcome these problems. The red herring of instant relief from our trials does not lend itself to the development of patience in our trials. It is the lessons learned from "remaining under" the pressure of a given situation that produce Christlike character in our lives. This is what Paul means in Romans 5:3–4 when he tells us that "we also exult in our tribulations, knowing that tribulation brings about perseverance; and perseverance, proven character; and proven character, hope."

Rebuking the Devil?

Many people are being led astray by deliverance teachings that promise instantaneous victory over one's problems by a timely rebuke of the Devil. This teaching misleads people from the biblical path of exercising endurance or patience in meeting their trials. As a result, many believers are not developing the kind of proven character that they need to handle trials.

This character-building approach is illustrated by Paul's thorn in the flesh (2 Cor. 12:7–10). The thorn is described as "a messenger of Satan to buffet me—to keep me from exalting myself" (v. 7). It is possible that this messenger was a demon. The Greek word for "messenger" is *angelos,* the word for "angel." Deliverance teachers today view this kind of situation as something that is out of keeping with the will of God, and they would seek to rebuke this "messenger of Satan" and run him out of town by giving him two black eyes in the process. But this was not Paul's response. Instead, he "entreated the Lord three times that it might depart from me" (v. 8). Yet, God did not grant Paul's request. But do we not have power in the name of Jesus? Yes, we do, but it is to be exercised within the will of God. The Lord was more interested in building Christlike character in Paul as a true display of His power (v. 9) than in putting on the kind of fireworks display that many people today are calling "power encounters."

Within certain circles today, it is common to hear a speaker lash out against Satan with various rebukes. Often, the speaker will rebuke Satan in the area of health, wealth, and peace of mind. It is not unusual to hear more preaching against Satan and the demonic powers than to hear preaching on Christ and His resources. Many people become so concerned with what the Devil is doing that they take their eyes off the Lord.

We must realize that believers are never instructed to rebuke the Devil or his demons. The New Testament views rebuking as the sole prerogative of Jesus as an expression of His lordship and sovereignty over the spirit realm.[2] The only acceptable condition for a believer to rebuke is when he lovingly corrects a brother who has fallen into sin (Luke 17:3; 1 Tim. 5:20). Throughout the New Testament, rebuke is understood as the sole prerogative of the Lord, and this is why Michael said when he was challenged by Satan, "The Lord rebuke you" (Jude 9).

Marks of a False Prophet

Second Peter 2:1-9 describes and denounces false prophets who will be active within the church until the second coming of Christ. Peter exposes their self-centered motives and conduct in the first three verses and then pronounces their condemnation in the next six verses. The rest of the chapter concludes with a description of their characteristics. One characteristic that the contemporary church would do well to note is found in verse 10: "Especially those who indulge the flesh in its corrupt desires and despise authority. Daring, self-willed, they do not tremble when they revile angelic majesties." The earlier context indicates that these self-willed false prophets were engaged in reviling fallen angelic majesties—demons. Remember that this is characteristic of false prophets, so it is a warning for Christians not to engage in such practices.

Peter goes on to explain this practice in greater detail in verses 11 and 12. He notes that "angels who are greater in might and power do not bring a reviling judgment against them before the Lord" (v. 11). Angels know better than to do such foolish things as rebuking or reviling other angels. They have much greater strength and power than the most powerful human being, yet they know better than to engage in such practices. Certainly God's holy angels cannot be justly accused of not being involved in spiritual warfare, but for them, as it should be for us, it is a question of being properly involved.

Jude 8-9, in a similar warning about false teachers, gives a specific example of this kind of incident. Jude uses almost identical language when he notes that the false teachers "defile the flesh, and reject authority, and revile angelic majesties" (v. 8). How do they do that? He tells us that "Michael the archangel, when he disputed with the devil and argued about the body of Moses, did not dare pronounce against him a railing judgment, but said, 'The Lord rebuke you'" (v. 9). This passage is telling us that even Michael, the highest-ranking elect angel, would not rebuke the Devil; yet many Christians today do it regularly. The text says "did not dare," which means that doing such a thing was so unthinkable for Michael that he would not even come close to it. Michael did not even say what we hear many people saying today: "I rebuke you, devil, in the name of the Lord!" Michael simply said, "The Lord rebuke you." Unlike many modern Christians, Michael knew that rebuking was a prerogative of the Lord alone!

With not one but *two* warnings in Scripture against such practices, we must ask, "Why do so many Christians and Christian leaders regularly engage in such practices?" Both passages give us the answer: they are acting out of ignorance. "These, like unreasoning animals, . . . reviling where they have no knowledge, . . ." (2 Peter 2:12). "These men revile the things which they do not understand . . ." (Jude 10).

This verse is an example of ignorance of God's Word leading to wrong practice in the area of spiritual warfare. No wonder many Christians are growing weary and dropping out of the battle! Many of them are following leaders who are leading them on wild-goose chases through beliefs and practices that open them to *attacks* from the enemy rather than the advertised protection from the enemy. A believer in Christ can develop true maturity only through genuine biblical training, which teaches us to keep our eyes upon Christ and not be preoccupied with the demonic powers.

Training for the Big Game

The book of Hebrews was written to Jewish believers who had trusted Christ as their Savior. As time passed, some of them were starting to "drift away" (2:1) from Christ back into the comfort and familiarity of Judaism. The writer of Hebrews demonstrates the error of this thinking by showing that the old (Judaism) was merely temporary, and he looked forward to the fulfillment in Jesus the Messiah. Jesus the Messiah fulfilled the shadows of Old Testament ritual in His ministry; therefore, five warning passages are issued to the Jewish readers, showing that if they grow impatient with Christ and His work, a return to the old way will lead only to judgment because they then have no Messiah who actually took away sin. After showing that the new things in Christ are superior to the old things in Judaism, the writer of Hebrews notes how the saints from the Old Testament never received these promises in their lifetimes but faithfully continued in their trust of God (Heb. 11). By the time the writer gets to Hebrews 12, he is telling the Hebrews, and us, that if their brethren displayed such faith and endurance without having seen Jesus the Messiah, their faith should be even greater because they, and we, are able to look back to Jesus as our example. This fact forms the context for understanding Hebrews 12.

A good friend of ours was a pro football player who was a starter on a winning Super Bowl team. He told us how this is the ultimate test for a pro athlete because the importance and national interest of such a game provides a powerful incentive for any player to prepare and perform at his best. A similar picture is painted in the first two verses of Hebrews 12. The stands are packed with "so great a cloud of witnesses surrounding us" (12:1), which are the Old Testament saints from chapter 11. The players are readying themselves by laying "aside every encumbrance, and the sin which so easily entangles us" (12:1). The hindrances in the race are said to be sin generated by each believer, not external demonic attacks. The resolve carried into the contest consists of running the race "with endurance" (12:1). The Christian life is not a sprint, but a marathon that requires endurance, which, in turn, requires training and resolve.

The Right Example

Hebrews 12:2 pictures the runner in the starting blocks fixing his eyes on Jesus. On *Jesus,* not on Satan and the demonic powers! *Christ* is our example because He has run the race before us and is the model of how to run the race properly. Three things furnished Christ's motivation and should be ours as well. First, He emphasized "the joy set before Him." His orientation was not on the present pain of the race but on the joy that would result when He finished the race. He was *future*-oriented, not present-oriented. Second, He "endured the cross." He did not let the suffering aspect of His mission knock Him out of the race because of His future orientation. Third, He was "despising the shame." The world viewed His death as a shame, an embarrassment. But Christ despised that. When He endured and finished the race, He "sat down at the right hand of the throne of God." The glory comes after we have endured the pain of the race; then we are able to sit down and receive the glory.

Next, we are told to "consider Him who has endured such hostility by sinners against Himself, so that you may not grow weary and lose heart" (12:3). *Consider* means "to contemplate, to think about." In context, it implies that we are to sit down and think through a strategy that will enable us to run this race of endurance successfully. How are we to develop the character and internal fortitude to complete such a race? By modeling our own race strategy after the one that Christ ran. There is a twofold purpose for this plan. The first purpose is that we "may not grow weary" or become discouraged. This often happens to a runner who starts a long race. Early in the race, he begins to realize that it is going to be a long, tough haul, and soon he becomes discouraged and begins to think about dropping out of the race. The second purpose is that we might not lose heart or suffer from low morale, which could also lead to dropping out of the race.

Over the last few years, we have talked with many Christians who have become discouraged with the "quick-fix" approaches to spiritual warfare in which they were taught to *rebuke* Satan rather than *resist* him to handle their problems. When this strategy didn't work, they become discouraged and dropped by the wayside. Often, these people didn't really want to quit the race; they simply had not received the proper training or developed the kind of maturity and character necessary to endure the tough battles. Their basic problem was that they had been on a spiritual diet of ice cream and cookies and their exercise program had amounted to watching games on television while relaxing in their easy chair.

Hebrews 12 goes on to speak of the need to develop discipline and maturity in our lives if we are to complete the race properly, as those in the stands have already done. This training "yields the peaceful fruit of righteousness" (12:11). Godly character takes time to develop through practice and discipline.

Helping the Weak

When I (Thomas) was in Army boot camp we often went on long marches. Our goal was for the whole company to complete the march successfully. If one man dropped out, then we did not complete our mission; therefore, the strong were encouraged to help the weak by carrying their packs or helping them make it to the finish so that the company as a whole could make it to the finish line. Likewise, some Christians are stronger than others, and we are admonished in the New Testament to help those within the body of Christ who are weak. Repeatedly, the New Testament says that the cause of their weakness is sin in the person's life with which they have not properly dealt. Such sin hinders a Christian's spiritual development, rendering him spiritually weak (Heb. 12:1).

The danger we face is growing weary in the struggle. The writer to the Hebrews exhorts us to consider Jesus so that we will not grow weary and lose heart. The Greek word for weary here occurs in two other important passages, Revelation 2:3 and James 5:15. In both the Hebrews and the Revelation passages, the word clearly is used in contrast to endurance. The same is true in the James passage. Unfortunately, the passage has traditionally been understood as teaching something about healing physical sickness. We recognize that this is a debated passage, but we believe that it—when properly understood and applied—offers great hope to the believer whose endurance is failing.

Can All Illness Be Healed?

Many people have struggled with the traditional explanation of James 5:13-16, which focuses on physical sickness. The reason for this struggle is that verse 15, "the prayer offered in faith will restore the one who is sick," appears to be an unconditional promise but often seems to be unfulfilled.

On July 7, 1952, my (Robert) mother was stricken with polio. I was born less than a month later, and I have never seen my mother walk. When I was a child, with the faith of a child, I regularly prayed that God would heal her so that she could walk again. This prayer was never answered. Later, I realized that God does not always answer a prayer for healing. However, James 5:15, if it is talking about physical disease, indicates that God will always heal. Another well-known case of God's not healing someone is that of Joni Earickson Tada. She writes that many Christians have prayed for her, anointed her with oil, and laid hands on her, yet she is still a quadriplegic to the glory of God. In light of these and many other situations in which God has not healed, we must be open to the possibility that this passage might not be talking about physical healing at all, but spiritual healing instead. We all recognize that many sick people for whom we pray never recover and even die. Is this true because we lack faith or because God is not faithful? Or could it be that the sickness mentioned here is something other than physical illness?

The word translated "sick" in verse 14 ("Is anyone among you sick?") has two meanings in the Greek. At its root is the idea of *weakness*. In some places, the weakness is physical (Matt. 10:8; Luke 4:40; John 4:46), and in other places the weakness is spiritual (Rom. 6:19; 8:26; 2 Cor. 12:5, 9–10). The *context* determines whether the meaning is spiritual or physical. In James 5, two different Greek words are translated "sick." The first word is in verse 14 and translates the Greek *asthenes*. The next verse translates the Greek word *kamno* as "sick." Because *kamno* clearly means to be spiritually weary (Heb. 12:3; Rev. 2:3), we learn that James did not have in mind *physical* weakness but *spiritual* weakness.

This fact is further supported by the fact that the entire thrust of James, especially this last chapter, is on patience (5:7–8, 10) and endurance (5:11). The example that James used to illustrate his point is from the Old Testament, where Elijah persevered in his confrontation with Ahab (1 Kings 17:1). If James were talking about healing a *physical* disease, that same chapter in 1 Kings provides a much better illustration: Elijah's restoring life to the widow's son.

Excellent biblical grounds exist for understanding this passage to be talking about what to do if and when a believer is growing weary. First, he is to lean upon more mature believers and their prayers. He is to call upon the elders to have them pray for him. Furthermore, if there is sin in his life, sin that entangles him and destroys his endurance, he is to confess that sin (James 5:16). The result is that he will be "healed." Again we find that the original Greek word used here is also found in our other endurance passage, Hebrews 12, where we find the writer concluding his exhortation to endurance by saying, "Therefore, strengthen the hands that are weak and the knees that are feeble, and make straight paths for your feet, so that the limb which is lame may not be put out of joint, but rather be healed" (vv. 12–13). The context makes clear that the writer is using a physical-healing figure of speech to describe what must take place in the body of Christ when a brother or sister is weary of the struggle: He must be lifted up, he must lean on the stronger Christian, and he must be strengthened in his faith.

The Scriptures are consistent in stating that the solution to struggle in the Christian life is based on prayer—a recognition of our submission to God and reliance upon His strength rather than our own strength. We must confess and turn from sin in our lives as we move toward obedience to the truth. When we are weak, we should cry out to God, as David did many times as recorded in the psalms. We should also seek the counsel of more mature Christians to encourage and help us along the way, as we have seen in James 5.

Patience in Action

As we have already seen, the epistle of James has much to say about patience and endurance. James begins his letter with the admonition to be joyful through trials because this produces endurance in the life of the faithful believer (1:2–4). Toward the end of the epistle James returns to the theme of endurance or patience and cites three examples of patient endurance needed to handle our trials (5:7–11). Some of us may be happy to know that there are limits on how long believers are expected to patiently endure; we must only be patient "until the coming [rapture] of the Lord" (5:7). After that event the race is over, and patience and endurance no longer be required of Christians.

The first example of patient endurance is illustrated by the farmer who has to wait on rain for his crop to grow into a harvest (James 5:7–8). Then the Old Testament prophets are presented as "an example, brethren, of suffering and patience . . . who spoke in the name of the Lord" (5:10). These men had to suffer during their lifetime for giving a prophecy that would not be fulfilled in their lifetime. This act took patient endurance.

James also reminds us, "You have heard of the endurance of Job and have seen the outcome of the Lord's dealings, that the Lord is full of compassion and is merciful" (5:11). Job had to trust God to vindicate him and bless him even though he was engaged in one of the most severe attacks from Satan in the history of the world. So the life of Job is a model of a believer handling a satanic attack with endurance and patience. Now let's look at what occasioned Satan's encounter with Job.

The Patience of Job

When I (Thomas) was a teenager, a group of us would pile into a car and go cruising. This activity is still common for many young people who are looking for potential excitement. In the first chapter of Job, the Bible tells us that Satan does some cruising of his own and that God gives even Satan access to His presence (Job 1:6). Much of Satan's time is spent cruising the earth looking for Christians who do not know how to resist Him by submitting to divine authority.

When God asked Satan, "From where do you come?" Satan replied, "From roaming about on the earth and walking around on it" (1:7). The Hebrew word translated "roaming" is used to describe the way a lion roams an area looking for his prey. When the lion locates a potential victim, he stalks his prey and, at just the right time, moves in for the kill. This is the same description used to explain Satan's activities when the Lord asked him about a certain individual, Job. "Have you considered My servant Job?" the Lord challenged. Apparently Satan had, because he shot back, "Does Job fear God for nothing?" Today we might say something like, "He's only in it for the money." But to demonstrate that Job served God because he loved God for who He is and not just for the benefits that Sugar Daddy provides, God allowed Satan to attack Job to such a severe degree that the very name *Job* has become synonymous with undeserved suffering.

The apostle Peter must have had the Job passage in mind when the Holy Spirit moved him to picture Satan, the Devil, as one who "prowls about like a roaring lion, seeking someone to devour" (1 Peter 5:8). What did Peter prescribe for the believer in light of Satan's persistent harassments? We are to be persistent in our fight against him. Peter says that the hard times through which Satan puts us do not result in aid to Satan's cause; instead, godly resistance to Satan produces Christlike character and maturity, giving a battle-tested stability to our lives (vv. 9–11).

Response for Persevering Believers

How does Peter instruct a Christian to react to Satan's attacks? Not by talking about how we are going to run the Devil out of town or give him a black eye. Rather, Scripture says that we are to *resist* him (1 Peter 5:9). James 4:7 and Ephesians 6:11, 13–14 repeat this command. This is what the Bible specifically and repeatedly says is to be our strategy when Satan attacks us. Scripture does not tell us to develop from experience a formula of rebuking, binding, insulting, or arguing with Satan and the demonic powers. Instead, we are to follow God's explicit instructions on this issue. By habitually following God's Word, we will see the Lord bring stability and character into our lives, including the type of endurance that we need to engage in spiritual warfare without fainting in the day of battle.

11

WAR'S END

I saw an angel coming down from heaven, having the key of the abyss and a great chain in his hand. And he laid hold of the dragon, the serpent of old, who is the devil and Satan, and bound him for a thousand years, and threw him into the abyss, and shut it and sealed it over him, so that he should not deceive the nations any longer, until the thousand years were completed.

—Revelation 20:1–3

After Satan led his rebellion against God, during which he recruited one-third of the angels and all of humankind, God launched a counterattack. He enlisted believers from Adam's descendants, those whom He has called out from the darkness of their sin to be a part of His coming kingdom. The battle, which involves the eternal destiny of humanity, is moving rapidly toward its grand climax. Although Satan and his minions are a defeated foe as a result of Christ's work on the Cross, the war still rages. Some of the hottest battles are yet to come. How will the war end, and what significance does that hold for believers today?

The Two-Stage Conquest

God's victory over Satan is being worked out historically in two stages. *Stage one* was accomplished on the Cross. At that time, Satan's defeat was ensured, his destiny certain. But defeated though he was, he still has power to operate, so much so that he is still called the "god of this world" (2 Cor. 4:4). His ultimate defeat will be accomplished in *stage two,* during the second coming of Christ. At this time, Satan will be defeated and bound in the bottomless pit for one thousand years, after which he will be released for a short while, only to be defeated again and thrown into the lake of fire for eternity (Rev. 20:1–3, 10).

Because we live in the interim between stages one and two called the church age, we must determine what our strategy toward Satan should be. We have seen that in the current church age we, as believers, are to engage in spiritual warfare *defensively* by standing against Satan. We do so solely on the basis of our position in Christ, which Christ gained for us at His first coming, when His humiliation brought about the forgiveness of our sins. Ultimate victory will be accomplished at His second coming, when, in glory, He will sweep Satan and his demons from the field of battle and remove them from the realm of human activity. Meanwhile, Christians are to remain faithful in their defensive position, standing firm in the faith.

The defensive posture toward Satan and his demons appears to have been part of God's plan for His creatures even before the fall of man. God told Adam to subdue and rule over the *earth* (Gen. 1:26), not the heavens. When God placed man in the Garden, He told him to cultivate and keep the garden (2:15). Many Bible scholars have pointed out that the word for "keep" *(shamar)* includes the idea of guarding. The implication is that Adam was to guard against an intrusion, which we know from Genesis 3 was Satan. As God's creature, man has always been in the position of defending himself with God's Word. Apparently, for a creature to go on the offensive against Satan is to usurp a divine prerogative that is reserved for God alone. The creature's posture is trust in God by taking a defensive stance.

Wrong Strategy

The last decade has seen the rise of many people teaching that the church of Jesus Christ is to take up an *offensive* strategy against Satan and the demonic powers before Christ returns. This error is the result of a poor understanding of God's purpose for both this age and the age to come and is a failure to distinguish the threefold aspect of Satan's defeat. From the earliest times in history, Satan has attempted to deceive God's people into doing something that is good (in this case, launching an offensive attack against Satan and the demonic powers) but engaging in it wrongly or prematurely. Satan tempted Adam and Eve with a promise of knowledge, something that they would have received from God anyway had they not been arrogant and presumptuous. However, they believed that they could have it on their own terms, and this assumption resulted in humanity's being cast into sin. Satan later tempted Christ unsuccessfully with the kingdoms of this world, something that Christ will end up with anyway (Rev. 11:15).

In a military briefing, I (Thomas) was once told that the Russian offensive strategy was to attack in three waves. The first wave would strike, initiating the attack. The second and third waves were held in reserve, waiting for the time when the battle would become fierce and the momentum of the attack was being slowed. Because of our inferior numbers, we Americans have countered with a strategy that is designed to make the Russians think prematurely that they have met large pockets of resistance that necessitate deployment of their second and third waves. This strategy of premature deployment is designed to trick the Russians into expending their energy and resources in fighting a phantom enemy. Then, when they have spent themselves, the Americans can move in and exact a fatal blow. This strategy is similar to what Satan is attempting to do to Christians who try to go on the offensive before our General—Jesus Christ—has decided on such a plan.

When Satan tricks Christians into expending their time and energy in wrong directions, he has achieved a temporary victory, and that is why it is important to know how the war will conclude. It will terminate during the final seven years of history (the Tribulation) with a series of the most spectacular events the world will ever see. Part of those events will include both direct combat between Jesus Christ and Satan and battles between the holy angels and the demons. Jesus Christ will be victorious. Only by understanding this fact can we live effectively as Christians today and avoid being duped by Satan into premature deployment. As believers, we must not fall into the trap (as many people within the church are doing today) of substituting Satan's strategy for God's plan.

Two major errors are being advocated today that often lead to improper strategies in spiritual warfare. The first error relates to the *means* of our spiritual warfare, which we have already discussed at length. The second error relates to the *timing* of Christ's ultimate victory, which we will explain in the rest of this chapter.

Binding Satan and Demons?

In chapter 6, we dealt extensively with this error, but we will mention it again further to drive home the point that this is an error relating to both *timing* and *means*. First, the *time* when Satan and the demons will be bound is in the *future,* not in the present, as Revelation 20:2 tells us: "He laid hold of . . . Satan, and bound him for a thousand years." The Bible describes our current strategy as resisting Satan (Eph. 6:11; James 4:7; 1 Peter 5:9). Second, God will not be using believers to round up Satan and put him out of commission by binding. Instead, the *means* that God will use is stated clearly in Revelation 20:1, where it says that "an *angel* coming down from heaven, having the key of the abyss and a great chain in his hand" will do the honors. Therefore, the idea that believers have removed Satan and his demon armies from spheres of influence because they have prayed for Satan's binding is unbiblical.

Inherited Curses?

This error of timing misinterprets Scripture from a past era and wrongly applies it to present circumstances. It is the view that occult powers or curses are passed from parent to child. Those who advocate this view usually quote Exodus 20:5: "You shall not worship them or serve them; for I, the Lord your God, am a jealous God, visiting the iniquity of the fathers on the children, on the third and the fourth generations of those who hate Me." Proponents of this view believe that if a parent's or grandparent's curse or occult power is not specifically uncovered and removed by renouncing it, a Christian can be oppressed by such a past curse which would include "demonization."[1]

For at least two reasons this view is an inaccurate interpretation and application of the passage. First, when a person becomes a Christian, he is delivered from all of his sins, including occult sin, because a Christian cannot be demon possessed. *The Bible does not recognize occult sin as a special category of sin that has not been dealt with by the Cross.* Remember, everyone is born under the authority of Satan (Col. 1:13) and has Satan working through him (Eph. 2:2). Second, it is wrong to assume that Exodus 20:5 refers to God's "visiting the iniquity of the fathers on the children" because of *inheritance* rather than because each successive generation decides to follow in the footsteps of their parents. Ezekiel 18:2-20 says that God curses each Israelite individual for his *own* sins and not specifically because of something that his ancestors might have done. God specifically states in verse 4 that "all souls are Mine; the soul of the father as well as the soul of the son is Mine." God goes on to state that if the son does right, in contrast to the parents' sins, including occult sins, then "he shall surely live."

This kind of "I-inherited-it-from-my-parents" view is also a popular explanation for all kinds of aberrant behavior within many Christian psychology circles as well. It is used to avoid personal responsibility and to explain mental and emotional disease, chronic sickness, all sorts of female problems from miscarriage to premenstrual syndrome, marriage and financial problems, and rebellious teenagers. But the idea that a Christian might have to be delivered specifically from a curse or occult power that salvation in Christ has not covered is not found in Scripture. In fact, *not one example exists in the entire Bible of a saved person's being under a satanic curse that had to be broken by Christian exorcism or distinct confession.* The only curses that the Bible treats as effective are those uttered by God. This attempt to shift responsibility for current failures to someone else is reminiscent of Adam's attempt to shift to Eve the blame for his sin.

The passages used to support generational cursing derive from the Old Testament (Exod. 20:4-7; 34:6-7; Num. 14:17-19; Deut. 5:7-10) and are all directed to Israel. In the context, these curses are part of the cursing and blessing pronouncements in the Mosaic Covenant directed to Israel. Those who obeyed God would be blessed; those who violated the covenant would be disciplined, or "cursed." Because these statements applied only to Israel under the Old Covenant, these curses have no application today (Rom. 7:1-6; 10:4; Gal. 3:19; 3:24–4:7). Furthermore, because these curses derive from God as discipline on the disobedient, we know that the way to avoid the wrath of God is through faith in Christ (Rom. 5:8).

The nature of the curses in the Mosaic Law was to recognize that parents pass on certain traits and teach patterns of life to their children. When parents have rejected Christ and mire themselves in paganism, idolatry, and the occult, they teach these sins to their children. The result is the transfer of rebellion from one generation to another. But this fact does not remove from the subsequent generation their own responsibility for sin. In fact, the Bible teaches just the opposite. No matter what false religion is passed on by one generation to another, the children decide to accept or reject it. They are punished ("cursed") for their own decision to follow the rebellious path of their parents. Jewish expositor Umberto Cassuto speaks strongly against the possibility of this "ancestral principle" interpretation.

> In regard to the fearful threat of punishment that will be inflicted upon the children and children's children, various apologetic interpretations have been advanced, which it is not possible to accept. It has been suggested, for example, that we should see here an allusion to the transmission of parental qualities to the character of the children and children's children, but this is merely a modernization of the verse; . . . The difficulty exists, however, only for those who overlook the fact that the verse, in its simple signification, is directed to the entire nation as a single entity in time throughout its generations. Since a man, and particularly an Israelite, grieves over the tribulation of his children and grandchildren not less? nay, even more? than over his own affliction, the Bible issues a warning, so as to keep man far from sin, that in the course of the nation's life it is possible that the children and grandchildren will suffer the consequences of the iniquities of their father and grandfather. (emphasis added)[2]

This concept of the transfer of curses or demons is prevalent within animistic religions but not biblical Christianity.

> This doctrine . . . rests on the assumption that our vulnerability to demonic influence derives from physical or symbolic contacts or contiguity with some object, word, or person rather than on moral, spiritual and doctrinal grounds—an assumption which is at the heart of magic and animism—but which biblical Christianity nowhere propagates.[3]

Other deliverance teachers claim that any Christian with an occult past must specifically renounce those sins or he will not be free. In other words, salvation is not enough, there must also be a separate, postsalvation deliverance from presalvation occult sins. Yet if this is true, then Christ's work is not sufficient, and salvation does not truly break the tyranny of the sin nature (Rom. 6:6–7; 17–18). If their position were true, then we would need to specifically go back and name all our sins in order to be saved. But this is completely contrary to the entire teaching of Scripture that Christ died for all sin—past, present, and future—and that every believer is delivered from all of his sins at the instant of salvation.

Those who teach the ancestral inheritance principle quite naturally and logically also teach that a postsalvation deliverance is necessary in order for the believer to really be free from the impact of one's ancestral past. However, the idea that a Christian might have to be delivered specifically from a curse or occult power which salvation in Christ would not have taken care of is not found or implied anywhere in Scripture. This notion is even more far-fetched when one considers the fact that the individual did not even commit the sin. In fact, there is not one example in the entire Bible of a saved person being under a satanic curse, which had to be "broken" by Christian exorcism or distinct confession. On the other hand, one example of demonic deliverance by Christ in the New Testament seems to imply that the ancestral inheritance principle is totally off base.

John 9 records the incident of Jesus' healing a man who was born blind. Apparently, Christ's disciples believed wrongly that the man's blindness was a result of the sin of his parents, just as many people wrongly believe today. Perhaps those Jews two thousand years ago misinterpreted the same passages that are being cited in our own day to come to their false conclusion. Notice the dialogue in John 9:2–3: "And His disciples asked Him, saying, 'Rabbi, who sinned, this man or his parents, that he should be born blind?' Jesus answered, 'It was neither that this man sinned, nor his parents; but it was in order that the works of God might be displayed in him.'"

Regarding this "curses" approach, Dr. John Hannah makes the following perceptive comment:

> Christians do face demonic opposition, for which God has provided the appropriate spiritual armor (Ephesians 6:10ff.). We must put it on and utilize it to the fullest extent. However, we do *not* need some additional procedure for dealing with evil curses, for which there is no scriptural warrant. This is a mixture of Christianity with Zoroastrianism, Eastern mysticism, and black magic *voodoo*). We do well to remember the old fable of the "tar baby and the rabbit"![4]

Dominion Theology

The 1980s witnessed the rise of the idea that because we are now in the kingdom, we should take dominion over Christ's enemies, in essence running them out of town.[5] This thinking has been around for a long time, but it has become dominant in many circles today. This error stems from the wrong view that we are currently in the kingdom/millennium instead of the church age. Once again, proponents of this view confuse the characteristics of the future with those of the present. Those who hold this view suggest that because Satan and the demons will be gone during the kingdom, the church's responsibility is to take the offensive and "run them out of town." They tell us that if we will do this, territories that have been under the control of demons and evil spirits will be liberated, and this result will greatly facilitate evangelism, social reform, and godly political progress.

This view could be viewed as something similar to Christian

ghostbusters. If there is something weird in your neighborhood, and if you know the right group to call, you can exterminate your neighborhood of demons and evil spirits. With the Devil and his crowd out of town, then you can get down to the important business of solving the world's problems. Whatever happened to simply preaching the gospel and trusting God the Holy Spirit to do His work?

The April 1990 issue of *Charisma* magazine featured cover stories on how to defeat "territorial spirits." John Dawson, author of a new book, *Taking Our Cities for God,* contributed an article titled "Winning the Battle for Your Neighborhood: How you can drive away the demon forces now dominating the streets where you live."[6] Steven Lawson wrote on the subject "Defeating Territorial Spirits: Battles against evil spiritual forces controlling our cities can be waged and won."[7] Lawson gave many examples of dealing with territorial spirits, usually along the lines that a Christian ministry was ineffective in a particular area until the Christians tuned in to the fact that territorial demons were in control. Once they did prayer battle, they were able to identify these strongholds and force the demons to give up their territory. They allege that this action resulted in the outbreak of spiritual revival.

C. Peter Wagner of Fuller Seminary's School of World Mission sees the defeating of territorial spirits as central to fulfilling Christ's Great Commission. Wagner suggests that certain countries, such as Japan, that have had a low response rate to the gospel compared with similar countries could be bound by territorial spirits. If some brave soul could discern the location and nature of these spirits and break their stronghold, then such action could lead to a harvest of souls in Japan.[8]

Although it is certainly true that the demonic realm has within it a form of organization (Eph. 6:12), it does not follow from this fact or any other biblical evidence that demons can interfere with our sovereign God's work of evangelism. God can save His elect through the preaching of the gospel no matter what the spiritual climate. He is sovereign! In addition, the idea that we can run these so-called "territorial demons" out of town is based on an error in timing. This kind of offensive tactic is invalid during the church age, which is a time when God is "taking from among the Gentiles a people for His name"

(Acts 15:14). The offensive defeat of Satan and the demonic powers is something that awaits the end times, and will be accomplished not by Christians but by Christ Himself and His holy angels. This kind of dominion teaching impatiently confuses God's defensive strategy for believers during this age with the offensive strategy of Christ and His angels during the age to come.

Restoration Teaching

Another teaching derived from dominion theology is the idea that the Lord cannot and will not return until the body of Christ has reached some kind of unity, which will contribute to increased power within the church, thereby leading to the greatest revival that the world has ever seen. Sometimes related to these views is the idea that Christians must submit to certain leaders and their teachings so that they will have phenomenal power and influence when apostolic Christianity is restored and the revival of the "latter rain" begins, probably in the early decade of the new century.

Many of these teachings sprang up in the late 1940s through Pentecostals such as Franklin Hall and William Branham, and they were disseminated from meetings held at Sharon Orphanage and Schools in North Battleford, Saskatchewan, in early 1948. The leading Pentecostal denomination, the Assemblies of God, declared these and other teachings stemming from that source to be heresy, and the movement died down for a while. But in recent years many bits and pieces of these teachings are rising to the surface like scum on a pond.[9]

Many of the teachings are based upon alleged revelations received by various leaders in the movement who are considered to be prophets and apostles. Unfortunately, when they try to support their views from Scripture, they repeatedly take passages that refer to God's unfulfilled future restoration and blessing of Israel in the last days and wrongly apply it to the church. Acts 3:19-21 is an example of their misunderstanding of the *timing* for the fulfillment of that passage. Shortly after the Day of Pentecost, Peter preached a second major sermon to the Jews in Jerusalem, showing that Jesus was their promised Messiah. He concluded with an explanation that only when Israel (not the church) received Jesus as their Messiah would the promised kingdom come:

Repent therefore and return, that your sins may be wiped away,
in order that times of refreshing may come from the presence
of the Lord; and that He may send Jesus, the Christ appointed
for you, whom heaven must receive until the period of restoration of all things about which God spoke by the mouth of His
holy prophets from ancient time. (Acts 3:19–21)

Certain key phrases must be properly understood in the context in
which Peter spoke them. "Times of refreshing" (v. 19) is a description of the millennial kingdom promised to Israel in the Old Testament. This time would come when Israel accepted their Messiah
(Matt. 23:37–39; Zech. 12:10). The "period of restoration of all things"
(v. 21) is a term used by the Old Testament prophets to refer to the
restoration of Israel at the end times (Jer. 15:19; 16:15; 24:6; 50:19;
Ezek. 16:55; Hos. 11:11). Nowhere does the Bible speak of the church
ever being restored. The Bible reveals nothing of a great revival, a
latter-day rainstorm that will be produced by a "perfected" body of
Christ or some kind of restoration of a "superspiritual" brand of Christianity shortly before Christ's second coming. The New Testament
does not comment directly one way or the other about an increased
or decreased rate of conversion at any point in the church age. However, it *does* teach that there will be increasing apostasy as the age
progresses (2 Tim. 3:1–17), hardly an environment that is produced
by a church in revival!

Much of the false teaching related to the restoration-and-overcomer
concepts lies behind the contemporary teaching about spiritual warfare. This teaching often revolves around the theme that you need
the special insights that a given teacher or ministry espouses to defeat Satan and the demonic powers so that you can become one of
God's special end-time warriors.

Colossians 2:18 warns believers about getting involved in "the worship of the angels, taking his stand on visions he has seen, inflated
without cause by his fleshly mind." Because we are in a spiritual
warfare with the demonic powers, we must take seriously the Bible's
sober warnings against falling prey to false doctrine that is being propa-
gated by "false apostles, deceitful workers, disguising themselves as

apostles of Christ" (2 Cor. 11:13). True biblical discernment is an essential ingredient for Christians who desire to grow to spiritual maturity and be champions for Jesus Christ.

Doctrines of Demons

Paul warns believers in 1 Timothy 4:1,

> The Spirit explicitly says that in later times some will fall away from the faith, paying attention to deceitful spirits and doctrines of demons.

What does the term *later times* mean? It very likely refers to the "later times" of the current church age. Notice that Paul did not say "in these last days," as the writer of Hebrews did to refer to the whole church age (1:2). Paul used a different expression to convey the clear idea that the Holy Spirit is talking about the "later times" of the current church age. Therefore, the Holy Spirit is giving a dual warning for the church in our day: first, not to "fall away from the faith," and second, do not pay "attention to deceitful spirits and doctrines of demons." We have already called attention to the problem of apostasy in the church today. The second warning is especially interesting in light of the fact that those within the church who depart from the faith are said to be especially open to demonic teachings.

We think that it is significant that both biblical terms for the demonic realm are used in this verse: *spirits* and *demons*. A clear contrast is drawn between what the Holy Spirit is saying explicitly and what "deceitful spirits" and "demons" are saying. The Holy Spirit's teaching that the "later times" will be characterized by apostasy in the church is strengthened by the addition of the term *explicitly*, so that there is no mistaking what He is trying to say. However, many people today in these "later times" who repeat this Spirit-inspired warning about the increase in apostasy are accused of being negative, polemic, and divisive and of obstructing the work of the Holy Spirit. Yet, simultaneously, these critics are teaching concepts that can be proved from the Bible to be error. This passage would lead us to believe that they are "paying attention to deceitful spirits and doctrines of demons." "Deceitful spirits" are the agents that Satan uses to generate these teachings, which are then described as "doctrines of demons"—that is, doctrines that come from demons.

The Tragedy of Spiritism

This problem is illustrated in the life of King Saul in the Old Testament (1 Sam. 28). Early during his reign as the king of Israel, Saul disobeyed God and strayed from the faith. God withdrew the ministry of the Holy Spirit, which gave to the king of Israel guidance and direction to know God's will in important matters of governing the nation. When Samuel died, Saul no longer had access to God's guidance for the nation. Toward the end of Saul's life, he wanted to know whether he should engage in a battle with one of Israel's enemies, but God would not speak to him. In his distraught condition, Saul turned from God and His clear warning in the Law not to consult mediums (Deut. 18:10–12), and he visited a medium in Endor so that he could consult with Samuel. The next day, God killed Saul and his sons in battle as a result of Saul's resorting to spiritism.

Too many people today are engaging in a form of "spiritual warfare" that involves carrying on conversations and discussions with demons. In fact, some such people are teaching as fact information that they have learned from demonic sources, whether explicitly from a demonic statement or implicitly from the way they operated. Some people are being told the names of demons, the hierarchical order of demons, and how many and which demons supposedly rule over certain territories.[10] Other examples of information learned from demons sometimes include what the demon is doing, why he is inhabiting a particular person, his intents and purposes, and general conversations. Because demons are liars and deceivers, how can anyone ever trust anything a demon would say? To engage in such practice is to come close to being involved in spiritism.

Walter Martin described spiritism as "the masquerade of demonic forces, who pretend to be departed spirits with the intent of deceiving through the power of Satan those foolish enough to believe the testimony of demons in preference to the authority of the Word of God Himself."[11] Because spiritism involves unauthorized communication with demons, this abomination is a very real possibility for those who are practicing the new spiritual warfare. This approach seems twice as risky in light of the many biblical warnings for believers to stay away from such things (Exod. 22:18; Lev. 19:26, 31; 20:6, 27; Deut. 18:9–12; Isa. 8:19).

Demonic Dangers

Many of the current teachings on spiritual warfare promise great benefits to the church if they are followed. They promise a great hope in the area of evangelism—the greatest ingathering of souls in the history of the church. They also promise believers greater freedom and increased spiritual power. Unfortunately and tragically, when these teachings are examined in the light of Scripture, this new spiritual warfare seems closer to fitting the description of the final apostasy during the end times of the church age. In addition, the new spiritual-warfare theology increasingly appears to fit the description of the false religious system headed by the false prophet in the coming Tribulation. Apparently, Satan and his demons are giving many advocates of the new spiritual warfare the types of "power" experiences they are seeking as a means to deceive them. Because these advocates tend to emphasize only the demonic realm (and that from a false perspective), they are open to Satan's attacks in the realm of the flesh and, especially because of lack of discernment, the influence of the world system and its false teachings.

The apostasy of the last times during the church age leads to and helps prepare the world for the coming false religion during the Tribulation. As we look at some of the passages describing characteristics of this final deception, many aspects of the new spiritual warfare apparently are increasingly similar to the characteristics of this coming false religion. Notice that these attributes that we are about to list could be called "occult sins." The false teachers are not noted for wanting to *take away* from the Word of God by denying God's Word, as evil as that error is, but for wanting to *add to* Scripture in the name of the Lord.

In Matthew 7:21–23 our Lord says, "Not everyone who says to Me, 'Lord, Lord,'" will enter the kingdom of heaven" (v. 21a). This statement is followed by the response of the people who are condemned, who boasted of three activities that they thought should qualify them to go to heaven: "Did we not prophesy in Your name, and in Your name cast out demons, and in Your name perform many miracles?" (v. 22). These are the very areas in which the new spiritual warfare claims achievements and are major emphases in many of the teachings found within the new spiritual-warfare movement. However, our Lord's sobering reply was a command to depart from Him because "I never knew you" (v. 23). According to Christ, true spirituality is evidenced not by power signs but by genuine Christian character (v. 20).

In 2 Corinthians 11:13–15, Paul warns believers that Satan and his demons are subtle and seductive in their dealings with Christians. Demons are able to disguise themselves as angels of light and servants of righteousness. Many people who are involved in the new spiritual-warfare movement give lip service to this notion, but they seem open to information learned from any experience with the supernatural realm or any person who claims to speak in the name of the Lord no matter how much his teachings and lifestyle differ from those of the Bible.

The Final Apostasy

The apostasy of the last days is not a failure to believe in miracles. Instead, the apostasy will be characterized by an unbiblical emphasis on the miraculous and supernatural. A passage that describes this phenomenon is 2 Thessalonians 2:1–12. Paul states that the future deception will include the following demonic activities. There will be a false spirit or message or letter (v. 2); there will be deception (vv. 3, 10); the deception will be persuasive because of the activity of Satan, which includes all power (miracles) and signs and false wonders (v. 9); and God will send a deluding influence (v. 11).

Matthew 24:24 describes the Tribulation as a time to be on the lookout for "false Christs and false prophets," who "will arise and will show great signs and wonders, so as to mislead, if possible, even the elect." Notice that these *false* signs and wonders are called "great," which means that they are highly impressive displays. However, their purpose is to mislead, not to edify.

Revelation 13 includes a description of the religious false prophet who performs "great signs" (v. 13), which includes the ability to deceive "those who dwell on the earth because of the signs which it was given him to perform in the presence of the beast" (v. 14). This kind of occult power will be impressive to those who are not biblcally discerning and who think that just because something is miraculous it must be of God.

The book of Revelation describes that the major reason for rejecting Christ during the coming Tribulation consists primarily of occult sins, including the worship of demons and idols as well as sorcery (9:20–21). In 16:14, we see "spirits of demons, performing signs, which go out to the kings of the whole world." Babylon the great is said to be "a dwelling place of demons and a prison of every unclean spirit" in 18:2. The world during the Tribulation will be preoccupied with Satan and the demonic realm, but believers are supposed to be preoccupied with our Savior, the Lord Jesus Christ.

Victory with Christ

The Bible teaches that Christ Himself will gain the final victory over Satan at His Second Coming. Scripture also tells us that upon His return, the saints will rule with Him in victory. This fact is made especially clear in the seven letters to the churches in Revelation chapters 2 and 3. These letters are written to church-age believers and contain specific commendations that will be the basis for future rewards. Even here the Christian is seen as resisting the evil generated by Satan and the demonic powers by remaining true to the Lord in a defensive posture. Spirituality in the sight of God is measured by transformed thinking and character, not by metaphysical power. The eternal rewards and positions of leadership are given on the basis of achieving true victory over the enemy by remaining faithful to the Lord's Word.

Revelation 2:25–27 is typical of what the Lord expects of His children. In Thyatira, believers are expected to "hold fast until I come" (v. 25). When Christ returns, He will take believers to rule over the nations with Him (v. 26). This event is still in the future, but future status is gained through present faithfulness to God and His Word. Revelation 3:21 offers a similar promise to Christians.

The war will end with Christ Himself exercising victory over Satan and the demonic powers. What a glorious victory that will be! But we must not get trapped into thinking that we can experience that victory in this age. In the current church age, the believer is called to evangelism and spiritual warfare on a threefold front: the world, the flesh, and the Devil. We are not to *take dominion* but to *stand firm*. We are not to *run the Devil out of town* but to *resist him*. As believers in Christ, we are called upon to resist the Devil by focusing upon Christ until He returns from heaven and takes us home.

SUCCESSFUL SAINTS

Be strong in the Lord, and in the strength of His might.
Put on the full armor of God, that you may be able to
stand firm against the schemes of the devil. For our struggle
is not against flesh and blood, but against the rulers, against
the powers, against the world forces of this darkness, against
the spiritual forces of wickedness in the heavenly places.

—*Ephesians 6:10–12*

I (Thomas) recently heard a nationally known televangelist preach a sermon. He began by looking fiercely into the camera and saying, "I rebuke you, Satan, and bind you by the blood!" I took out a piece of paper and divided it in half. Every time the televangelist made a reference to Satan and demons, I noted it; every time he talked about Christ, I noted that, too. It turned out that his sermon was not supposed to be about Satan but about the Christian life, yet this televangelist mentioned Satan and the demonic realm about twice as often as he did our Lord Jesus Christ!

This kind of preoccupation with Satan is becoming all too common in Christian circles today. We certainly believe that demonic activity is real and should be taken seriously. In fact, we have written this book precisely because the Bible takes this subject seriously and gives specific instructions for dealing with the Devil. Our goal is to help the church of Jesus Christ look upon spiritual warfare from the perspective of God's infallible Word and not from the perspective of rationalism or experience.

The Bible views spiritual warfare as a conflict that is fought on three fronts: the world, the flesh, and the Devil. Unfortunately, the common practice today is to major on Satan and demons while neglecting the other two fronts. We have seen that the enemy within—the flesh, the sin nature—is just as evil as and is to be taken just as seriously as the worst demon from hell. Christians tend to be weakest in understanding how Satan influences them through his use of the world's thought system. It is in these areas of confrontation that believers must be especially on their guard.

The New Testament gives us a specific strategy for handling the attacks of the Devil, whether by land (the flesh), sea (the demonic realm), or air (the world). This biblical framework is more than sufficient to equip us to resist Satan and to stand firm while enduring through prayer.

On this basis, we can understand how to handle some of the situations that we noted in the opening chapter. You might want to read them again to refresh your memory about the details involved and the questions raised.

Answers to the Questions

In answer to the first question, pressures in life should be dealt with by realizing that Christians should act responsibly in every situation. If we succumb to the pressures of the moment because of self-absorption, self-indulgence, self-pity or other invalid reasons, we will never develop the type of resistance to the temptations of the sin nature and the thought systems of the world that we need to please the Lord. First Corinthians 10:13 assures us,

No temptation has overtaken you but such as is common to man; and God is faithful, who will not allow you to be tempted beyond what you are able, but with the temptation will provide the way of escape also, that you may be able to endure it.

Sue was not looking to the Lord for deliverance from the situation.

She had adopted the worldly thinking of arrogance that she was entitled to certain pleasures even if it meant financial irresponsibility. All too many people have perpetuated ungodly habits by saying each time, "Just one more time."

In the second example, José and Maria are to be commended for wanting to see friends and relatives come to faith in Christ. One can hardly pray too much, but it is possible to pray wrongly and for the wrong things. God has made clear in His Word that Satan and the demons will not be run out of town or from the earth until Christ and His angels accomplish this feat at the Second Coming. José and Maria should not be misled into thinking that we must sterilize an environment of the demonic powers before God can save people or bring revival. Christ's strongest language during His earthly ministry was directed against "fine, church-going people" who were just as blinded by Satan as were demon-possessed people. Jesus told the religious leaders of His day, "You are of your father the devil, and you want to do the desires of your father" (John 8:44). All unsaved people are in a sense equally blinded by Satan (Eph. 2:2). God uses the same dynamics to save all people who are deeply into sin; He has no special gospel or unique approach for those who are demon possessed.

Because Julia was a Christian, she could not be demon possessed. Satan and demons can influence a believer but not against the individual's will. Demons can tempt and exert influence, but each believer ultimately makes his or her own decision whether to sin or to resist. Flip Wilson's famous statement "The devil made me do it" is biblically incorrect when it is applied to believers. The quick-fix solutions that deliverance practitioners offer sound alluring, especially if we have struggled for a long time over a particular sin. However, this is not the biblical way to solve problems. A believer in this situation usually just needs to keep learning scriptural principles, applying them consistently, walking by means of the Holy Spirit, and growing in his Christian life because spiritual maturity equips a Christian to handle his problems in a godly way.

The Bible contains absolutely no indication that a believer can be bound by occult curses. Like Frank's friend, many people today interpret events in their lives as the products of a curse. Yet, if this were possible, the New Testament would have provided us clear warnings and instructions on how to deal with such curses. Interestingly, curses are common fears of those who traffic within the occult world. The superstition that a Christian can be cursed and must have the curse discovered and broken before he can have spiritual victory is now being taught in many Christian circles, but the Bible clearly teaches that because we are in Christ He protects us. Believers should be concerned about the influence of the teachings and beliefs from the occult but not about their spells. The same principle would apply to Fred and Linda's situation concerning the lady's worry about bringing a demon into the church.

In the fifth example, Carl should not participate in occult practices no matter how much they are said to be scientific or neutral because they are based upon accepting false views of God, man, and change. Many Christians need to be warned in this area. Many motivational seminars and psychological techniques have their roots in the occult. These methods are often whitewashed using neutral terminology, but this cover-up does not change their basic nature.

The only times the New Testament speaks about lust, murder, and anger, it is always as a product of the flesh or our sin nature. Bob and Bill would be wrong to interpret their problems as the products of evil spirits. Scripture clearly states that "each one is tempted when he is carried away and enticed by his own lust" (James 1:14). Demons might be involved in the temptation process in the same way that an amplifier projects a voice, but the Bible teaches clearly that the flesh is our primary culprit.

Christ's payment for sin deals effectively with all of the sin in a person's life when he becomes a believer. To say that a person must go through a separate step of deliverance for occult sins, as Sandy was told, is not found in the Bible. Once again, superstition might suggest such a notion, but the Bible does not.

The Sure Word of God

We are calling on the body of Christ to reject the proliferating superstitions in Christendom. These beliefs are the products of human thoughts and experiences, but they cannot be verified from the Bible.

Possibly the fact that so many people have recently been converted out of the occult explains why spiritual warfare in many circles increasingly resembles a "tit-for-tat" battle between two sorcerers. But the Bible says that our minds are to be renewed by *God's Word itself*, not by the Word of God as interpreted from a non-Christian framework, especially a framework that has much in common with the occult.

As believers in Jesus Christ we have been called to fight Satan and the demons through spiritual warfare, but our commissioning and orders come only from Holy Scripture. The Holy Spirit, who inspired the Bible through its human authors, does not say one thing in the written Word and then contradict Himself through a new teaching that is claimed to have come from the Holy Spirit. As Peter noted, "We have the prophetic word made more sure, to which you do well to pay attention . . ." (2 Peter 1:19). When a contradiction occurs between human teachings and the Bible, we have no choice as members of the family of God who have sworn allegiance to our Lord except to follow the sure Word of God. Won't you join us as we seek to faithfully serve our Lord and Savior Jesus Christ until He returns?

> We've heard the call
> Of the Lord of Hosts:
> Fight the good fight of faith—
> Be strong in the Lord.
> Gird your armor on
> When your enemies assail,
> For He is a strong deliverer
> All power is given unto Him.
> Go fight! Go fight!
> Fight the good fight of faith.
> —Author unknown

NOTES

Chapter 2

1. C. Peter Wagner and F. Douglas Pennoger, eds., *Wrestling with Dark Angels* (Ventura, Calif.: Regal Books, 1990), 84–85.
2. Ibid., 85.
3. Ibid., 76.

Chapter 3

1. See D. R. McConnell, *A Different Gospel* (Peabody, Mass.: Hendrickson, 1988), for a detailed analysis of how these metaphysical, mind-science ideas have infiltrated Christianity. When Christians have an impoverished and nonbiblical understanding of suffering, they become vulnerable to false doctrines that shift responsibility away from the individual or diminish the reality of suffering, misery, and despair in this life because we live in a fallen world. One consequence of this kind of thinking is to blame someone else or something else (such as demons) for personal suffering, addictions, and heartache.
2. Quoted by Cyril Bibbly, *T. H. Huxley* (New York: Horizon Press, 1960), 84.
3. Job 38:4–7.
4. Gordon Wenham, *Genesis*, vol. 1 of *Word Biblical Commentary* (Waco: Word, 1987), 136ff.; Umberto Cassuto, *Genesis*, vol. 1 (Jerusalem: Magnes Press), 291–292; and Stephen C. Lovelady, "The *bene-ha'elohim* Pericope: A Biblical and Theological Study" (Master's Thesis, Trinity Evangelical Divinity School, 1986).
5. Some people have taught that they are the spirits of a pre-Adamic race or the souls of the wicked who have died, but no basis exists in Scripture for this opinion.
6. Allan Ross, *Creation and Blessing: A Guide to the Study and Exposition of Genesis* (Grand Rapids: Baker, 1988), 132.

Chapter 4

1. Lewis Sperry Chafer, *Systematic Theology* (Dallas Seminary Press, 1948), 2:77.

2. Ibid., 47–48.
3. Much of the information on Babylon is taken from Charles A. Clough, *Dawn of the Kingdom* (Lubbock, Tex.: privately printed, 1974), 14–16.
4. Dave Hunt and T. A. McMahon, *America: The Sorcerer's New Apprentice* (Eugene, Ore.: Harvest House, 1988), 107–245.
5. Paul B. Clingen, "A Portrait of Satan in Ezekiel Twenty-Eight" (master's thesis, Dallas Theological Seminary, 1954), 39.
6. Much help in this section was gleaned from Allan S. Maitha, "The World: Enemy of the Believer" (master's thesis, Dallas Theological Seminary, 1970).
7. Ibid., 99–100.
8. Ibid., 81.

Chapter 5

1. Robin Bruce Lockhart, *Reilly: Ace of Spies* (New York: Penguin, 1984).
2. Ernest De Witt Burton, *A Critical and Exegetical Commentary on the Epistle to the Galatians*, in *The International Critical Commentary* (Edinburgh: T & T Clark, 1977), 306.

Chapter 6

1. Eugene Merrill, "Theology of the Pentateuch," in *Biblical Theology of the Old Testament*, ed. Roy B. Zuck (Chicago: Moody, 1991), 17–18.
2. Sidney Page, *Powers of Evil: A Biblical Study of Satan and Demons* (Grand Rapids: Baker, 1995), 270.
3. Friedrich Buchsel, *Theological Dictionary of the New Testament* (Grand Rapids: Eerdmans, 1964), 2:60.

Chapter 7

1. Matthew 4:24; 8:16, 28, 33; 9:32; 12:22; 15:22; Mark 1:32; 5:15–16,18; Luke 8:36; John 10:21.
2. C. Fred Dickason, *Demon Possession and the Christian* (Chicago: Moody, 1987), 37–35; and Clinton E. Arnold, *Three Crucial Questions About Spiritual Warfare* (Grand Rapids: Baker, 1995), 75–79.
3. Matthew 11:18; Luke 7:33; 8:27; John 7:20; 8:48–49 ("to not have a demon"), 52; 10:20.
4. Merrill F. Unger, *Demons in the World Today* (Wheaton: Tyndale House, 1971), 102.
5. John Wimber, *Spiritual Warfare* (Anaheim, Calif.: Mercy Publishing/ Vineyard Ministries International, 1989), 98.
6. Cited by Willem Berends, "The Biblical Criteria for Demon-Possession," in *The Westminister Theological Journal* 37, no. 3 (spring 1975): 342. First published in R. H. Robbins, *The Encyclopedia of Witchcraft and Demonology* (New York: Crown Publishers, 1959), 395.

7. Neil T. Anderson, *The Bondage Breaker* (Eugene, Ore.: Harvest House, 1990), 174.
8. Unger, *Demons*, 102.
9. Dickason, *Demon Possession*, 89.
10. I. Howard Marshall, *The Epistles of John* (Grand Rapids: Eerdmans, 1984), 251–52; Stephen S. Smalley, *1, 2, 3 John*, vol. 51 of *Word Biblical Commentary* (Waco, Tex.: Word Books, 1984), 302–3; and John R. W. Stott, *The Epistles of John* (Grand Rapids: Eerdmans, 1964), 191–93.
11. Dickason, *Demon Possession*, 94. Dickason attempts to obfuscate the passage by throwing out several interpretations and then concluding that the passage just is not clear. If this same methodology is applied to the rest of Scripture, then nothing can be known because there are a plethora of contradictory interpretations of almost every verse in the Bible. In our opinion, the exegetical confusion is predetermined by presuming the validity of clinical observations.
12. Zane Hodges, "1 John," in *The Bible Knowledge Commentary*, ed. Roy B. Zuck, John F. Walvoord (Wheaton: Scripture Press, 1983), 903.
13. Walter Bauer, William F. Arndt, and F. Wilbur Gingrich, *"hapto,"* in *A Greek-English Lexicon of the New Testament and Other Early Christian Literature*, 2d ed., ed. F. Wilbur Gingrich and Frederick W. Danker (Chicago: Univ. of Chicago Press, 1979), 102–3. This source suggests that the nuance is to touch for the purpose of harm; it is also likely that the verb is a synonym for *echo*, another common word in possession narratives.
14. Smalley, *1, 2, 3 John*, 303.
15. Bauer, Arndt, and Gingrich, *Greek-English Lexicon*, 102–3.
16. Dickason, *Demon Possession*, 147.
17. Ibid., 186.
18. Ibid., 175.
19. Merrill F. Unger, *Biblical Demonology* (Wheaton: Scripture Press, 1952), 100.
20. Unger, *Biblical Demonology*, 117.
21. Unger, *Demons*, 113.
22. Unger, *Biblical Demonology*, 100.
23. Ibid.
24. Wimber, *Warfare*, 100.
25. The anarthrous (no article) use of *diabolos* here is comparable to the anarthrous use of *theos* in John 1:1 and emphasizes the quality of the noun, its essence or attribute. Thus, Jesus is making a clear statement at this early stage that Judas is already indwelt by Satan.
26. In the Greek, two different words are used for *washing*. The first word, *luow*, is the same word the LXX uses to describe the head-to-toe bath of the High Priest at his consecration, which is analogous to the believer's salvation. This bath symbolizes the judicial cleansing of sin that occurs

at the believer's salvation. The cognate noun describes the "washing of regeneration" in Titus 3:5.

Chapter 8

1. Ed Murphy, "My Daughter Demonized," in *Equipping the Saints* 4 (winter 1990): 27–29. The story is a summary of this article, and all quotes are taken from it.
2. This is not a cop-out. Much goes on in this life that we are unable to explain because we do not have all of the data. Therefore, believers must rely exclusively on the veracity of God's Word and not experience. We know little, if anything, about what goes on either in the invisible spiritual warfare around us or in the recesses of sinful, carnal human souls. To draw dogmatic conclusions based on limited experience invites calamity. Only when the truth of God's Word becomes more real to us than our experiences, emotions, circumstances, and situations do we "walk by faith, not by sight" (2 Cor. 5:7). This faith is not a faith in faith, a faith in feelings, or a faith in intuition but an unshakable reliance on the truth conveyed in the Scripture alone.

Chapter 9

1. James 5:16. See Peter Davids, *Commentary on James,* in *New International Greek Testament Commentary* (Grand Rapids: Eerdmans, 1983), 196–97.

Chapter 10

1. Some of the material in this section, including the reasons why Christians suffer, is adapted from Charles Clough, *Laying the Foundation* (Lubbock, Tex.: Lubbock Bible Church, 1973), 64–66.
2. Gerhard Kittle, ed., *Theological Dictionary of the New Testament* (Grand Rapids: Eerdmans, 1964), 2:625–26.

Chapter 11

1. C. Fred Dickason, *Demon Possession and the Christian* (Chicago: Moody, 1987), 162–63.
2. Umberto Cassuto, *A Commentary on the Book of Exodus* (Jerusalem: Magnes Press, 1967), 243. See also C. F. Keil and Franz Delitsch, "The Pentateuch," vol. 1 of *Commentary on the Old Testament* (1875; reprint, Grand Rapids: Eerdmans, 1975), 116–17.
3. Robert J. Priest, Thomas Campbell, and Bradford A. Mullen, "Missiological Syncretism: The New Animistic Paradigm" (paper read at the annual meeting of the Evangelical Missiological Society, Chicago, Ill.: November 17–19, 1994), 22. Quoted in David G. Moore and Robert A. Pyne, "Neil Anderson's Approach to the Spiritual Life," *Bibliotheca Sacra* 153, no. 609 (January 1996): 82.

4. John David Hannah, "The 'Curses' Syndrome—An Evaluation," unpublished paper delivered at the Evangelical Minister's Fellowship, Houston, Texas, Spring, 1985, p. 3.

5. For critiques of these movements, see H. Wayne House and Thomas Ice, *Dominion Theology: Blessing or Curse?* (Portland: Multnomah, 1988); Hal Lindsey, *The Road to Holocaust* (New York: Bantam Books, 1989); Dave Hunt, *Whatever Happened to Heaven?* (Eugene, Ore.: Harvest House, 1988); and Albert James Dager, *Vengeance Is Ours: The Church in Dominion* (Sword Publishers, 1990).

6. John Dawson, "Winning the Battle for Your Neighborhood: How you can drive away the demon forces now dominating the streets where you live," *Charisma*, April 1990, 57.

7. Steven Lawson, "Defeating Territorial Spirits: Battles against evil spiritual forces controlling our cities can be waged and won," *Charisma*, April 1990, 47.

8. C. Peter Wagner and F. Douglas Pennoger, eds., *Wrestling with Dark Angels* (Ventura, Calif.: Regal Books, 1990), 89.

9. See Albert James Dager, "Latter-Day Prophets: The Kansas City Connection," *Media Spotlight* (1990). See also Thomas Ice, "What is Dominion Theology?" *Biblical Perspectives* 1, no. 3 (May–June 1988).

10. Wagner and Pennoger, *Wrestling with Dark Angels*, 76, 84-5.

11. Walter Martin, *The Kingdom of the Cults* (Minneapolis: Bethany Fellowship, 1965), 199-200.

Comments or questions can be addressed to Robert Dean Jr., at rdean@prestoncitybible.org. Those who wish more information also can visit the website at www.prestoncitybible.org.

Robert Dean Jr. is the pastor of Preston City Bible Church, Preston City, Connecticut.

Thomas Ice is the Executive Director of the Pre-Trib Research Center in Arlington, Texas. He is the author of more than twenty books on biblical prophecy. Both Ice and Dean are known for their skill in presenting the teaching of Scripture clearly, accurately, and practically while interacting with the issues of our time.

To find out more about the Pre-Trib Research Center, visit them on the World Wide Web at www.timlahaye.com.